# Differentiating Instruction *for* Students With Learning Disabilities

SECOND EDITION

WILLIAM N. BENDER

# Differentiating Instruction *for* Students With Learning Disabilities

**BEST TEACHING PRACTICES FOR GENERAL AND SPECIAL EDUCATORS**

SECOND
EDITION

A JOINT PUBLICATION

Council for
Exceptional
Children

CORWIN PRESS
A SAGE Publications Company
Thousand Oaks, CA 91320

*For information:*

Corwin Press
A Sage Publications Company
2455 Teller Road
Thousand Oaks, California 91320
www.corwinpress.com

Sage Publications Ltd.
1 Oliver's Yard
55 City Road
London EC1Y 1SP
United Kingdom

Sage Publications India Pvt. Ltd.
B 1/I 1 Mohan Cooperative
    Industrial Area
Mathura Road, New Delhi 110 044
India

Sage Publications Asia-Pacific Pte. Ltd.
33 Pekin Street #02-01
Far East Square
Singapore 048763

Printed in the United States of America on acid-free paper.

*Library of Congress Cataloging-in-Publication Data*

Bender, William N.
Differentiating instruction for students with learning disabilities: best teaching practices for general and special educators/William N. Bender. — 2nd ed.
        p. cm.
"A joint publication with the Council for Exceptional Children."
Includes bibliographical references and index.
ISBN 978-1-4129-5445-7 (cloth)
ISBN 978-1-4129-5446-4 (pbk.)
    1. Learning disabled children—Education. 2. Individualized instruction. I. Title.

LC4704.5.B46 2008
371.9′043—dc22                                    2007011193

This book is also available in audio through the Recording for the Blind & Dyslexic. For more information on how to obtain a copy, contact (866) 732-3585 or www.RFBD.org.

08   09   10   11   10   9   8   7   6   5   4   3   2

| | |
|---|---|
| *Acquisitions Editor:* | Allyson P. Sharp |
| *Editorial Assistants:* | Mary Dang and David Gray |
| *Production Editor:* | Astrid Virding |
| *Copy Editor:* | Gretchen Treadwell |
| *Typesetter:* | C&M Digitals (P) Ltd. |
| *Proofreader:* | Dennis W. Webb |
| *Indexer:* | Ellen Slavitz |
| *Cover Designer:* | Michael Dubowe |
| *Graphic Designer:* | Karine Hovsepian |
| *Illustrator:* | Nathaniel Schiel |

# Contents

# About the Author

 **William N. Bender** earned his PhD from the University of North Carolina in 1983. Prior to this, he taught eighth- and ninth-grade students in the public school system for several years. Since he has been in higher education, he has published more than sixty research articles and twelve books in education and special education. He specializes in differentiated instructional strategies and disciplinary strategies for students with disabilities, particularly learning disabilities, emotional disturbance, and attention disorders, in the general education classroom. He is recognized as a national leader on instructional tactics and distance education. His combination of practical strategies and easy humor leads to a demand for numerous workshops each year on various topics in education. He would like to receive your comments on this work and invites e-mail from both educators and parents nationwide at williamneilb@aol.com.

# Acknowledgments

Corwin Press gratefully acknowledges the following reviewers:

Eloisa E. Alfonso
Exceptional Student Educator
DCPS Teacher
Miami, FL

Mary Ann Beckman
Director of Special Education
Arrowhead Special Education Cooperative
Hartland, WI

Carla Fry
Elementary Principal
Woodlands Elementary
Ponca City, OK

Wendy A. Harriott
Assistant Professor
Monmouth University
West Long Branch, NJ

Patricia McCoy DeLancey
Special Educator
Sumrall Elementary School
Sumrall, MS

David M. Sable
Director of Special Education
Radford City Schools
Radford, VA

# Introduction

Students with learning disabilities, as a group, are some of the most courageous students I have ever dealt with. I have taught students with learning disabilities, directly and indirectly, for more than twenty-five years and, although I have seen my share of behavioral problems from these students, it is wise to reflect for a moment on what the ultimate cause for those problems may be. These students are continually frustrated in their learning endeavors by the difficulty of the assignments given them, and misbehavior is often the result. Furthermore, students with learning disabilities may be ridiculed by their peers; they are often the victims of overt bias, ignorance, and outright hostility from peers (and, even in this day and age, from some teachers).

Still, most students with learning disabilities do not demonstrate highly disruptive behavior problems, and most generally manage to confront their particular disabilities, compensate for them in some fashion, and move forward with their learning and their lives in productive ways. I am always humbled when I begin a project such as this book, simply because of the continuous courage and dedication I see in the students that this book is ultimately designed to help. I sincerely hope that this text may make their learning somewhat easier and their lives a bit simpler.

Thus, the ultimate purpose of this text is to highlight a variety of differentiated instructional strategies (Gregory & Chapman, 2002; Tomlinson, 1999) that work for students with learning disabilities in the special education and the inclusive general education classroom. As educators, we all realize that most students with learning disabilities spend almost all of their school day in inclusive general education classes (Mastropieri & Scruggs, 1998), and consequently, teachers need differentiated instructional strategies that are proven to work for these students in those classrooms. Fortunately, research has proceeded over the past two decades, and we can now state fairly definitively that a number of instructional strategies will work for students with learning disabilities (Vaughn, Gersten, & Chard, 2000). Thus, the ideas presented here are, for the most part, research-proven ideas, and although not exhaustive, these strategies do represent the best practices to date for students with learning disabilities. Implementation of a variety of these strategies in the special education class or the inclusive class will focus the efforts of both teachers and students on academic success and will result in higher overall academic achievement for students with learning disabilities, as well as greater satisfaction in the class generally.

This book is not intended as an introduction to learning disabilities, and no information on characteristics of these students is presented, except as an explanation of why a particular tactic is effective. Also, although this book includes some summaries of the latest research, this is not intended as a comprehensive research review. Furthermore, a number of these strategies have been explored over a longer period of time—self-monitoring is one example, and the research cited does include some of the initial and seminal references for this and other tactics. However, the major focus is not an exhaustive exposition of available research but rather a working knowledge of how and why these strategies are so strongly suggested for students with learning disabilities.

> Students with learning disabilities, as a group, are some of the most courageous students I have ever dealt with.

The differentiated instruction concept will serve as the primary model for this text, and the strategies described in each chapter will be presented within the context of that model (Gregory & Chapman, 2002; Tomlinson, 1999; Tomlinson et al., 2002). I have used the term "strategies" for effective, yet somewhat involved, instructional procedures, and I use the term "tactic" for quickly implemented instructional ideas. Furthermore, the content/process/product structure of the differentiated instructional concept will be explored for the instructional strategies that are recommended herein (Tomlinson, 1999), and thus the differentiated instructional construct will serve as a background for the entire text. Many reflective exercises for teachers will focus on relating the recommended strategies herein to the differentiated instructional model of teaching.

Chapter 1 presents the concept of differentiated instruction and the basis for that concept in multiple intelligences literature and the emerging research on brain compatible instruction. Foundation differentiated instructional concepts such as tiering and cubing are also presented. Chapter 2 presents the relatively new concept of universal design and how that concept impacts the structure of the inclusion classroom to facilitate differentiation. Chapters 3 and 4 involve supporting students academically, using a variety of metacognitive and/or scaffolded learning techniques that allow teachers to differentiate the learning process for students with learning disabilities. Chapter 5 describes a series of tutoring techniques that may be employed in the inclusive classroom to assist the teacher in providing differentiated instruction for all the students in the class in a timely fashion. Chapter 6 presents the new concept of response to intervention: performance monitoring to facilitate differentiation, as well as a variety of differentiation assessment models.

Chapter 7 is a more focused chapter that demonstrates the application of many of these strategies in the area of reading instruction for the elementary and middle grades. Because reading disabilities are some of the most common disabilities among students with learning disabilities, I felt that a chapter that specifically addressed reading was essential in this text, and although writing or math disabilities negatively affect some students with learning disabilities, reading is—for most students with learning disabilities—more critical, and no text can address all types of disabilities. Finally, Chapter 8 presents suggested guidelines for implementing differentiated instruction.

In addition to the focus on differentiated instruction, another subtle yet important theme that runs through the book involves relationships. I believe that the most important single factor in the learning process is the relationship between a teacher and a pupil and that this critical relationship—not strategies or instructional tactics—provides the basis for effective instruction. Perhaps because this book focuses on a wide variety of instructional strategies and tactics, I felt a need to make this statement up front—that the basis of effective teaching is a caring relationship. For learning to take place effectively and efficiently, students must be absolutely convinced that the teachers care for them and that the students' learning and, more fundamentally, the students' well-being are at the heart of the teachers' interest. Only from that caring position will teachers be effective in motivating students to involve themselves in their learning. Furthermore, and perhaps in a more basic sense, only from that caring perspective will teachers be motivated to implement the strategies required by the differentiated instruction concept. This relationship theme is apparent in certain sections of the text, such as the self-management section, in which a teacher motivates a student to begin attending to his or her own attention and/or learning behaviors. Also, in using scaffolded instruction, the teacher must attend intimately to the student's learning to determine when to withdraw the scaffold or support the student's learning efforts; this instructional decision can be based only on intimate knowledge and understanding of a student's learning technique, and thus a relationship between the teacher and the pupil is critical. Again, the single most important aspect of learning in today's classrooms is the relationship between a pupil and a teacher, and based on a rich relationship, the strategies identified herein will enhance student learning and allow students with learning disabilities to shine!

Finally, I hope that both the special educator and the general educator realize that almost all of these strategies will work as well for students with other disabilities, as well as for many of the other lower achieving students in the class. Thus, teachers are encouraged to experiment with differentiated instruction, adapt these strategies to their specific situation, and generally make differentiated instruction work. Again, these strategies and tactics truly represent the "best practices" for students with learning disabilities today and, as such, should dominate our instructional efforts.

> The most important single factor in the learning process is the relationship between a teacher and a pupil, and this critical relationship—not strategies or instructional tactics—provides the basis for effective instruction.

# What Is Differentiated Instruction? 1

Students with learning disabilities (LDs) have a way of challenging almost every general education teacher because of the learning characteristics that are displayed by many kids with learning disabilities. As every veteran teacher realizes, students with learning disabilities may be less engaged in the learning task, unable to cope with multiple instructions, and poorly organized in their thinking and work habits. Approximately 75 percent of students with learning disabilities are males, and because males are more physically active than females at many age levels, the mere volume of physical activity shown by males with learning disabilities in the typical classroom can enhance the difficulties of teaching these students. When these deficits are coupled with fairly severe academic deficits, the result can be a student who is very challenging for general education teachers. In my workshops nationally, I've found that teachers are hungry for tactics and ideas that work for these challenging students.

The concept of *differentiated instruction* is based on the need for general education teachers to differentiate instruction to meet the needs of diverse learners in the general education class; this includes students with learning disabilities as well as a number of other disabilities.

Differentiated instruction may be conceptualized as a teacher's response to the diverse learning needs of a student (Tomlinson, 1999, 2001; Tomlinson & McTighe, 2006, pp. 1–82). Teachers must know the learners in the class, understanding not only such things about each learner as the learning style and learning preferences but also showing a concern for each student by tailoring instruction to meet the needs of each individual student. In creating the concept of differentiation, Tomlinson incorporated a wide range of recent research on how diverse students learn, including Dr. Howard Gardner's concept of multiple intelligences and the more recent instructional suggestions emerging from the brain compatible research literature (Gardner, 2006; Goleman, 2006; Moran, Kornhaber, & Gardner, 2006; Sousa, 2006; Tomlinson, 1999; Tomlinson et al., 2002). With this emphasis on diverse learning styles as a backdrop, Tomlinson encouraged teachers to personalize the instructional activities in order to challenge students with a highly interactive, challenging, and interesting curriculum. Teachers are thereby encouraged to consider students' unique learning styles and then differentiate the educational activities presented in the class to provide for those divergent learning styles. In particular, Tomlinson encouraged differentiation in three areas:

1. *Content* (what is learned)

2. *Process* (how the content is taught)

3. *Product* (how the learning is observed and evaluated)

The learning content involves what students are to master and what we want the students to accomplish after instruction (Tomlinson, 1999, pp. 1–65; Tomlinson et al., 2002, p. 46). The content may be delineated in state-approved curricula, in scope and sequence charts (i.e., objectives grouped by subject area and grade level), in state or national standards, or in the curriculum material itself. In most cases, the teacher will not be able to control the specific content that must be covered, but he or she will have control over how to modify that content for presentation to the students based on the learning styles of the students, and in that modification process, some content will be emphasized more than other material (Tomlinson, 1999).

> The concept of differentiated instruction is based on the need for teachers to differentiate instruction to meet the needs of diverse learners in the general education class.

The learning *process* involves how the student interacts with the content, and those learning interactions will in part be determined by the various learning preferences of the students (e.g., is this student an auditory learner, a visual learner, a learner who needs concrete demonstrations?). Because of the diversity of learning styles and preferences demonstrated by students today, the differentiated classroom will typically involve a wide array of activities to address the different learning needs of everyone (Gregory & Chapman, 2002, pp. 9–17; Tomlinson et al., 2002, pp. 46–59; Tomlinson & McTighe, 2006, pp. 1–25). These learning processes may include some of the following:

- *activating the learning*—the introductory activities that focus on the material to be learned, relate that material to previously mastered material, let the student know why that material is important, and describe what students should be able to do once they learn

- *learning activities*—involve the actual instructional activities for the students, such as modeling, rehearsal, choral chanting, movement associated with the content, and/or educational games
- *grouping activities*—both individual and group-oriented learning activities should be planned as a part of the learning process

Different learning needs require differentiated instruction.

Finally, the learning *product* will be of paramount importance because demonstrations of learning allow the teacher to determine the students who have mastered the material and those who may need more time and continued instruction (Tomlinson, 1999, pp. 1–65). Again, the learning styles of the students in the class will help determine what types of products the teacher may wish to accept as demonstrations of learning (Gregory & Chapman, 2002, p. 20). In the differentiated learning classroom, it would not be uncommon for a given unit of instruction to have four or five different types of culminating projects that students may choose in order to demonstrate their knowledge of the topic. Art projects, role-play mini-dramas for groups of students, library or Web-based research, multimedia projects, paper-and-pencil projects, written reports, or oral reports all represent excellent projects that students may complete to demonstrate their knowledge. This assessment component is discussed more completely in Chapter 6.

Using this model of differentiated instruction, the teacher will constantly modify his or her classroom organization, curriculum, instructional methods, and assessment procedures to address the individual learning needs of the students in the class (Bender, 2005, pp. 1–40; Gregory & Chapman, 2002, pp. 1–37; Tomlinson, 1999). Furthermore, the teacher's relationship with, and knowledge of, the students in the class will be the basis for the differentiations in instruction, and so the relationship between the teacher and the pupil is critical. Only a solid positive relationship and fairly complete knowledge of the student's learning styles and preferences can provide an effective basis for differentiated instruction (Marzano & Marzano, 2003).

# FOUNDATIONS OF DIFFERENTIATED INSTRUCTION

## Multiple Intelligences: One Foundation of Differentiation

Dr. Howard Gardner's work on intelligence in children (Gardner, 2006; Moran, Kornhaber, & Gardner, 2006; Stanford, 2003) has refocused how educators understand student learning, and the concept of differentiated instruction is founded in part on this body of work (see Tomlinson, 1999). Essentially, Gardner has now postulated nine different intelligences, which he refers to a nine relatively independent but interacting cognitive capacities (Moran, Kornhaber, & Gardner, 2006). These intelligences are presented below.

*Verbal-linguistic:* An ability to understand and use spoken and written communications, abstract reasoning, symbolic thinking and conceptual patterning. Individuals with this strength make excellent poets and attorneys. This intelligence is highly emphasized in schools.

*Logical-mathematical:* Ability to understand and use logic and numeric symbols and operations, recognize patterns, and see connections between separate pieces of information. These individuals tend to excel in math and related fields such as computer programming.

*Musical:* Ability to understand and use such concepts as rhythm, pitch, melody, and harmony. These individuals often are highly sensitive to sounds, and will excel in music composition, but note that this intelligences does not necessarily mean the individual has performing talent in each of these areas.

*Spatial:* Ability to orient and manipulate three-dimensional space. Judgments based on spatial intelligence allow some individuals to shoot a basketball through a hoop 30 feet away with relative ease. These individuals can excel in architecture, mapmaking, and games requiring visualization of objects from differing perspectives.

*Bodily-kinesthetic:* Ability to coordinate physical movement, or use the body to express emotion. Students with this strength often excel in athletics.

*Naturalistic:* Ability to distinguish and categorize objects or phenomena in nature, master taxonomy, or demonstrate extreme sensitivity to nature. The ideal occupation for a person with this strength is zoologist.

*Interpersonal:* Extreme ability to understand, interpret, and interact well with others. Students who seem to "come alive" when working in small group work represent this type of learner, and the ideal occupation for this person include politics and/or sales.

*Intrapersonal:* Ability to understand and use his or her own thoughts, feelings, preferences, perceptions, and interests. This ability can assist persons in any job, since self-regulation is one component of success in almost every task. These persons succeed in reflective professions (e.g., authors) and entrepreneurship.

*Existential:* Ability to contemplate phenomena or questions beyond sensory data, such as contemplations of the infinite. This is the more recent of these intelligences described, and there are still questions about the reality of this as a separate intelligence.

Clearly, these abilities exist in almost everyone to some degree, and almost everyone demonstrates strengths in several different intelligences (Moran, Kornhaber, & Gardner, 2006). Focusing on these intelligences and planning activities with these in mind will, it is believed, result in a wider array of educational activities in the classroom, and various researchers are proposing that teachers should consider these in planning every lesson.

We should point out that Gardner's work represents one *theory* of intelligences, and that even the existence of these nine separate intelligences has not been validated (Sousa, 2006). In fact, subsequent research may show that, in reality, only five or six of these nine, in fact exist. Still, Gardner's work has highlighted several points on which almost all educators agree. First, students do seem to learn in highly diverse ways, and knowledge of these different ways of learning can offer the opportunity for teachers to build instructional activities that involve a number of varied capabilities. It was in this realm that Tomlinson utilized multiple intelligences theory as the basis for advocating increased differentiation in curricular activities. Second, expanding the range of educational activities in the traditional classroom will, in all likelihood, result in enhanced learning. For these reasons, many practitioners have advocated use of this multiple intelligence construct for educational planning purposes (e.g., Bender, 2005; Gregory & Chapman, 2002; Sousa, 2006; Stanford, 2003).

However, another caution on multiple intelligences is in order. Some educators, when presented with these nine intelligences, immediately began to plan nine different versions of a single instructional lesson, and that type of "reductionistic" thinking was not Gardner's intent (Moran et al., 2006). Rather, these capacities are viewed in terms of relative strengths and weaknesses that interrelate to each other. Some students demonstrate a particularly strong intelligence in one area, whereas others seem to demonstrate strengths in a "cluster" of intelligences.

In terms of planning an individual unit of instruction, and sometimes even an individual lesson, teachers can take this multiple intelligences concept and devise an interesting array of highly diverse educational activities, with the various activities targeted to the strengths of the different learners in the class. Teaching Tip 1.1 presents a sample of the types of activities that might be used in a third- to fifth-grade mathematics unit which would tap strengths in each of these nine intelligences. In a two-week unit on fractions, teachers should be able to implement each of these instructional ideas, as either individual or small group work.

**Teaching Tip 1.1**

### A Sample of Instructional Ideas Based on Multiple Intelligences

| | |
|---|---|
| Verbal-linguistic | Write a description of several fractions, and/or draw a picture to illustrate each. |
| Logical-mathematical: | Describe and evaluate a recipe, then multiply it by two to serve twice as many people. |
| Musical: | Use a chant to learn the steps in reducing fractions, or to memorize multiplication or division math facts. Have students write a "rap" about how to reduce improper fractions. |
| Spatial: | Visualize large objects, and mentally divide them into fractional parts. Draw those objects and fractional parts of them. |
| Bodily-kinesthetic: | Mount a large circle on the wall, from the floor to approximately head high. Have a student stand in front of the circle and use his or her body to divide the circle into fractions. Standing with hands by one's side, the body divides the circle into halves—head to foot. Holding one's arms out straight to each side divides the circle into fourths, etc. |
| Naturalistic: | Explore the core of an apple, cutting it into fractional parts. |
| Interpersonal: | Playing musical chairs, discuss the improper fractions in the game (i.e. five persons circling four chairs is the improper fraction of 5/4). Another idea is to have pairs of kids create fractional parts together by cutting up circles/squares. |
| Intrapersonal: | Have these introspective children keep a daily journal of each experience in their home lives where they experience fractions (e.g., "I wanted more cake last night, so I ate ½ of the part that was left over"). |
| Existential: | Have this child reflect on the relationship between one person and the groups to which he or she belongs ("I am 1/22 of this class, and 1/532 of this school, while our class is 22/532 of this school"). Write down these reflections and share them with the class. |

One additional point may be made here. While some teachers and schools have implemented multiple intelligence instruction at the level of unit planning, others have actually begun to teach these different intelligences to their students. For some students, this can be quite empowering, and here is an example. I recently dealt with a young man in a mentoring session, and he explained to me that he didn't wish to complete college because, "I can't learn right." In attending a local technical college, he'd failed a course, because, as he explained, "I don't make notes right." When I asked him how he succeeded in high school courses, he explained that his notes were not checked in high school. At long last, I asked him to show me his notes, and once I saw them, I understood.

> For many students, learning about different intelligences can be quite empowering, since many students learn in a nonlinguistic fashion.

This young man was a spatial learner who needed to see relationships between his concepts in graphic form—his notebook was a collection of "notes" developed as spontaneously produced graphic organizers or semantic webs. In that form of note-taking, rather than outline notes, one demonstrates relationships between facts and broader concepts in the form of a graphic. In short, because he took his notes graphically rather than in a linguistic/outline fashion, he considered himself less capable. In fact, in his entire public school career, no teacher had ever explained that his learning strength was an "acceptable" way to make notes; consequently he felt somewhat like a failure because he didn't make notes in outline form, when he knew that most others did.

In this example, it would have been quite empowering for schools to literally have taught the multiple intelligences to this young man. He would have then learned that his note-taking/learning style was not a "failure" but a fairly common procedure. Further, perhaps he could have learned to perfect that strength and become more efficient at note-taking in semantic web fashion. In short, schools did this young man a disservice by not teaching him about his learning strength. Once I did explain that to him, he was quite motivated to read a bit about the various intelligences, and his style of note-taking became "acceptable" in his own mind; his confidence increased, and he returned to his technical degree.

For this reason, many teachers who move into differentiation likewise begin to teach their students about these intelligences. In perhaps a 30-minute lesson, these teachers define the intelligences for the class and provide various examples of them. They may also download a brief "Multiple Intelligences Inventory" from the Web and allow students to complete it and thus begin to identify their own intelligences. However, the emphasis on intelligences doesn't end at that point after teaching about this topic once. Rather, throughout the year, when those teachers begin a new instructional unit, they challenge their students with a prompt like, "Think about your learning strengths before you decide which of these projects to do for this unit."

> Do you need to increase student performance to meet AYP? In a day when teachers are forced to meet adequate yearly progress, differentiation of instruction—and attending to students' learning strengths—provides one way to empower students and greatly enhance learning in the classroom.

Giving students such choices among assignments (at least some limited choices) and having them base those choices on their learning strengths can result in students taking more responsibility for their work (Caine & Caine, 2006). In turn, this is quite likely to lead to enhanced learning performance; to paraphrase Sternberg (2006), when we teach students in a way that matches how they think, they do better in school. In point of fact, even if Gardner's intelligences are refined and/or redefined in the coming years, having students begin to think in this fashion about their own strengths results in high impact teaching. Thus, differentiation based on multiple intelligences can result in enhancing learning, and in a day when teachers are forced to meet adequate yearly progress, differentiation provides one way to greatly enhance learning in the classroom.

## Brain-Compatible Instruction: Another Foundation of Differentiation

While related in a general way to the concept of multiple intelligences, the literature on brain-compatible instruction is much more solidly grounded in the neurosciences (Bender, 2005; Caine & Caine, 2006; Sousa, 2006). However, like multiple intelligences, the instructional ideas stemming from the neurosciences provided Tomlinson with another foundation for differentiated instruction (Tomlinson, 1999). Brain-compatible instruction, sometimes referred to as brain-based learning, has emerged only within the last ten years and is based primarily on improvements in the medical sciences (Caine & Caine, 2006; Leonard, 2001; Sousa, 2001, pp. 1–25). In fact, much of our increasing understanding of the human brain has come from the development of the functional magnetic resonance imaging techniques (a technique that is sometimes represented in the literature as the fMRI). This is a nonradiological technique—and thus a relatively safe brain-scanning technique—that has allowed scientists to study the performance of human brains while the subjects concentrated on different types of learning tasks (Richards, 2001). The fMRI measures the brain's use of oxygen and sugar during the thinking process, and from that information, physicians can determine which brain areas are most active during various types of educational tasks (Sousa, 1999, pp. 1–20). For example, specialists have now identified brain regions that are specifically associated with various learning activities such as language, reading, math, motor learning, music appreciation, or verbal response to questions in a classroom discussion (Sousa, 2006).

Caine and Caine (2006), two leaders in the field of brain-compatible instruction, refer to learning in terms of "cognits," which are defined as organized configurations of brain cells that activate together and result in a unified thought. These may range from simple cognits, which represent a single fact, to much more involved cognits that might be activated to handle more complex information. From this perspective, the teacher's role is to provide instructional experiences that are rich in learning potential, and thus develop more and/or increasingly complex cognits.

For example, having a student complete a written problem involving the addition of negative 2 plus positive 3 activates a number of different cognits within the brain, and thus can result in learning. However, having that same students "walk through" the same addition problems using a number line of positive and negative integers on the floor activates many more cognits within the brain, and thus results in higher impact learning—both increased understanding and enhanced memory. Further, Caine and Caine (2006) have specified the types of high impact activities students should engage in when presented with new material in the class. Students should

- undergo sensory and emotional experiences tied to the content, because sensory and emotional tags associated with content learning enhances memory
- make associations with previous knowledge and their own experiences
- articulate questions and develop a focus that leads to planning their activities on the content
- perform some action related to understanding the content, or produce some product associated with it
- be challenged with high quality curricula that are minutely more challenging than tasks the student is known to perform independently

While this single text cannot present the exciting array of recent findings from the neurosciences, several additional discoveries bear directly on discussions of the ways students experience learning in the classroom. First, within the last several years, a set of neurons commonly called "mirror neurons" have been identified within the human brain (Goleman, 2006; Sousa, 2006). These neurons allow human beings to create internal, mental simulations of what is going on in the minds or emotions of other people in their environment. Thus, when two people interact, their minds are actually influencing each other (Goleman, 2006), and they are likely to increasingly reflect each other's moods and emotions. In fact, they are quite likely to begin to "match" each other on such things as voice volume, voice tone, emotional intensity, or even facial expression and body language, depending on the degree and level of intensity of the interaction. Thus, when teachers or students are unhappy in the context of an educational activity, the other students in the class are somewhat predisposed to reflect that in their own moods, emotions, and possibly even their actions (Sousa, 2006; pp. 23).

Next, brains perform at their best when they are highly motivated and involved and experiencing "manageable" stress (Goleman, 2006). Should a student experience too much stress (e.g., when presented with a math problem he or she cannot do, and expected to perform that problem on the dry-erase board in front of the whole class!), energy is shunted into the emotional centers of the brain, and the cerebrum or "cognitive area" of the brain actually demonstrates reduced brain activity. Thus, higher order thinking—which takes place in the cerebrum—decreases when students are overstressed.

With these neuroscience concepts in mind, it is easy to understand why some instructional environments don't work for many students, including many students with learning disabilities. Taken together, what these findings suggest is that if students do not experience their learning as a warm, positive environment that challenges them at an appropriate level—a level of task which, while challenging, is at least within the realm of the possible for them—those students will actually become less capable of learning, as the brain activity in the cerebrum decreases. Thus, every teacher is obligated to ask, "How do all of my students—particularly students with learning disabilities or other learning challenges—experience learning in the context of my classroom?"

In addition to these issues raised by the neurosciences, other researchers have suggested that the research on brain-compatible instruction has developed to a point where specific teaching suggestions may be made. On the basis of this growing understanding of how students learn, teachers across the nation have begun to restructure their classroom practices based on these guidelines (Moran, Kornhaber, & Gardner, 2006; Sousa, 2001; Sylwester, 2000). Although various authors make different recommendations, the ten tactics for a brain-compatible instruction classroom, presented in Teaching Tip 1.2, represent the accumulated thought in this area (for additional suggestions, see Gregory & Chapman, 2002; Moran, Kornhaber, & Gardner, 2006; Richards, 2001; Sousa, 2006; Stanford, 2003; Sternberg, 2006; Sylwester, 2000; Tomlinson, 1999).

### Teaching Tip 1.2

**Ten Tactics for a Brain-Compatible Class**

1. Provide a safe, comfortable learning environment.
2. Provide comfortable furniture.
3. Provide water and fruits to students.
4. Structure frequent student responses.
5. Pair physical movement to learning tasks.
6. Use visual stimuli for increasing novelty in the learning task.
7. Use music and rhythms for learning.
8. Provide adequate wait time.
9. Give students choices.
10. Use students to teach each other.

### REFLECTIVE EXERCISE: A PREDICTION EXERCISE

Prior to reading the discussion below about the ten brain-compatible instruction tactics, review the list in Teaching Tip 1.2 and make predictions concerning how these tactics may be tied to the emerging brain-compatible research. Read the information below to check your predictions.

*A Safe, Comfortable Environment.* Research on learning has demonstrated that the brain serves as a filter on several levels. First, the brain selectively focuses on sounds, sights, and other stimuli that threaten our safety, often to the exclusion of other stimuli. A second priority is information resulting in emotional responses, and only as a last priority does the brain process information for new, non-threatening learning tasks (Sousa, 2001, p. 43). Thus, based on this filtering or prioritizing brain function, several implications for the classroom come to mind. Clearly, students must not be distracted by a sense of danger in their learning environment; they must feel safe and comfortable in order to be prepared to focus on new material (i.e., the school curriculum) that, by its very nature, is usually not threatening. For students who come from violent homes or communities, who may be picked on at school, or who may frequently feel punished by the school environment, learning new material will be almost impossible. However, physical safety is not enough; for students to feel comfortable, students must feel emotionally secure. Thus, a positive personal relationship with the teacher is paramount. Only in the context of such a comfortable, caring relationship will students with learning disabilities turn their attention to mastering new tasks.

Of course, this holds serious implications for students with learning disabilities because some students may suffer from a sense of frustration in certain classrooms. Students with disabilities may even experience some school classes as "hostile terrain" in which they are frequently punished by either their continuing failure in learning tasks or by the teacher. Clearly, this classroom environment will not support strong academic success for those students.

> The brain selectively focuses on sounds, sights, and other stimuli that threaten our safety, often to the exclusion of other stimuli.

*Comfortable Furniture.* As a part of structuring a comfortable learning environment, many teachers bring "house furniture" into the classroom and set up reading areas with a sofa and perhaps several comfortable chairs. Lamps are also used in brain-compatible classrooms for more "homelike" lighting, and some research has suggested that lighting closer to the red end of the light spectrum functions like a "wake-up" call for the brain.

A moment's reflection on the hardness of the wooden desks in most of our nation's classrooms—desks in which students must sit in for up to five hours each day—makes this a critical concern for many teachers. How would any adult like to sit in those wooden desks for five or six hours each day for an entire year? A different type of furniture can make our classrooms more user-friendly and facilitate learning.

*Water and Fruits.* Research has shown that the brain requires certain fuels—oxygen, glucose, and water—to perform at peak efficiency (Sousa, 2001, p. 20). Up to one-fourth of the blood pumped in our bodies with each heartbeat is headed for the brain and central nervous system, and water is critical for even blood flow. Furthermore, water is essential for the movement of neuron signals through the brain (Sousa, 2001, p. 23). Finally, we now know that fruits are an excellent source of glucose for the brain, and research has shown that eating a moderate amount of fruit can boost performance and accuracy of word memory (Sousa, 2001, p. 22). Thus, in brain-compatible classrooms, individual water bottles are usually present on the desks for students to take a sip whenever they need to; water is not a once-an-hour privilege in the brain-compatible class. Also, many teachers offer light fruits as snacks.

*Frequent Student Responses.* Students will learn much more when work output is regularly expected from them because students are generally much more engaged in the process of learning when they must produce a product of some type (again the differentiated instructional emphasis on the products of

Brain-compatible classes use comfortable furniture.

learning!) (Gregory & Chapman, 2002, pp. 37–46). For this reason, students must be required to do assignments, either in the form of class work or homework on any new material that is presented. The frequency of work expected from the students will be a major determinant of how much information students retain. However, the required work output doesn't have to be an entire page of problems—more frequent output of only a few problems each time will be much more useful in the learning process for students with learning disabilities (Sousa, 2001). More frequent, shorter assignments also give the teacher additional opportunities to check the students' understanding of the concepts covered.

*Learning With Bodily Movements.* Have you ever wondered why motor skills such as swimming or riding a bike are usually remembered forever, whereas the skills involved in speaking a foreign language are quickly forgotten if not constantly practiced? The emerging research on the human brain has addressed this question concerning motor learning versus higher order cognitive learning, and two findings have emerged. First, learning of motor skills takes place in a different area within the brain—the cerebellum, which is a more fundamental level—than learning of languages. Second, the brain considers motor skills more essential to survival. Because our ancient ancestors often had to run away

**Teaching Tip 1.3**

---

**Movement-Based Instruction in Higher Grades**

Carolyn Chapman (2000) shared a movement-based instructional technique for the upper grades, using movement to illustrate a map of the world. The body parts coupled with the following movements represent the locations of the seven continents and the equator. While facing a map of the world on the wall, students should be taught to do the following movements from memory.

1. Left arm/hand extended, palm open. While left hand is out, reach over with right fist, touch left palm, and say, "This is North America, where we live."

2. Now move right fist to touch forehead and say, "This is Europe."

3. Stick right hand out, palm open, touch that palm with left fist, and say, "This is Asia."

4. Put both hands on hips and say, "This is the equator."

5. Put hands together over one's belt to make a diamond (i.e., left thumb touching right thumb, left fingertips touching right fingertips) and say, "This is Africa. Part of Africa is above the equator and part is below it."

6. Stick left leg out and say, "This is South America."

7. Stick right leg out and say, "This is Australia."

8. Point to the floor between the feet and say, "This is Antarctica; very cold down there."

---

SOURCE: Adapted from Chapman, C. (2000, March 16). *Brain compatible instruction*. Paper presented at a nationwide telesatellite workshop, Tactics for Brain Compatible Instruction, Bishop, GA.

from predators or, alternatively, had to hunt for their own food, motor movement has been prioritized by the brain as a survival skill (Sousa, 1999; 2006). Consequently, motor skills, once learned, are remembered much longer than cognitive skills such as language usage. This suggests that whenever possible, teachers should pair factual memory tasks with physical movements. For example, various spelling works may be taught by moving the arms and legs to the shape of the letters in the word. Even in the upper grades, various memory tasks can be represented by physical movement, and this will greatly enhance retention for students with learning disabilities as well as most other students. An example of this movement technique for learning the location of the continents is presented in Teaching Tip 1.3. This modification involves a change in the process of learning for students who seem to do better with physical movement as a learning support. The contents of other maps can easily be represented with body parts, as can various other learning tasks (e.g., parts of a business letter).

Because our ancient ancestors often had to run away from predators or, alternatively, had to hunt for their own food, motor movement has been prioritized by the brain as a survival skill.

I recently assisted a student teacher in a secondary class to develop a movement technique for demonstrating the living processes at the cellular level in the human body. The lesson required an instructional demonstration that represented a cell involved in the processes of protecting the cell from bacteria while letting in various enzymes. Initially, three big male students stood together facing inward and locked their elbows tightly to represent the cell wall. We then pointed out that "the cell wall is very strong to protect the cell." Next, we selected a bacterium (i.e., another student) to try to break into the cell, with the cell wall holding that bacterium out. "Cell walls protect the cell from bacteria." Finally, we had a student, representing the friendly enzyme, move toward the cell wall to gain entrance. For our demonstration, we used one of the young women in the class, and the cell wall let that person in without delay. "Cell walls let in food and friendly enzymes." As you can see from these several illustrations, the only limit on the use of this technique in the upper grades would be the limit of the teacher's creativity.

*Learning With Visual Stimuli.* Although teachers have known that visual stimuli often enhance learning, this commonsense insight has been confirmed by the brain-compatible instructional literature (Sousa, 1999). Teachers should use color enhancements, size, and shape enhancements in developing lesson materials posted in the classroom because the human brain and central nervous system are specifically attuned to seek out novelty and differences in stimuli (Sousa, 2001, p. 27). Thus, highlighting the topic sentence of the paragraph in a different color for students with learning disabilities can be of benefit for them in describing the topic of the paragraph. Likewise, using different colors for different parts of speech (red for nouns, blue for verb, green for adjectives, etc.) can facilitate learning. However, to make color an effective learning tool, the teacher and the student (or the class) should specifically discuss why certain aspects of the material are colored differently and the importance of those colored items. Many computer-assisted instructional programs are making use of this technique today and include color highlights to teach syllabication and other reading skills. Again, this represents a modification of the learning processes for students with learning disabilities.

*Using Chanting, Rhymes, and Music.* Because music and rhythms are processed in a different area of the brain from language, pairing facts to be learned to a musical melody, or a rhythmic chant, can enhance learning. Most adults, on reflection, can remember the song that was frequently used to memorize the ABCs—the tune to *Twinkle, Twinkle Little Star*—and many students used that same song for other memory tasks in the higher grades—the periodic table or division math facts. Again, teachers have used this insight for a number of decades, but the emerging research on the human brain has documented the basis for enhanced learning when music and rhythms are used.

*Wait Time.* Students have learned that teachers will often call on the first one or two students who raise their hand after the teacher has asked a question in class. Thus, all that students with learning disabilities have to do is remain "invisible" for a few seconds (i.e., not raise their hand and not look toward the teacher), and the teacher will usually call on someone else. On average, teachers will wait only one or two seconds before calling on someone for an answer, and this period of time between the question and when an answer is called for is defined as "wait time" (Sousa, 2001, p. 128). However, students process information at different rates, and the brain research has demonstrated the importance of waiting for a few seconds (perhaps seven to ten seconds) after asking a question, prior to calling on someone for the answer. This increased wait time gives students who process information more slowly and deliberately a period of time to consider their answer and, it is hoped, raise their hand to volunteer a response to the teacher's question. For this reason, adequate wait time can be a critical component of learning for students with learning disabilities, many of whom do process information more slowly than others in the class.

*Student Choices.* Sylwester (2000) emphasized the use of choices for students. In short, if teachers want their students to make reasonable and informed choices when they are not in the context of the school, teachers must offer choices and coach students in making informed choices within the context of the classroom. Such choices may involve the options for demonstrating competence or understanding a set of facts or other choices among assignments on a particular topic.

*Using Students to Teach Others.* It has often been noted by veteran teachers that having students explain new information to other students can enhance learning, and the emerging research on the human brain has once again supported this instructional procedure. Teachers should get in the habit of presenting some information (the brain research suggests presenting new information at the beginning of the period for between ten and twenty minutes) (Sousa, 2001, p. 90) and frequently pausing during that presentation and then asking students to reflect on the new information together. The teacher should present information for two to three minutes, get to a stopping point, and then say something such as the following:

> All students with learning disabilities have to do is remain "invisible" for a few seconds (i.e., not raise their hand and not look toward the teacher), and the teacher will usually call on someone else.

> Turn to your learning buddy beside you, and take turns explaining the four points I just made. Let me know if you uncover any disagreements in what each of you heard.

The teacher should then move around the room for one to two minutes, listening to the discussions between the students and checking that the students do have a correct understanding of the information just presented. This instructional procedure will result in much higher retention than merely presenting new information in a lecture format because students will have to take personal responsibility for the material as they explain it to their peers.

## WHY SHOULD I MOVE INTO DIFFERENTIATED INSTRUCTION?

Before planning a differentiated lesson, however, we should consider the "Why" of differentiation. Why should teachers expend this effort to move into more diversified instruction? The best answer to that question—an answer which teachers across the nation respond quite positively to—is the extreme academic diversity in today's classes. In understanding differentiation, teachers need to conceptualize how differentiated lessons are unique from the more traditional lessons and the more traditional lesson plan, which was rooted in the "effective schools" and "effective teaching behavior" literature of the 1970s (Bender, 2005, pp. 27–29). The traditional lesson plan is a lesson plan format that is quite familiar to every teacher; it would typically present a series of instructional phases that were originally referred to as the "phases" of a lesson. These included: orientation to the lesson, initial instruction, teacher-guided practice, independent practice, check, and reteach.

It is interesting to note that, other than Tomlinson's work on differentiation, no theorist has reconceptualized how to develop a lesson plan during the last 35 years or so. In short, the traditional lesson plan is still found in almost every teachers' manual, in almost every subject across the public school years. Further, we should note that this lesson plan was developed at a time when classes were much less academically diverse than today. Specifically, researchers of the late 1960s and 1970s who developed the traditional instructional plan based their work on the types of classrooms and the types of students who were then prevalent in the public schools, and in that context of relatively homogeneous classes, the traditional lesson plan worked very well. For example, if a teacher taught in Grade 5 in the early 1970s, he or she could realistically assume that most of the students in that class were working on reading and math somewhere between grade level 3 and grade level 7—a very limited range of academic diversity indeed, by today's standards. While there would have certainly been some differences in the children's math or reading skills, there was a fairly narrow level of academic diversity within the class. Moreover, much of the effective schools research took place in classrooms prior to the full implementation of Public Law 94–142 in 1978; thus many students with special needs were excluded from the classes in which the traditional lesson plan model was developed. Specifically, students with learning disabilities were often educated for some portion of the school day in resource rooms, and students with other disabilities were not in the general education class at all during those years.

In contrast, in today's fifth-grade class it is quite likely that students' achievement levels in reading and math range from grade level 1 up through grade level 10 or 11. Our nation has made a commitment to educate all students in the general education class to the extent possible, and today's teachers face that fact daily in the highly diverse general education classroom. In spite of this increase in the range of academic skills present in the typical classroom, educators have not effectively re-conceptualized how teachers should conduct lessons to meet the demands of this increased academic diversity.

> Teachers will never see less diverse groups of kids in their classes than they see today; in contrast, academic diversity in the class is quite likely to increase over the next few years, as it is in our broader society. This is the best reason to differentiate instruction in the classroom.

Once teachers grasp that the traditional lesson plan in their instructional manuals is outdated by 35 years and doesn't fit well with today's highly diverse classes, it becomes a priority to learn how to differentiate in order to meet the needs of a more diverse group of learners. In point of fact, teachers will never see less diverse groups of kids in their classes than they see today; indeed academic diversity in the class is quite likely to increase over the next few years, as it is in our broader society. Thus, teachers need to offer a much wider array of instructional activities, in order to accommodate such diversity in the general education and special education classroom.

## PLANNING A DIFFERENTIATED LESSON

At this point, we should examine lesson planning for differentiated instruction. In a quest for simplicity, teachers should begin with the traditional lessons available to them in the teachers' manuals. As late as 2006, also every teacher's manual includes some version of the traditional lesson plan and thus some version of the concept of different "phases" in a lesson. While the terms may change from one curriculum to another (e.g., some texts use essential questions, "hook 'um activities" or "activate their understanding" rather than "orientation to the lesson," as one example), the fact is teachers have been encouraged to plan their lessons for the past 30 years around the concept of the traditional lesson plan. Further, that traditional lesson plan involves several specific assumptions as follows: (1) They all need the same instruction, (2) they are all at the same general instructional level, (3) all of their students will work together in a series of whole class activities, and (4) they will all move through these phases of instruction at the same rough pace. In today's highly diverse classes, these are no longer valid assumptions.

Consider these other assumptions that underlie this lesson plan. The fundamental assumption is that all students would follow this main line of instructional activities and that this sequence would facilitate learning for every student. Second, use of this traditional lesson plan presumed a relatively small level of academic diversity. For example, in order for this type of group instruction to work, one had to assume that students in Grade 5 were functioning somewhere around the Grade 5 level in mathematics—say between grade levels 3 and 6. Next, this lesson is based on the assumption that all students could and would learn in the same fashion if the teacher presented an appropriate lesson activity for each concept or construct to be mastered.

> Teachers have been encouraged to plan their lessons for the past 35 years on a set of assumptions that are no longer valid for today's highly diverse classes.

As Tomlinson (1999) stated so succinctly, the increasing diversity of students, diverse learning styles, and of learning needs in the general education classroom has effectively outdated the set of assumptions on which the traditional lesson plan is based. In fact, the traditional format has never truly worked for many students even in relatively homogeneous classes. For advanced students, this instructional sequence often leads to boredom in the early steps on any particular type of problem, since many advanced or gifted students may already have mastered the content prior to the teacher's initial instruction. Thus, those students would tend to be off-task by the time the teacher begins the later phases of the instructional lesson, and they might even begin to disrupt others in the class. For students who are more challenged, this model of instruction often failed to engage them because they may not have had the prerequisite skills necessary for the lesson. Consequently, many of those students demonstrate both off-task and disruptive behaviors, since they are bored with material that they cannot learn and are not engaged with the lesson activities. Therefore, as a result of teachers attempting to follow this series of direct instructional steps, many students in the typical class were bored and often misbehaved, and of course managing those problems takes the teacher's time away from delivery of the lesson activity to the other students in the class.

## A Differentiated Lesson Plan Example

In order to provide a comparison model of a differentiated lesson, imagine the following instructional lesson in Ms. Wheland's third-grade math class. The class includes 22 students, five of whom are special education students; two of those students have learning disabilities, with an overlay of hyperactive behavior. In addition, two of the other students in that class are gifted students. In schools today, this would seem to be a typical class. In this scenario, Ms. Wheland is teaching a math lesson concerning the aggregation of data, the creation of a tally table, and the eventual formulation of a frequency table summarizing those data.

The chart presented in Teaching Tip 1.4 shows a traditional lesson on the left and a series of differentiated lesson activities on the right for the same lesson. To begin this lesson with an attention-grabbing orientation activity, Ms. Wheland might ask students to identify their favorite dinosaur, since dinosaurs have become big Hollywood stars recently. She would hold up a picture of one of the five most recognizable dinosaurs and have a student at the dry-erase board begin to tally how many students like the T-Rex, the allosaurus, the raptor, or the stegosaurus. Once she has several sets of tally marks on the dry-erase board beside each of these, she may then say something like, "How can we summarize these data so they make sense?" Ms. Wheland would then ask for suggestions from the class, and she will eventually develop a frequency table with dinosaurs in one column, tally marks in the second column, and numerals in the third column (i.e. the actual count of the tally marks for that dinosaur). After this brief orientation activity, the traditional direct instruction lesson would suggest that Ms. Wheland begin to teach about tally tables, and ultimately frequency tables, using several more examples.

The differentiated lesson plan, however, offers an alternative approach. For example, it is possible that, after the orientation to the lesson and prior to initial instruction, some of the students have already mastered the concept. During the orientation phase of the lesson, several students may have looked ahead in the text and seen several examples of tally tables and frequency tables, and those students may have compared those to the ongoing example with the dinosaurs above. In short, even before the lesson is taught some students may already have grasped the ideas and concepts, and thus they may need a more challenging lesson. In the differentiated classroom, even

> Even before the lesson is taught some students may already have grasped the idea and may need a more challenging lesson, leading to differentiation of class activities.

## Teaching Tip 1.4

### A Traditional Lesson and Modifications for Creating a Differentiated Lesson

| Typical Phases of a Traditional Lesson | Differentiated Lesson Activities |
| --- | --- |
| *A. Introduction*<br>Cover tally tables and frequency tables | After the intro, break out one group (Omega group) to create a tally table on the floor, then rejoin main group |
| *B. Teacher-Guided Instruction*<br>Teach tally tables vs. frequency tables | Tear out a second group (Beta group) Complete Step 2 Activity to stand in the tally table on floor sorted by favorite singers |
| *C. Teacher-Guided Practice*<br>Have main group complete practice worksheet | Have two groups work together to evaluate each other's work |
| *D. Independent Practice*<br>Have students complete the Independent Practice | Omega and Beta groups rejoin mainline instruction or move into another enrichment activity |
| *E. Check*<br>Have Omega and Beta groups describe their activities to the entire class: continue with check activity | Reshuffle all students and reselect students who have it, and do enrichment activity |
| *F. Reteach Content as Necessary* | |

at this early stage in the lesson, Ms. Wheland would offer some differentiation in the lesson tasks.

Rather than continuing into the initial instruction phase for everyone in the class, Ms. Wheland can probably identify some students who have already mastered the concept. In other words, some of the more advanced students do not even need to be taught the lesson! Ms. Wheland can quickly check her assumptions with a quick assessment question or two directed to the group (e.g., "Do you think you could structure a tally table to collect data, and then transfer those data to a frequency table?"). For the students who indicate they could, she would tear out these students and provide some group work as an alternative instructional activity (Bender, 2005). Moreover, in differentiated classes, she might also place a few children who do not understand in that differentiated group, under the assumption that, if that group works together on a similar task, the students who know the content will be "teaching" the student who doesn't understand it.

### The Omega Group

We'll call the first group of students working on that differentiated activity the Omega group; this is the first group of students torn out of the mainline traditional lesson. Of course, you may use any terms you like to name these groups, as long as the names for the groups are nonsequential and thus do not indicate a quantitative or qualitative judgment on the skills or the intellect of the group. For the first activity of the Omega group, Ms. Wheland may hand them a preselected assignment sheet for a group work activity involving structuring such a frequency table. These five students would then be instructed to move to a separate section of the room to begin their group project.

In a differentiated lesson, the good news is that teachers usually don't have to create these alternative activities; these group project alternatives are usually described in the teacher's manual as "enrichment" activities or "reteaching" activities. Ms. Wheland, thus, provides a set of directions for that assignment as well as any necessary materials to the Omega group. For our example, imagine that she copied the following activity out of the math teacher's manual:

> This activity requires some floor space (15′ by 15′) and a roll of masking tape. Students will place masking tape on the floor to develop an outline for a frequency table. The rows will represent choices of students' favorite color for tennis shoes (teachers should select five specific colors as options). One column will be used for preferred color (red shoes, white, black, green, or blue shoes). The second column will be used for students to stand beside their preferred color of shoe, and the third for the numbers representing the count of persons preferring the various colors. Use the masking tape to develop an appropriate five by three grid for this activity.

Based on a set of instructions such as this, the students in the Omega group should be provided with a roll of masking tape, and then should do this activity in one corner of the room. Given that the next instructional phase—the teacher directed phase—typically takes approximately 15 minutes, the group activity for Omega group should be planned with that time frame in mind. The Omega group students would have to jointly plan what the frequency table would look like (remember they have a model on the dry-erase board), including how big the boxes are going to be in order to hold various groups of students, and how the categories in the tally table should be organized.

In this activity, the box on the left is the "category" box, where pictures of shoes of different colors are placed, and that box need be only large enough to accommodate the pictures. In contrast, the box in the middle must be large enough for a number of students to stand in, as they stand by their preferences. The box on the right end will hold only a digit or two that summarizes the data in the middle box, so it can be somewhat smaller. The point is that the Omega group has to figure all of this out—including the number of categories and the relative size of the boxes—while working as a group.

Given the considerations in designing this floor grid, it is possible for the Omega group to make a mistake in their work. For example, while the Omega group may develop a five-by-three grid, they may forget to consider the relative size of the boxes. Specifically, rather than merely a set of tally marks—as in the earlier example on the dry-erase board—the grid on the floor must include a second column of boxes that are large enough to hold a number of students. Thus, the challenge of making this grid is a more complicated activity than the example in the lesson orientation. This activity, while focusing on the lesson of data aggregation, is more intellectually demanding than the lesson activities offered to the mainline instructional group.

### The Mainline Instructional Group

It is relatively easy in this classroom scenario to note the differentiation of lesson demands. After only a two- or three-minute orientation to the lesson and prior to having "taught" the lesson, Ms. Wheland has two groups of students in her class—the Omega group and the mainline group—the group of students who were not torn out for the differentiated activity. As the Omega group does its work, Ms. Wheland will engage in teacher-led initial instruction as she normally would for the mainline instructional group. She may use a variety of activities from the instructor's manual, but she should make certain that a variety of activities are offered that are engaging and as interesting as the work the Omega group is doing.

Further, in order to hold the student's attention, Ms. Wheland should consider reorienting the class furniture a bit. If she placed the Omega group in the front left corner of the classroom, she should then move to the back right corner and tell the mainline instructional group to, "Turn your desks around so you can see the floor activity we'll be doing." By doing that move, she accomplishes two critical things:

1. She has oriented the mainline instructional group to have their backs to the Omega group—and thus both groups are more likely to pay attention to their assigned task; and

2. She has placed herself in a position to lead instruction for the mainline instructional group and still visually monitor the Omega group.

We should now consider the differentiated activities Ms. Wheland is using in the class. In a math class of 22 students, if she selected five students for the Omega group, only 17 students would remain in the mainline instructional group during the initial instruction, and they are likely to be more homogeneously grouped. Consequently, Ms. Wheland's instruction is likely to be more highly targeted to those she is teaching in the mainline group for the following reasons:

- Ms. Wheland's teaching will be more focused for this mainline group.
- Ms. Wheland will be less distracted by the gifted or advanced students who would be bored had they remained in the mainline instruction.
- Ms. Wheland is more likely to make eye contact more frequently with 17 students as compared with 22 students. Thus she will have a better sense of the level of understanding of this reduced number of students.

- Finally, Ms. Wheland's examples during this teaching phase are more likely to be on target for these students than if she were still working with the entire class.

This is, of course, the main strength of differentiated instruction—it is strategically targeted instruction aimed at the learning needs of individual students in the class, and encourages the teacher to offer more highly targeted instruction. In this sense, differentiated instruction is "higher impact" instruction than merely following the traditional lesson plan from the teacher's manual.

### The Beta Group

However, merely offering one group of students a different task does not constitute differentiation, and we should consider what happens after Ms. Wheland completes the initial instruction for the mainline instructional group. By 20 minutes into the lesson, Ms. Wheland will have completed both the lesson orientation and the initial instructional phase for the mainline students. Also, the Omega group will probably have completed its work in designing the grid on the floor. Thus, at this point in the traditional lesson it is probably time to form another group for another differentiated activity. Again, with a few judicious questions, the teacher can again identify a second group of perhaps five or six other students from the mainline group who now understand the data aggregation concept and do not need the next phase of the traditional lesson—teacher-guided practice. We'll call this group the Beta group. Again, Ms. Wheland would select this group from the mainline instructional group and provide a differentiated assignment.

For example, this group may be provided the assignment to work with the Omega group to "test out" the large frequency table grid that has been developed. The Beta group could be given two or three frequency table assignments based on student preferences for (1) favorite musicians, (2) favorite video games, or (3) favorite presidents. Of course at this point in the lesson, the Omega group will also need another assignment. It would be perfectly appropriate to use them to work with the Beta group to develop these activities for later classroom use. However, Ms. Wheland may wish to give them a separate assignment that involves writing several data aggregation problems for subsequent classroom use, or she may merely invite them to rejoin the mainline group of students for the next 15 minutes or so.

Again, we should consider what is happening in Ms. Wheland's class at this point in the lesson. First, note that Ms. Wheland's class will be quite differentiated only 15 minutes or so into the day's lesson. Specifically, after she oriented the students to the lesson, she tore out the Omega group, and after the initial instruction phase, she tore out the Beta group. Thus, after 15 to 20 minutes, five students in the Omega group will be doing a second tear out assignment, the Beta group will be testing the grid on the floor with several sample problems, and the mainline instructional group will include only 11 students who are receiving highly targeted, direct instruction from Ms. Wheland. Again, Ms. Wheland's instruction will be increasingly focused on these students in the mainline group who have not yet grasped the idea, and these students in turn will get the additional attention that they need from the teacher. Thus, differentiated instruction is very effective, strategically targeted teaching (Bender, 2005).

We should note here that many practitioners miss this critical aspect of differentiation; some believe that differentiation is a "rehash" of multiple intelligences instruction or merely good brain-compatible instruction. Nothing could be further from the truth. In fact, the very essence of differentiation is provision of highly divergent instructional activities targeted to the learning capabilities and styles of the learners. Thus, good "differentiation" takes place before the class even begins—when a teacher is carefully planning lesson activities and critically thinking about which activities might work best with particular students.

> The very essence of differentiation is provision of highly divergent instructional activities targeted to the learning capabilities and styles of the learners.

## How Much Differentiation Is Appropriate?

Often teachers feel a bit overwhelmed when they first consider implementing differentiated instruction. They may be concerned with the time it takes to plan multiple activities for the class, and certainly relying on the traditional lesson plan is easier than planning a dynamic, differentiated lesson. Sometimes, in doing workshops on differentiation, I'm challenged by teachers who state, "You can't teach that way; there aren't enough hours in the day to do all of that planning!"

In response, teachers should know that not every daily lesson needs to be highly differentiated. First, many whole class activities can and do actively engage learners with various learning styles. Activities such as gaming activities, video/computer–based presentations, interactive simulations, role play, and many other whole class activities are excellent instructional activities for the entire class, and when a teacher is using these activities, little differentiation will be necessary. Thus, as a general guideline that does make this approach to teaching more possible, teachers should consider planning and implementing a differentiated lesson only for some of the days in a given instructional unit; I typically recommend that two or three days per week should be differentiated in a given subject area, while other highly engaging, whole class activities may be used on the other days.

Another version of that same time constraint issue involves the question of "How many groups should I plan for in the class?" It is difficult to address the question concerning how much differentiation is needed in any specific class or during any specific lesson. There is no obvious rule for how many different groups should be formed in any class for any particular lesson, but there are several points we can consider that teachers may use as guidelines. First, the differentiated lesson format presented here requires that a teacher create a differentiated group after each of the first two or three phases in the traditional lesson. Thus, differentiated groups would be formed after the orientation to the lesson, after the initial instruction phase, and perhaps, after the teacher-guided practice phase as well. When various veteran teachers have implemented this differentiation in general education classrooms, they indicate that, pending appropriate selection of kids for the various groups, teachers can manage up to three differentiated groups of kids in the class.

The second point involves not overdoing it! To be specific, at some point in every lesson, this process of continual group formation breaks down. For example, after the teacher completed the initial instruction and tore out the Beta group, he or she would be working with a mainline group of students who have not grasped the concept after the initial instructional phase. According to the traditional lesson plan, these students would move into teacher-guided practice. However, if the students still do not have the basic concept at that point, why would any teacher force them to move into the next instructional phase? In fact, for students who do not grasp a concept after initial instruction, the teacher should move directly to the "reteach" phase anyway and perhaps present the concept in a different way. Alternatively the teacher may wish to try a peer tutoring approach at that point, and see if the peers of the child lacking comprehension can explain the concept more effectively to the challenged student.

Also, it is possible that there is some confusion among some of the members of the Omega and Beta groups. While initially believing that they understood the concept, it is possible that some of them did not have an adequate grasp of the idea after all. Thus, some of those students may need to rejoin the mainline instructional group.

As these examples show, in a differentiated class, the instructional groups are quite fluid, frequently formed for specific short term tasks, and then merged again into the mainline instruction. Teachers should never be reluctant to form a differentiated group for brief specific activities or to re-include those same students in the mainline instruction should that become necessary. This fluid differentiation is the very substance of a differentiated lesson.

## Guidelines for Planning a Differentiated Lesson

With these ideas in mind, we can now identify the general guidelines for modifying a traditional lesson in order to transform it into a differentiated lesson. Note that these are merely guidelines, and that every teacher should, based on his or her understanding of the individuals in the class as well as the demands of the subject content, adapt these to the specific needs of the students. These guidelines are presented in Teaching Tip 1.5.

## Results of Differentiation

Teachers who have chosen to move into differentiation for instruction have generally found that many of the anxieties they had about such instruction did not materialize. For example, many teachers are initially concerned about the issue of management of varied groups within the classroom. Of course, every class includes some students who, at least initially, should not be selected for less supervised differentiated activities, since their behavior patterns necessitate close teacher supervision. However, teachers typically find that after the class as a whole gets accustomed to this learning format, even those behaviorally challenged kids can participate meaningfully in tear out activities. In fact, one teacher provided me with the following idea of how to get a child with verbal aggressive tendencies to participate in a differentiated group. After she moved to differentiated instruction for three days a week, she continued to

## Teaching Tip 1.5

### Guidelines for Planning a Differentiated Lesson

1. *Subdivide early and often.* The teacher in a differentiated class should provide many differentiated activities. In fact, teachers employing differentiated instruction will subdivide their class much earlier in the lesson than is usual in the direct instruction model, and will do so much more frequently. For this reason, differentiation offers the most effective instructional option for students at all levels of ability in the class. When teaching within a differentiated instructional lesson, teachers should form either a homogeneous group or a heterogeneous group of students for an alternative instructional activity after each phase in the traditional lesson plan. For heterogeneous groups, teachers should select some students who have grasped the concept and some who haven't, by exercising judgment concerning who can work effectively in a group and who can or will work together.

2. *Never plan just one activity when you need two or three!* The academic diversity in today's elementary classes often necessitates the presentation of the same content in multiple ways, so I suggest that each time a teacher plans one activity, he or she plans at least one more and subdivides the class, with some students doing one and some doing the other. While creative teachers can always generate interesting instructional ideas, many ideas can be found in today's teachers' instructional manuals, and certainly instructional manuals of the future will feature differentiated lessons rather than a traditional (or mainline) of lesson activities. These differentiated ideas today are typically included as "enrichment" or "alternative teaching" ideas. In most cases, teachers merely need to select these activities from the curriculum ideas presented.

3. *Use the various differentiated activities more than once in the unit.* In the example above, the Omega group was the first to develop a frequency table on the floor. On subsequent days within that unit of instruction, other students in other groups may also be challenged with that activity. Further, it is perfectly acceptable for a particular student to be included in several groups doing the same activity. That would merely be a good example of a repetitive instructional technique!

4. *Modify alternative activities to address different multiple intelligences.* The teacher in the example above, while using the grid activity in her class, provided an activity that emphasized several intelligences, including spatial, logical/mathematical, and interpersonal. Can this activity be modified and subsequently used to involve other intelligences? If the assignment were to blindfold a student, and have him or her provide verbal directions for the formulation of the grid on the floor without watching the process, could linguistic intelligence be strengthened?

5. *Use what you have in the local community!* Using examples in the students' community can involve students more and motivate them to complete the math. For example, in farming communities, tying math problems to local crop sales can be quite effective. For students in urban areas, describing math problems in terms of the types of clothes or tennis shoes that are in vogue can motivate students more than simply using whatever math problems are on the page. If students live near a major historical park, teachers should consider history examples that could be tied to that local resource, with an emphasis on something like, "What national history took place in our town?"

*(Continued)*

(Continued)

Teachers in every field should use examples from the community whenever possible. One interesting type of assignment for some differentiated groups is to rewrite each of the math word problems in a particular unit using some local example. The others in the class can then use those problems for their practice work. This results in more "authentic" learning than some of the math problems presented in the standard math texts.

6. *Tie students in emotionally.* We now know that, prior to learning, the student must sense emotional safety in the learning environment. Further, if teachers can tie the content of a lesson to an emotional hook, students will become more involved in the content. Discussions of sociology in terms of the various racial groups in the community might be one illustration of this idea.

7. *Use differentiated instruction for inclusive classes.* While including students with significant disabilities in general education classes is not new, the use of differentiated instruction as a basis for inclusion is. The overall fit between inclusion and differentiated instruction is almost perfect; again we owe another tribute to Carol Tomlinson, PhD, for her groundbreaking work on this concept. Teachers should jointly plan to use differentiated lessons in inclusion classes. Moreover, with both a general educator and a special educator in the class, the monitoring of the differentiated groups is much more easily managed!

8. *Continue some traditional lessons.* I encourage teachers not to attempt differentiated lessons each and every day. While lectures seem ineffective with many students today, other aspects of traditional instruction work wonderfully, including group project activities, whole class discussions of video- or media-based examples, student presentations, and independent student research. These instructional activities should always be an important component of learning in the elementary classroom.

One question I am frequently asked is, "How often should teachers differentiate?" I usually tell teachers to aim for a highly differentiated lesson structure perhaps three days each week, and on the alternate days utilize more traditional instructional procedures, such as those mentioned above. I believe that this will provide an appropriate mix of activities and will create an effective classroom learning environment where the needs of all students can be met. I also find that teachers respond to this suggestion positively; while teachers have a difficult time seeing themselves teaching three or four groups of students in different tasks during each 15-minute segment each day of the week, they can see themselves doing this two or three days each week and using other effective whole-group tactics on the other days.

9. *Teachers should "test the waters" of differentiated instruction tentatively.* Once a teacher decides to attempt differentiated instruction, he or she should try this approach in a successful class—a classroom that seems to be working well. The teacher should also initially do this in an area of the curriculum that students know well. This will effectively increase the teacher's comfort zone, and will be more likely to result in a pleasant teaching experience than trying this new teaching paradigm in a challenging class. Also, testing this idea in a class that is not presenting challenges is more likely to result in initial success. After that, teachers can expand into other, more challenging classes. Moreover, teachers who have moved into this slowly, and have seen it work as both they and the students grow to understand this instructional system, have stated that teaching is simply much more fun this way!

exclude him, knowing he would eventually ask, "Why can't I ever work over there?" That not too subtle request put the teacher in a perfect negotiating position to work with that child. Thus, the teacher

- waited until the child requested to be placed in a differentiated group
- negotiated with the child about his or her problem behavior

Finally, because the training of most teachers in schools today was formulated on the traditional lesson plan model, some teachers cannot bring themselves to believe that learning will take place in differentiated groups. Some teachers even view these unsupervised groups as disasters waiting to happen. However, experience with this type of instruction will show the inaccuracy of these fears. Even highly skeptical teachers, upon trying this approach, have subsequently stated that, once they moved to a differentiated instruction format, they found that students do learn from each other in the differentiated groups, and that this instructional format results in increased student learning overall.

Finally, the ultimate reason to undertake differentiation stems from the fact that this is highly effective teaching. All teachers who are under pressure today to address the state standards based curriculum that is now mandated by every state department of education should consider differentiation as one approach. This learning format will result in improved instruction compared to whole class, traditional instruction. The chart in Teaching Tip 1.6 lists the typical results reported by teachers once they begin the transition to a truly differentiated classroom.

## SEVERAL DIFFERENTIATED INSTRUCTIONAL IDEAS

### Cubing

As an example of the type of differentiated instructional modification that typifies the differentiated classroom, several authors have suggested the idea of cubing (Cowan & Cowan, 1980; Gregory & Chapman, 2002; Tomlinson, 2001). Cubing is a technique that will assist students to consider a concept from six points of view, by giving students suggestions on how to conceptualize a particular concept. While envisioning the six sides of a cube, the student is told that each side represents a different way of looking at the idea (as presented by Gregory & Chapman, 2002, pp. 1–15).

| Cube Sides | Function | Use Terms Like |
| --- | --- | --- |
| Side one | Describe it | recall, name, locate, list |
| Side two | Compare it | contrast, example, explain, write |
| Side three | Associate it | connect, make design |
| Side four | Analyze it | review, discuss, diagram |
| Side five | Apply it | propose, suggest, prescribe |
| Side six | Argue for/against it | debate, formulate, support |

### Results of Differentiation Reported by Teachers

1. *Provision of Varied Instruction.* This approach offers the most effective instructional option for presenting appropriate instruction for all students in today's classes.

2. *Increased Involvement of Advanced Students.* The advanced kids in this procedure will be more challenged and thus less likely to get bored and engage in problem behaviors.

3. *Varied Behavior Management Concerns.* Management of an increased number of instructional groups will be a concern, and the teacher should move into differentiation slowly for this reason. However, students who would otherwise be bored with traditional lessons will be more engaged in this instructional model, and it is possible that these behavior management results will effectively even things out for the teacher in the differentiated lesson.

4. *Improved Instruction for Those Who Need It.* As the mainline group gets smaller, the instruction for that group is likely to improve, since the teacher is concentrating on a smaller group. Thus, the teacher is providing increased support for the students who really need the help on a particular lesson. This will tend to increase learning—thus increasing test scores—on average for the entire class.

5. *Provision of the Best Instruction for Everyone.* Differentiated instruction encourages teachers to offer the most effective enrichment/instruction to kids across the ability spectrum. Teachers must make the mainline group activities as varied, as novel, and as exciting as any of the alternative assignments for the tear out groups.

6. *Effective Use as a Model for Inclusive Instruction.* Teachers can readily see the comfortable fit between the use of multiple differentiated groups and the demands of the inclusive classroom. Differentiated instruction provides one of the most effective models for inclusion of students with learning disabilities that is currently available.

7. *Teachers Become Used to Teaching This Way.* Once teachers try this instructional model, particularly if they test this model in an academic area within their comfort zone, they typically find that they enjoy this type of teaching. While all teachers differentiated to some degree, teachers who devote themselves to this approach often state that they would not like to return to teaching in a traditional fashion.

Using this idea of cubing, the same concept is looked at from six different perspectives, and the various levels of knowledge of different students may be addressed in this context (e.g., some students consider initial descriptions of the concept, whereas others are involved in analysis of it). In the differentiated classroom, the teacher will intentionally construct his or her lessons based on this cubing concept, and that will emphasize to the students that concepts covered in this fashion are multidimensional and must be considered in a more complex fashion. In studies of President Kennedy's and President Johnson's response to North Vietnam's and China's growing influence in the nation of

South Vietnam, the various sides of the cube would suggest that students should do the following:

| | |
|---|---|
| Describe that response | Buildup of U.S. troops in Vietnam |
| Compare the response | To French buildup of troops fifteen years earlier |
| Associate the response | To other presidents' attempts to limit power of other nations in other regions (e.g., President Wilson's response to Germany in 1916) |
| Analyze the response | Discuss the reasoning of Presidents Kennedy and Johnson |
| Apply alternatives | Suggest how other presidents chose to limit influence at other times (e.g., the Jefferson administration's response to pirates around the African coast) |
| Argue the response | Debate the wisdom of Kennedy's and Johnson's response |

In using this cubing concept, the lessons will be differentially aimed at one or more aspects of the cube, and students will be exposed to instruction based on a broad array of activities (Gregory & Chapman, 2002, pp. 1–56). Thus, the differentiated classroom is founded on a variety of lesson formats, learning processes, and products that are developed by the students.

## Tiering

Another concept that is central to differentiation is the concept of tiering instruction, or offering instruction on the same content at varied levels of challenge (Bender, 2005; pp. 34–36). Tiered instruction involves differentiation of work expectations based on the needs and capabilities of the individual student. It typically involves setting a series of lesson plans and activities in place that allow for some variation of the content. For some students with learning disabilities, mastery of an exhaustive set of standards will not be either possible or practical in the instructional time allowed, particularly given the series of time constraints and expectations involved in today's standards-based curricula. Thus identification of, and tiered instruction on, a subset of critically important standards may serve the student as a "rubric" for understanding of other additional content. Further, this may offer the option of having those students master that subset of the content, as opposed to mastery of none. Thus, the student will be in an enhanced academic position. Note that this does not mean eliminating content from the required standards-based curriculum; rather, it involves increased emphasis on critically important content, with the expectation that those concepts become a solid backdrop for further mastery of each standard.

Tiered lessons may be formulated according to a variety of options (Bender, 2005). Variation may be built into lesson plans in terms of variation in

- The challenge level of the tasks required. Teachers may require some students to concentrate on the first, basic standards for a given unit, while moving on to more challenging standards for other students.

- The teaching/learning process for the task. Some students may respond to problems modeled by the teacher, whereas others may respond better to problems modeled by a peer study-buddy.
- The learning product. Students with a learning strength in music may need rhythms or chants to assist in memory tasks, while students with strengths in spatial orientation/kinesthetic may need an art project or movement task respectively. More examples of this type of instruction are provided in Chapter 2.

Upon first hearing of the concept of tiered lessons, many teachers express concern about the amount of time that it takes to develop tiered lesson activities, and this is a valid concern; it does take more time to plan one's instructional unit based on tiered lessons on some of the days in that unit. However, teachers quickly realize two things that make this form of instruction worth their while. First, in developing several tiered variations of instructional activities this year, the teacher will already have them developed for the same unit next year. Second, teachers can frequently use students to develop some of these instructional activities (e.g., having a group of students develop a skit that demonstrates the critically important content in an instructional unit). Finally, once teachers offer tiered instructional options during some of their lessons, they will find an improved response from the students to those lessons and behavioral management concerns will tend to decrease somewhat; this, in turn, frees up more of the teacher's time for actual instruction and instructional planning.

With those advantages of tiering in mind, the guidelines for tiering are relatively simple and straightforward:

- Specify the multiple intelligence and/or learning style strengths of students, and tailor the lessons to a variety of learning styles (again, this is explained further in Chapter 2).
- Plan multiple lesson formats for some lessons in the unit (not for each lesson!). However, as one rule of thumb on "practice instruction" days, teachers should never plan one lesson for a group of students when several activities are required because of their varied levels of comprehension of the material.
- Offer multiple optional assessment plans, with student choice as to how they wish to demonstrate competence. Many alternative/authentic assessment options are available and should be offered. This is explored more fully in Chapter 6.

## WHAT'S NEXT?

With this overview of differentiation and these examples of differentiation tactics in mind, teachers can begin to see the emphasis on offering a wider array of highly engaging instructional activities than has historically been offered in the class; indeed almost any brain-compatible strategy or tactic can be a "differentiated" strategy if it is proven by research and results in a more engaging and diversified set of class activities. The remainder of this text focuses on various strategies and tactics that enhance the teacher's capability in differentiation. These strategies and tactics involve any number of instructional innovations that increase the variety and complexity of the academic activities presented for students, and thus will be of benefit for students with learning disabilities as well as for many other students in the general education class.

# Universal Design for Differentiation 2

*Organizing the Class for Differentiation and Personal Responsibility for Learning*

---

**Topics Included in This Chapter:**

- ✓ Universal Design
- ✓ Structuring the Classroom for Differentiation
- ✓ A Recommended Room Arrangement Model
- ✓ Teaching Tactics for Students With Learning Disabilities
- ✓ The Self-Monitoring Strategy
- ✓ The Responsibility Strategy

---

## UNIVERSAL DESIGN

When considering an increased emphasis on differentiation of instruction, teachers should reflectively evaluate every aspect of their teaching. In particular, the class should be organized in a way that will facilitate differentiated instructional activities, students working together, and personal responsibility for learning. One guiding principle available today to assist in such a reflective exercise is the concept of universal design. Universal design is a newly emerging concept that impacts how classroom educational activities are structured (Abell, Bauder, & Simmons, 2005; Acrey, Johnstone, & Milligan, 2005; Pisha & Stahl, 2005). The concept of universal design originally dealt with universal construction design to alleviate barriers for individuals with disabilities, but has now been expanded rather drastically to involve universal design for curriculum and assessment practices (Acrey, Johnstone, & Milligan, 2005).

As inclusive class placements for students with learning disabilities have become increasingly popular, more and more students with learning disabilities are included for longer periods of time in the general education class. Unfortunately, little change has been noted over the years in terms of how general education teachers delivered instruction (Abell, Bauder, & Simmons, 2005), and developing and understanding of universal design can assist all teachers in structuring their classes for increased differentiation.

Perhaps an example of universal design would help illustrate this important concept. Imagine a student with a learning disability—specifically a reading disability—as well as a vision problem. In short, reading is quite likely to be a significant challenge for that student. The principle of universal design would suggest that curriculum materials for that student should be designed such that his or her understanding of the content in the textbooks is not limited by virtue of that disability. In this example, the school should order textbooks that are available both in print and online, and presumably in the online version of the texts, the text size could be modified to make the print larger, which in turn would alleviate some of the negative effects of the vision problem. Moreover, texts could be equipped with various features to facilitate cognitive understanding, such as a feature allowing instantaneous access to definitions and/or verbal pronunciations of unknown words. Thus, this type of universally designed text could alleviate both the visual problems and the cognitive disabilities in understanding new vocabulary terms. Many states—Kentucky is one example—have now passed legislation designed to facilitate adoption of universally designed curricula (Casebier, 2002).

Universal design principles have been presented in a variety of ways (Abell, Bauder, & Simmons, 2005; Acrey, Johnstone, & Milligan, 2005), and these typically include several factors such as

- *Equitable Use*—the same means of use should be provided for all users, identical use where possible
- *Flexibility in Use*—options should include clear choices for users and adaptability of use
- *Simple and Intuitive Presentation*—use should be intuitively obvious, eliminate complexity, accommodate a wide range of literacy and language skills, and provide prompting and feedback on use
- *Perceptible Presentation*—information should be presented in several redundant modes such as visual, verbal, pictoral, and tactile
- *Tolerance for Error*—elements should be arranged to minimize hazards and errors
- *Appropriate Size and Space*—use should provide clear line of sight for important information and adequate space for the use of adaptive devices

When these principles are applied to school curricula, a number of instructional strategies have been recommended (Abell, Bauder, & Simmons, 2005; Acrey, Johnstone, & Milligan, 2005; Pisha & Stahl, 2005) including

- frequent summarization of big ideas and concepts
- implementation of scaffolded supports for instruction
- implementation of explicit instructional strategies based on clear goals and methods of instruction
- streaming of lecture notes and assignments for students online where possible
- use of digital books and text materials
- utilization of built-in academic supports (e.g., spell checker, grammar checker, calculator)
- use of electronic communications (teacher to/from student, and teacher to/from parents)
- provision of various assessment accommodations

With the universal design concept as a background organizer, this chapter continues with a focus on organizing the classroom for differentiation and then suggests two strategies for differentiation, both of which should increase a student's sense of ownership of his or her own learning activities, self-monitoring, and responsibility strategies. All of these organizational ideas and instructional practices are founded in the universal design concept, and teachers may expect to see that overriding concept as the governing factor for classroom organization and instruction for the next few decades.

## STRUCTURING THE CLASSROOM FOR DIFFERENTIATION

Well-structured lessons prevent boredom.

Most beginning general education teachers adopt a structure, organization, and instructional style for their class that is similar to the structure used by their cooperating teacher in their student teaching experience. These teachers arrange their desks in a similar fashion to their cooperating teacher, and many find that they teach in a similar fashion. Of course, this often allows a beginning teacher to implement a class structure that is appropriate and effective because most cooperating teachers are selected because they are believed to be effective teachers. In fact, most beginning teachers do not specifically reflect on their overall classroom organization until one or two years after they begin their career.

However, veteran teachers—teachers with two or more years of successful experience—tend to engage in a reflective process related to structuring their classroom and often improve on their room organization as well as their instructional technique. This reflection can be critical in dealing with students with learning disabilities because both instructional and disciplinary endeavors must begin with intentional structuring of the classroom to maximize effective instruction and minimize disruption. Students with learning disabilities do tend to function much more effectively in a highly structured environment, perhaps because disorganization tends to be one general characteristic of this group of students. Thus, regardless of whether the organizational issue deals with desk arrangement in the class or with the most effective method to study a particular section of the text, highly structured classes and assignments tend to facilitate learning among students with learning disabilities. When contemplating the instruction for students with learning disabilities, a teacher's first emphasis should be a general reflection and reconfiguration of the instructional space and instructional approaches to more easily differentiate the instruction in the class and thus accommodate the needs of students with learning disabilities in the differentiated classroom.

> Veteran teachers—teachers with two or more years of successful experience—tend to engage in a reflective process related to structuring their classroom and often improve on their room organization as well as their instructional technique.

## What Is Classroom Structure?

In helping teachers reflect on their classroom structure, the first issue concerns definition: what is classroom structure? Is it merely how desks are arranged, or does it also involve how assignments are structured and delivered, or perhaps how students spend their time? In my work, I have found it more effective to use an expanded definition of classroom structure. Of course, the first level of classroom structure involves how one organizes one's classroom furniture and equipment to create appropriate space for learning, and some consideration must be given to placement of desks, arrangement of computers, and so on. However, classroom structure in the differentiated classroom also involves several other levels of structure, such as how a teacher, as the instructional leader, structures the time of the students, as well as how the specific assignments are structured. High levels of organization within specific assignments will tend to result in better performance from students with learning disabilities, and this chapter, as well as several other chapters in this text, will include suggestions for specific structuring of assignments. Again, the overriding concept of universal design will guide these and subsequent chapters, and on that basis Teaching Tip 2.1 provides some additional thoughts on the components of classroom structure.

---

**Teaching Tip 2.1**

**Universal Design: Structuring the Classroom**

For our purposes in this text, classroom structure means the following:
- The arrangement of furniture
- The establishment of learning centers
- The arrangement of instructional computers and other devices
- The instructional grouping patterns for students
- The orchestration of students' learning time
- The structure of communication between teacher and students, as facilitated or restricted by elements of classroom organization
- The structure of the content of the lessons, the learning processes, and the instructional activities aimed at increasing the variety of learning activities

---

## A Self-Evaluation of Classroom Structure

Perhaps one way to get an understanding of how one structures one's classroom is to use an informal self-evaluation and look critically at the structural components of the class. A number of years ago, I saw the need for teachers to reflectively consider their class structure and, within that context, a variety of instructional techniques for students with learning disabilities. As a result, I developed the Bender Classroom Structure Questionnaire (BCSQ) (Bender, 1992). The indicators on the BCSQ were specifically selected to represent the types of instructional practices that encourage differentiated instruction and have been shown to facilitate effective inclusion of students with learning disabilities. This questionnaire has now been used in a variety of subsequent research investigations on how both special and general education teachers structure their classroom (Bender, 1992; Bender, Vail, & Scott, 1995). As a reflective exercise, teachers may wish to use this form and evaluate their classroom structure and differentiated instruction practices. The questionnaire is presented in Teaching Tip 2.2.

### REFLECTIVE EXERCISE: EVALUATION OF MY CLASS

Using the BCSQ, determine the number of instructional indicators that represent instructional tactics used at least once each week in your class. Consider which techniques you would like to use more frequently, and note some ideas on how you may implement those ideas this week.

**Teaching Tip 2.2**

## The Bender Classroom Structure Questionnaire

Name _____          Date _____

This self-evaluation rating is designed to measure various aspects of instructional environments in order to assist in making useful instructional improvements. It will take about fifteen minutes to complete. Please fill in each blank below, then rate your classroom on each question on the 5-point scale ranging from "only rarely" (i.e., less than once a month) to "almost always" (almost every day).

How many years have you taught school? _____

In what areas are you certified to teach? _____

How many years have you taught students with disabilities? _____

What is your current teaching assignment? _____

How many courses specifically on teaching students with disabilities have you completed?
_____

How many students with learning disabilities are in your class currently (during any one period)? _____

How many students total are in that class? _____

|  | Only Rarely | | | | Almost Always |
|---|---|---|---|---|---|
| 1. I keep the lesson moving along quickly | 1 | 2 | 3 | 4 | 5 |
| 2. The class reviews assignments when I return them | 1 | 2 | 3 | 4 | 5 |
| 3. Several students may be walking around in my class at any one time retrieving materials | 1 | 2 | 3 | 4 | 5 |
| 4. Students receive verbal praise from each other | 1 | 2 | 3 | 4 | 5 |
| 5. I encourage students to share various techniques that may help them memorize facts in class | 1 | 2 | 3 | 4 | 5 |
| 6. The class emphasizes correction of worksheets | 1 | 2 | 3 | 4 | 5 |
| 7. Students must raise their hand before standing | 1 | 2 | 3 | 4 | 5 |
| 8. I ask, "How did you learn that?" or some other question to focus on learning strategies | 1 | 2 | 3 | 4 | 5 |
| 9. I insist that doors be shut and students remain in their seats to minimize distractions | 1 | 2 | 3 | 4 | 5 |
| 10. New material is introduced fairly rapidly | 1 | 2 | 3 | 4 | 5 |
| 11. I suggest particular methods for remembering | 1 | 2 | 3 | 4 | 5 |
| 12. Peer tutoring is used to assist slower learners | 1 | 2 | 3 | 4 | 5 |
| 13. I emphasize the importance of working quietly | 1 | 2 | 3 | 4 | 5 |
| 14. I determine early in the year if a student needs the same concepts covered in different ways | 1 | 2 | 3 | 4 | 5 |
| 15. I use physical touch, such as a pat on the back, as a reinforcer | 1 | 2 | 3 | 4 | 5 |
| 16. I praise students for successful work whenever possible | 1 | 2 | 3 | 4 | 5 |
| 17. Students are encouraged to help each other informally on learning tasks | 1 | 2 | 3 | 4 | 5 |
| 18. I try to determine how students learn best | 1 | 2 | 3 | 4 | 5 |

|  | Only Rarely | | | | Almost Always |
|---|---|---|---|---|---|
| 19. I use reading materials that highlight the topic sentence and main idea for slower learners | 1 | 2 | 3 | 4 | 5 |
| 20. I individualize in my class when necessary | 1 | 2 | 3 | 4 | 5 |
| 21. Students are taught to use their own inner language to give themselves silent task instructions | 1 | 2 | 3 | 4 | 5 |
| 22. I use class privileges as rewards for work | 1 | 2 | 3 | 4 | 5 |
| 23. I use a specialized grading system that rewards effort for pupils with disabilities | 1 | 2 | 3 | 4 | 5 |
| 24. I use several test administration options such as oral tests or extended time tests | 1 | 2 | 3 | 4 | 5 |
| 25. Directions for educational tasks are kept simple and are demonstrated to achieve clarity | 1 | 2 | 3 | 4 | 5 |
| 26. Differential curriculum materials are selected based on the learning characteristics of particular students | 1 | 2 | 3 | 4 | 5 |
| 27. I routinely vary the instructional level for different ability children doing the same task | 1 | 2 | 3 | 4 | 5 |
| 28. Instructional materials are varied for different students | 1 | 2 | 3 | 4 | 5 |
| 29. I constantly monitor the on-task behavior of my students | 1 | 2 | 3 | 4 | 5 |
| 30. I individualize my class for low-ability students | 1 | 2 | 3 | 4 | 5 |
| 31. Visual displays and transparencies are used in class to aid comprehension | 1 | 2 | 3 | 4 | 5 |
| 32. Students use self-monitoring to record daily academic and behavioral progress | 1 | 2 | 3 | 4 | 5 |
| 33. A token economy is used for reinforcement | 1 | 2 | 3 | 4 | 5 |
| 34. I use the dry-erase board frequently to explain concepts | 1 | 2 | 3 | 4 | 5 |
| 35. I have a discipline plan in effect | 1 | 2 | 3 | 4 | 5 |
| 36. Cooperative learning groups are frequently used | 1 | 2 | 3 | 4 | 5 |
| 37. I use graphic behavioral contracts with students to improve behavior | 1 | 2 | 3 | 4 | 5 |
| 38. I use advance organizers to assist students in comprehension of difficult concepts | 1 | 2 | 3 | 4 | 5 |
| 39. Students complete direct daily measures of progress in class | 1 | 2 | 3 | 4 | 5 |
| 40. A set of class rules is on display in my class | 1 | 2 | 3 | 4 | 5 |

### Scoring the BCSQ

Scoring the BCSQ may be done either formally or informally. Because these techniques generally represent "best practices," a higher score on the BCSQ is more desirable and indicates that a teacher is employing the instructional techniques that should facilitate successful inclusion. To get a general score, one may merely total the circled score for each indicator, resulting in a score that ranges from 40 (the lowest possible score) to 200.

Bender (1992) reported that a group of 127 general education teachers in Georgia (from Grades 1 through 8) generated a total score of 143 (SD = 19) on this questionnaire. A group of 50 teachers from New Jersey (Grades 3 through 12) generated a score of 139 (SD = 19) on this scale. These general scores may provide some indication of how you provide varied instruction for students with learning disabilities in your class.

SOURCE: From "The Bender Classroom Structure Questionnaire: A Tool for Placement Decisions and Evaluation of Mainstream Learning Environments" by Bender, W. N. (1992). *Intervention in School and Clinic, 27,* 307–312. © 1992 by PRO-ED, Inc. Used with permission.

Use of this questionnaire will give teachers an initial sense of how well and how frequently they may be implementing various tactics and strategies that have been proven successful for students with learning disabilities in the inclusive general education class. Of course, no one would be expected to implement all of these differentiated instruction practices at any given time or in any one specific period. Still, students will be more successful in classrooms where a variety of these approaches are frequently implemented, and this tool will provide the caring, thoughtful teacher with one mechanism that can foster reflective thought on how one teaches. On the basis of this informal self-evaluation, we may now consider the various components of classroom structure.

## Instructional Grouping for Differentiation

In inclusive classes, teachers frequently teach eighteen, twenty-two, or twenty-eight students during each lesson, and to individualize the learning in any form, teachers many years ago began to form instructional groups within the class. Of course, differentiated instruction is based, in part, on effective grouping of students, as has been discussed previously. There are a variety of options available to general education teachers for structuring instructional groups (Gregory & Chapman, 2002, pp. 57–79). However, many teachers believe that the large numbers of students in the typical inclusive class necessitate whole-group instruction. In fact, this single teaching mode accounts for the largest percentage of the instructional time even in today's classrooms (Elbaum, Moody, Vaughn, Schumm, & Hughes, 2000). However, within the past decade, there has been some debate about the effectiveness of whole-class lecture/discussion as an instructional model, and research has suggested that small-group, teacher-led instruction may be a more effective instructional procedure for students with and without disabilities (Elbaum et al., 2000). Clearly, the general education classrooms should be structured to facilitate, as much as possible, various small-group instructional arrangements.

As illustrated in the differentiated lesson plan in chapter one, the differentiated class is characterized by small groups of students, either homogeneous or heterogeneous groups of students—doing tasks that are tailored to their particular learning styles or multiple intelligence strengths. However, students may likewise be placed in tutoring pairs. As an alternative grouping arrangement, research has also supported the use of students to tutor each other (Mortweet, et al., 1999; see also the subsequent chapter on peer tutoring). Even when students with special needs are involved in the tutoring, the research has been generally supportive. This is why a number of indicators on the BCSQ deal with varying the instructional group arrangement rather than always using a whole-group, teacher-led discussion. In fact, the differentiated classroom is characterized by a variety of instructional grouping patterns.

Recently, in many general education classes, the older instructional model of lecture/whole-group discussion seems to be giving way to more appropriate models of instruction that will benefit students with learning disabilities in their academic efforts, and classes that offer a variety of instructional grouping options will tend to be more successful for students

> Students will be more successful in classrooms where a variety of instructional approaches are frequently implemented.

with learning disabilities. However, as noted previously, there is still a place for whole-group instruction in the inclusive class. Activities such as morning exercises, simulation games, sharing time, multimedia instruction, class presentations, and social skills instruction seem to be activities that would be most effective as whole-group activities. Furthermore, these whole-group activities would require a space in the class—an area that allows all of the students to attend to the teacher at the same time. Consequently, any class will need to be physically arranged to accommodate a variety of instructional activities, including whole-group activities; teacher-led, small-group instruction; peer tutoring; and individual learning opportunities. These classroom arrangements will facilitate the teacher's ability to differentiate instruction.

### REFLECTIVE EXERCISE: HOW DO I TEACH?

1. What percentage of the time in my classroom do students spend listening to me deliver content?

2. What percentage of the time in my classroom are students engaged in group work on projects with their peers?

3. What percentage of the time in my classroom are students engaged in individual inquiry?

4. What percentage of time in my classroom are students engaged in creating products resulting from their learning?

# A RECOMMENDED ROOM ARRANGEMENT MODEL

Considerations of room organization for both inclusive general education and special education classes must be guided by concerns about the need to differentiate instruction, the types of activities planned, the number of students in the class, and the behavioral or academic problems demonstrated by those students. Both inclusive general education classes and special education classes, although involving different numbers of desks, may still be arranged based on a few straightforward considerations.

In an ideal classroom, space would be used to allow for varying instructional tasks at the same time. Although not every classroom has optimum space, Figure 2.1 presents an initial suggestion for arrangement of desks, learning centers, study carrels, computers, and so on in a general education classroom to facilitate differentiated instruction.

This suggested room arrangement includes areas for large- and small-group instruction, as well as individual seatwork, computer-assisted multimedia instruction work spaces for floor based activities, and work in study carrels. Perhaps the most notable feature is the semicircular desk arrangement. In this arrangement, students with challenging behaviors should be seated near the teacher, but not together, because they would model inappropriate behaviors for each other. Furthermore, using this arrangement, the teacher can more easily monitor students' behavior visually. Specifically, the teacher can visually monitor each student's work while assisting a particular child; he or she should merely remain outside or behind the semicircle. This arrangement allows the teacher to face almost all members of the class almost all of the time (even when leaning over a student's shoulder to assist on a particular assignment). This ease of visual monitoring will tend to improve behavior and assist students with learning disabilities in the class. A similar semicircular arrangement is also appropriate for special education classes, which generally include smaller numbers of students.

Again, to facilitate differentiated instruction for students with learning disabilities, a teacher must physically arrange his or her classroom to allow for instructional variations, and a variety of instructional areas will be necessary. These typically include various learning centers, a teacher's worktable, and a group work/social skills area. These areas will, of course, vary according to grade level, but differentiated instruction will make higher levels of success for students with learning disabilities more likely. Below are brief descriptions of the various instructional areas that may be appropriate in your class.

## Learning Centers

### Learning Center Structure

Learning centers should be included to allow for modifications and adaptability of instruction within the classroom context in almost every classroom setting because the activities and information in the learning center can provide one way to address the diverse needs of a wide variety of learners, including students with learning disabilities (Gregory & Chapman, 2002, pp. 105–110). For the elementary education classroom, learning centers in both reading/language arts and math would seem to be a minimum requirement. Other teachers, depending on their class grade level and teaching responsibilities, also include a center for science, social science, and/or other subject areas.

**Figure 2.1**    A Suggestion for Arrangement in a General Education Classroom

For secondary subject area teachers, various centers may be adapted for the subject content. Many history and/or social studies classes, as one example, may include versions of the following learning centers:

| | |
|---|---|
| Daily Living Center | Government Center |
| Commerce Center | International Relations |
| Political Center | Timeline Art Center |

As these examples suggest, in content areas (e.g., in this case, history) in departmentalized schools, the learning centers should be based on general concepts or issues within the topic that are not particular to a given unit of study. Thus, in the history centers mentioned above, the teacher would place materials in these centers that were appropriate for the various historical periods and/or different units of study, and although those materials may change when studies of one period conclude and another historical period begins, the learning center names and orientations remain constant throughout the year.

### Learning Center Materials

The materials that should be included in each learning center should be obtained on a continuous basis and subsequently labeled and organized in a way to facilitate the student's retrieval of appropriate materials. Students with learning disabilities should be taught how to obtain their own work materials from the learning center because this will assist them in the development of organization skills as well as instill an ability to focus on the specific task at hand. Thus, the learning centers must be a model of efficient organization of materials.

> A semicircular desk arrangement allows the teacher to face almost all members of the class almost all of the time.

Initially, in establishing a learning center, the teacher should inventory the class and the school's media center to get some idea of the educational materials already available. These may include books, charts or wall posters, bulletin board kits, computer software, educational games, manipulatives, and game boards for multiple uses. Most teachers develop sets of worksheets that may be used, either individually or by small groups of students, and place these worksheets in the learning centers as well. Remember, teachers should seek out the media specialist and inquire whether materials are available for long- or short-term loan to a particular class. In many cases, with special permission, the teacher may be able to check out materials for use for a week, a multi-week instructional unit, or a month. Teachers will also want some materials for lower level readers to use. This will enable almost all students to obtain assignments from the learning center.

In each learning center, teachers should provide some instructions for the students working there. Many teachers post "activity cards" on the wall in each learning center that instruct the students on the activities that must be accomplished to receive credit for completing the work in that center. To make these learning centers accessible for students with learning disabilities, teachers should keep the instructions for these activities simple and clear. Also, classes may have various levels of assignments present on these activity cards and instruct some students to complete the "Level 1" activities while others complete "Level 2" or "Level 3" activities. Again, such differentiated instruction must be provided to meet the needs of students with learning disabilities or other diverse learning needs.

## Teacher's Worktable and Desk

The teacher should have a worktable located such that the teacher can scan the entire room while working with one student or a small group of students at a time. This will greatly facilitate the teacher's use of small-group, teacher-led instruction, as the recent literature recommends. Although this requires that the worktable be located somewhere at the front of the room, it does not have to be the focal point within the front area. As long as the teacher has easy visual contact with all members of the class, any location toward the front of the class will do.

I generally recommend that teachers not use the teacher's desk as the worktable. The desk is typically used for writing assignments and grading papers at the end of the day, along with bookkeeping matters, such as lunch money collection and attendance records. Consequently, desks tend to be cluttered with a lot of noninstructional material—some of which may be confidential— and if students are working with a teacher on that desk, the opportunities for misbehavior are multiplied. In contrast, the worktable can be kept clear of everything except the instructional materials in use for the students working there. Also, with a worktable somewhere in front of the class (to ease the teacher's visual monitoring of students), the teacher's desk may be located at any place in the room.

## Group Instruction Area

Many social activities, such as sharing time, group games, or class projects, require or may best be facilitated by a group instruction area. In inclusive classes, this area may, of necessity, be the student's desk area because twenty-five or thirty desks do tend to fill up a room. However, in some smaller classes, the students may complete group projects on the floor in a nonfurnished, carpeted corner of the classroom. These group instruction areas generally include some nearby shelves for storage. A screen for viewing films together may also be placed here.

> Students with learning disabilities should be taught how to obtain their own work materials from the learning center because this will assist them in the development of organization skills as well as an ability to focus on the specific task at hand.

The teacher's desk usually doesn't have room for student group work.

## Computer/Multimedia Instruction Area

The use of computers and/or multimedia instruction (e.g., a language master that reads words) has increased rather dramatically in recent years. One would be hard-pressed to find a modern classroom without some multimedia equipment that facilitates learning. In fact, this provides teachers today with a critically important tool for offering differentiated instruction to students with learning disabilities, as well as other learners with special needs. In most general education classrooms, computers will typically be located along the wall, and the electrical outlets may determine where these are placed. In consideration of disciplinary issues for students with learning disabilities, the teacher should make certain that there is ample room between these instructional tools such that distractible and/or aggressive students cannot find too many opportunities for misbehavior. Generally, these should be located in study carrels that are designed for computers and prevent one student from observing another's work.

## Study Carrels

Study carrels are essential in classes that include students with learning disabilities because these students may be easily distracted by movement in the class. Generally, several study carrels can be lined up along one wall and may be used for individual seatwork for certain children. In some cases, the students feel better about using these areas if they are labeled an "office." If the class includes a student who is reluctant to work in a study carrel but would benefit from it, the teacher can create a "private office" environment for him or her, merely by labeling a study carrel. One important fact to remember is that if a student with a learning disability needs a place to work that is free of visual distraction, one must be provided to assist the student to remain task oriented.

In addition to limiting the visual distractions that may be present in the work area, teachers should note that many students with learning disabilities are quite disturbed by auditory distraction. Consequently, soft music played continuously in class becomes a type of background noise and may facilitate higher work output from those students. However, one person's relaxation music is another person's distraction. In some instances, teachers may wish to provide soft music through earphones to only one or two students. Regardless, teachers must be careful of the effects of such music on all of the students in the class.

## TEACHING TACTICS FOR STUDENTS WITH LEARNING DISABILITIES

As indicated previously, this entire text may be considered as a set of ideas for differentiated instruction, and each subsequent chapter presents specific instructional tactics for varying the instruction in the general education classroom. However, in addition to the class-structuring guidelines presented earlier and the ideas in the subsequent chapters, some general teaching tips for differentiating instruction can be offered as initial guidelines for teachers when challenged by students with learning disabilities.

First, the general structure of most classrooms can be greatly enhanced and can be specifically designed to facilitate active engagement by students with learning disabilities by following just a few simple guidelines. Ten tactics for fostering higher levels of attention are presented in Teaching Tip 2.3.

Next, consideration must be given to structuring lessons and developing alternative lessons for students with learning disabilities. Teaching Tip 2.4 presents ten tactics, described originally by Mathes and Bender (1997b), that can guide inclusive teachers in structuring lessons for students with learning disabilities.

### Ten Tactics to Foster Attention Skills

1. *Use a highly structured class.* In talking with students and giving instructions in the class, teachers should clearly differentiate between the "floor group work area" and the study carrel area. This will help students with learning disabilities understand your vision of the types of work to be done in each area, and higher structure will assist students with learning disabilities in their work overall.

2. *Display classroom rules.* Having a set of three to five positively stated class rules on display can alleviate many behavior problems. Rules that state what a child should do (i.e., "quietly complete your work") are usually best, and by referring to the rules when a student is misbehaving, the teacher can, in effect, differentiate himself or herself from the discipline process and make the misbehavior an infraction against the class (i.e., against the rules of the class).

3. *Post a daily class schedule.* Even for teachers in departmentalized schools with forty-five-minute periods, a posted schedule of the day's activities can greatly assist students with learning disabilities in understanding what they should be doing.

4. *Train on class cues.* Teachers should train students to recognize certain cues in the context of the classroom. Depending on the age level, some teachers have a small bell that they ring to get the attention of the class. Others use cue cards that are mounted in front of the class about how to begin a lesson ("get out the book," "get out your notebook," "get out your pencil," etc.). As the cue, the teacher may merely need to point to the chart.

5. *Use two desks.* Hyperactive students frequently get out of their seat without knowing why. For some students, assigning a second desk across the room gives them the ability to move from one to the other periodically (not every five seconds, of course!) without the teaching having to attend to an "out-of-seat" misbehavior.

6. *Use intentional distractions.* For some students with learning disabilities, movement is not only necessary—it is essential. For many of these students, providing them something to do with their hands may alleviate more disruptive movements in the class. This is the concept of "intentional distractions." In short, providing a child with a pen from which he or she can constantly remove and replace the cap provides something to stay busy with during a class discussion (and is usually much quieter than loud pencil tapping on the desk). For pencil tappers, teachers should demonstrate "quiet tapping" (which is tapping on the back of one's own hand). It provides more sensation/stimulation and is quieter than tapping on the desk.

7. *Keep desks clear.* Remind students to keep their desks clear and uncluttered, except for materials and texts used at the moment.

8. *Visually monitor students.* The teacher should arrange the class to allow for visually monitoring the students at all times. Provide verbal reminders to return to task, as needed.

9. *Provide color organizers.* Colored organizers can assist many students in organizing their assignments and notebooks. The teacher should work out a color-coded organization system appropriate for the students.

10. *Use peer buddies.* Setting up a peer buddy system in which pairs of students check each other's readiness to begin the next lesson can greatly assist students with learning disabilities in getting through transitions between lessons.

**Teaching Tip 2.4**

### Ten Tactics for Structuring the Lesson for Students With Learning Disabilities

Differentiated instruction focuses on the three components of content, process, and product. The tactics presented here offer teachers an array of possibilities to differentiate both the content and the process of instruction.

1. *Provide clear directions.* Providing clear, simple, instructions, particularly during transitions, can assist students with learning disabilities to focus on the learning task.

2. *Provide a lesson activity outline.* A lesson outline will help students focus on what will come next in the small-group or whole-class discussion. From the basis of this outline, the teacher should teach outlining and note-taking skills. This assists students with the learning process.

3. *Develop tiered activities.* To modify the instructional content, when a teacher develops a lesson, he or she should develop a minimum of two worksheets that present the same content at different levels. The use of alternative assignments that cover the same material is one cornerstone of differentiated instruction.

4. *Plan for frequent breaks.* Students who are hyperactive (including many students with learning disabilities) will need frequent opportunities to stand up and move around the classroom. Building thirty-second "stretch-breaks" every fifteen minutes or so into your class period can help alleviate many problems.

5. *Use physical activities.* For all students in public schools, learning is facilitated by movement. Even the learning of the highest achievers in senior high can be enhanced by movement. The emerging research on "brain-compatible education" has documented that the learning process can be greatly enhanced by movement, and if teachers can tie particular facts to a physical movement and have the class practice that movement, the students with learning disabilities will be much more likely to remember that fact. While some teachers feel that this type of movement-based instruction may be appropriate only in lower grades, a moment's reflection on the popular song/movement combination "YMCA" will indicate that even adults prefer learning associated with movement.

6. *Use clear worksheets.* Teachers should make certain that they do not unintentionally build distracters into the lesson by using cluttered worksheets or instructional materials. For students with learning disabilities who may be visually distracted, such worksheets can result in failure on the assignment.

7. *Decrease task length.* For some students with learning disabilities, a worksheet activity that involves fifty math problems will always appear to be an insurmountable assignment. However, if the teacher prints only fifteen math problems on the worksheet, the student will immediately attempt that assignment. The teacher may then give another worksheet with another fifteen additional problems on it.

8. *Check assignment notebook.* All teachers should require that students write assignments in a notebook, and while many do this, some teachers never check the notebooks. For students with learning disabilities, checking that they have written down the correct assignment can be critical, and the process of checking emphasizes the importance of noting the assignment due dates.

9. *Develop alternative assessments.* Looking at the product of student learning is a critical component of differentiated instruction, and students with learning disabilities, on some occasions, know more about a topic than a paper-and-pencil test can allow them to demonstrate. Teachers must develop and use alternative assessment practices, such as grading open-book homework or class work or using daily databased performance measures. These will be covered in a later section of this text.

10. *Turn to your partner and explain.* The idea behind "turn to your partner and explain this concept" is rooted in the truth that what one can explain, one understands. When conducting a lesson, at various points (perhaps every five minutes or so, when the class finishes a certain amount of material), teachers may have the students pair up and explain those several points to each other, as a comprehension check. Building this routine into the lesson can greatly enhance comprehension of students with learning disabilities.

## REFLECTIVE EXERCISE: USING DIFFERENTIATED INSTRUCTION

To better understand the overall construct of differentiated instruction, use the list of ten indicators in Teaching Tip 2.4 and identify each instructional modification as either a modification of content, process, or product. Then consider which of these tactics you are currently using in your own class.

## THE SELF-MONITORING STRATEGY

Throughout our nation's history, teachers have taken the perspective that education is a process done to and for students. Students have been viewed as passive recipients of the educational process, and active participation of students in planning their own learning has not been encouraged. Of course, this view was a serious problem for students with learning disabilities because these students are much more likely to become distracted and uninvolved in the learning process than other students.

In contrast, the concept of universal design would suggest that teachers teach in a fashion that encourages students to take personal responsibilities for learning. Daniel Hallahan and his coworkers, in their studies of students with learning disabilities, postulated that students must begin to plan a task and assume some personal responsibility for their efforts in attending to a task and learning (Hallahan, Lloyd, & Stoller, 1982; Hallahan & Sapona, 1983). Recent research on the human brain and learning has demonstrated the importance of "executive function." Executive function is the term that represents the thought processes involved in planning a task, or considering how to undertake a task, rather than specifically doing a task. Prior to actually initiating a task, successful students take a moment to consider what a task requires and how a task may be accomplished; this is executive function.

Educators now realize that the success of education is in large measure dependent on the responsibility students take for their own learning and behavior (McConnell, 1999), and the brain-compatible instructional literature has supported this view quite dramatically; students must be involved in their learning. Furthermore, students with learning disabilities must be intimately involved in the tasks of learning if learning is to take place. In short, it is very difficult if not impossible to teach anyone anything unless they are willing and motivated to learn. The self-monitoring strategy presented here addresses this requirement for individual responsibility for attending to the educational task. Self-monitoring also enhances the student-teacher relationship in a direct fashion; by implementing this strategy, teachers are asserting that students are responsible for their own behavior, and students will attentively understand this strategy as a sign of respect, as recommended by most theorists on class discipline today (Marzano & Marzano, 2003; Stipek, 2006).

The self-monitoring strategy involves teaching a student how to pay attention; attention in the context of the classroom typically means the ability to repeatedly check one's own orientation and focus on a particular task (McConnell, 1999). Whereas early research concentrated on the use of self-monitoring to enhance attention of students with learning disabilities (Hallahan & Sapona, 1983), more recent work has focused on using self-monitoring procedures to enhance classroom readiness behaviors (McConnell, 1999; Snyder & Bambara, 1997) or eliminate behavioral problems that may prevent learning (Shapiro, DuPaul, & Bradley-Klug, 1998). Each of these areas is discussed below.

> Teachers today know that education is an active process and requires student involvement.

## Self-Monitoring for Attending Behavior

Although teachers through the ages have often told children to "pay attention," very few teachers have ever taught a child exactly *how* to pay attention. The fact is, teachers tend to assume that students know what we mean by that frequently used phrase, "pay attention." However, experience with students with learning disabilities tells us that these students do not stay on task as well as other students; in short, students with learning disabilities do not really know how to pay attention. The attention problems and poor task orientation often noted among students with learning disabilities suggest this deficit in the skill of paying attention among these students. Thus, the initial application of self-monitoring procedures involves teaching students with learning disabilities how to attend to a learning task. This training procedure may be done in either the special education classroom or the inclusive general education classroom by following the steps below.

> Educators now realize that the success of education is, in large measure, dependent on the responsibility students take for their own learning and behavior.

*Identification of the Student.* As with all aspects of differentiated instruction, the first task of the teacher is to select the right strategy for the student. Again, this will depend on the teacher's relationship with the students, the teacher's knowledge of the students in the class, and the types of learning problems demonstrated by each student. In fact, there are several guidelines for identifying the type of students for whom self-monitoring may be an effective intervention. First, the self-monitoring strategy to improve on-task behaviors is intended for students with learning disabilities who demonstrate rather benign attention problems, such as poor task orientation or an inability to complete worksheets on time, rather than overtly aggressive behaviors. This strategy is not effective for children who do not perform their schoolwork because of violent behaviors or noncompliance in the classroom, though variations of self-monitoring procedures have shown some success, even with these severe behavior problems.

Second, self-monitoring should not be used when a student is being introduced to a new topic or learning task. This is not a strategy to be used during the initial instruction phase of learning. Rather, self-monitoring is most effective when a student is in the independent, drill-and-practice phase of learning. Seatwork and paper-and-pencil tasks in any basic skill area are appropriate. Also, self-monitoring is more effective for "speeding up" a student than for increasing the student's accuracy in problem completion.

*Components of the Self-Monitoring Tactic.* During a self-monitoring project, the student is trained to periodically ask himself or herself a very simple question— "Was I paying attention?"—to increase his or her attention skills. The only materials used in this self-monitoring procedure are (1) a "record sheet" on which the student will record his or her attention behavior and (2) a cue to record the behavior—usually a tape recorder with an audiotape of a bell that rings periodically. In making a record sheet, the question above should be printed on the sheet at the top, along with places to answer either "yes" or "no" to the question. This question provides the student with a simple memory technique that tells what should be done (i.e., paying attention to the worksheet and the problems it contains). Whenever the student is cued to consider his or her "attention behavior," the student should silently ask, "Was I paying attention?" He or she should then answer the question on the record sheet and return immediately to work. A record sheet is presented in Teaching Tip 2.5.

> Teachers tend to assume that students know what we mean by that frequently used phrase, "pay attention."

The second component of the tactic is an audiotape that will cue the student to ask the question and mark the record sheet. A cassette tape should be prepared by the teacher that presents a series of bell tones. The time interval between these bell tones should vary from ten to ninety seconds, but the average time interval should be around forty-five seconds. Teachers can easily make such an audiotape by sitting at a piano and recording a middle "C" (or any single note) at various intervals for approximately twenty minutes. The student will use the tape as the cue to ask the question above, mark an answer, and return to work. For inclusive classes, teachers may wish to have the student use headphones to listen to this bell tone to prevent disruption to other students during seatwork.

*Initial Instruction in Self-Monitoring.* Hallahan et al. (1982) also recommended a series of instructional steps by which the teacher actually teaches attention skills. On the first day, the teacher begins instruction by suggesting that the student could finish the work faster and

> The self-monitoring strategy to improve on-task behaviors is intended for students with learning disabilities who demonstrate rather benign attention problems.

## Self-Monitoring of Attention Record Sheet

Was I Paying Attention?

| YES | NO |
|-----|-----|
|     |     |
|     |     |
|     |     |
|     |     |
|     |     |
|     |     |
|     |     |
|     |     |
|     |     |
|     |     |
|     |     |
|     |     |
|     |     |

more accurately by learning how to pay attention better. This possibility is discussed with the student in an attempt to have the student accept responsibility for the self-monitoring procedures. The dialogue presented in Teaching Tip 2.6 was recommended by Hallahan et al. for this initial self-monitoring instruction.

## REFLECTIVE EXERCISE: REVIEWING THE DIFFERENTIATED INSTRUCTION COMPONENTS

Review the dialogue presented in Teaching Tip 2.4, and consider the three differentiated instructional components (content, process, and product). What specific teaching techniques are presented in this dialogue that represent one of these components of differentiated instruction? For example, the "modeling of attention and inattention" presented here would be one instructional example of modifying the processes used to teach self-monitoring. Can you see other examples of these three processes in this dialogue?

This dialogue presents a discussion of exactly what paying attention means. The teacher should sit in the student's desk and model eye contact with the educational task (worksheet, the reading book, or the blackboard). Also, the teacher may model several off-task behaviors such as staring out the window, playing with a pencil, or talking to other students. The student should then complete a work activity consisting of a set of problems in any subject area while wearing a headset and listening to the bell tone. Each time the student hears the bell, he or she should mark either yes or no on the recording sheet and return to work.

### Teaching Tip 2.6

#### Self-Monitoring Instructions

"Johnny, you know how paying attention to your work has been a problem for you. You've heard teachers tell you, 'Pay attention,' 'Get to work,' 'What are you supposed to be doing?' and things like that. Well, today we're going to start something that will help you help yourself pay attention better. First we need to make sure that you know what paying attention means. This is what I mean by paying attention." (Teacher models immediate and sustained attention to task.) "And this is what I mean by not paying attention." (Teacher models inattentive behaviors such as glancing around and playing with objects.) "Now you tell me if I was paying attention." (Teacher models attentive and inattentive behaviors and requires the student to categorize them.) "Okay, now let me show you what we're going to do. Every once in a while, you'll hear a little sound like this." (Teacher plays a tone on tape.) "And when you hear that sound, quietly ask yourself, 'Was I paying attention?' If you answer 'yes,' put a check in this box. If you answer 'no,' put a check in this box. Then go right back to work. When you hear the sound again, ask the question, answer it, mark your answer, and go back to work. Now, let me show you how it works." (Teacher models entire procedure.) "Now, Johnny, I bet you can do this. Tell me what you're going to do every time you hear a tone. Let's try it. I'll start the tape and you work on these papers." (Teacher observes the student's implementation of the entire procedure, praises its correct use, and gradually withdraws his or her presence.)

SOURCE: Hallahan, Lloyd, and Stoller (1982).

On the first day, the initial instruction in self-monitoring takes about fifteen or twenty minutes. This should be repeated (in a briefer form) for the first several days of self-monitoring. The student should use the self-monitoring procedure every day during the initial stage of instruction. This instruction will require ten to fifteen days. At that point, the teacher will have a number of work activities on which the student had the opportunity to finish the work in class; these successes should be pointed out to the student.

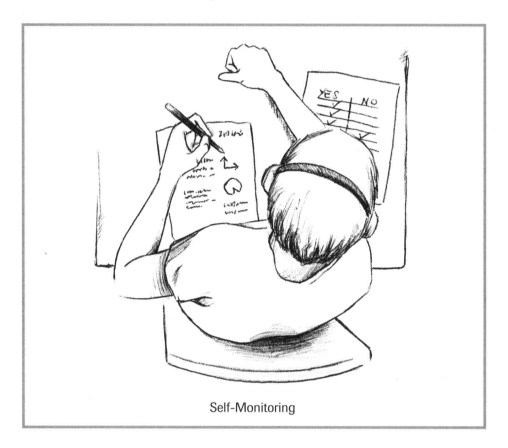

Self-Monitoring

*Weaning Procedures.* The goal of self-monitoring is the establishment of good attentional skills based on the "habits" of attention, rather than being outwardly dependent on behavior charts and tape-recorded bells. Consequently, teachers should wean the students from the record sheet and bell tone, leaving the "habit" of continually monitoring one's own attending behavior.

Initially, the teacher should wean the student from the bell tones. After a successful intervention period using the full self-monitoring procedure (usually ten to fifteen days), the teacher simply indicates that the student's success in attending to task has increased and that it is no longer necessary to listen to the taped bell sounds. During this weaning phase, the student is encouraged to continue monitoring on-task behavior by asking, "Was I paying attention?" whenever he or she thinks about it. The student should mark the record sheet, and if the student was paying attention, he or she should self-praise (e.g., give yourself a pat on the back!) and then return to the worksheet.

During the next weaning phase, the student is weaned from the recording sheet. The student is given instructions to ask the question whenever the thought occurs and to praise himself or herself for being on task and then to return quickly to the task. Generally five or six days are recommended for each phase of the weaning.

## Efficacy Research on Self-Monitoring of Attention

The research on self-monitoring has demonstrated that this procedure works for students across the grade levels in both special education and general education classes, making this an excellent strategy for the differentiated classroom in almost any school setting (Barry & Messer, 2003; McConnell, 1999; Shapiro, DuPaul, & Bradley-Klug, 1998; Snyder & Bambara, 1997). Next, this procedure may be taught to students in groups. Finally, research has shown that almost every student with a learning disability can improve his or her attention using this procedure (Digangi, Magg, & Rutherford, 1991). The on-task behavior of some students has more than doubled (from 35 to more than 90 percent), which is roughly like doubling the educational time in any given year for children with learning disabilities!

Research has now addressed a number of additional questions about the use of self-monitoring. First, for students with attention problems severe enough to warrant medication, this self-monitoring procedure can dramatically enhance attention skills above the effects of medication alone (Barry & Messer, 2003; Harris, Friedlander, Saddler, Frizzelle, & Graham 2005; Mathes & Bender, 1997a). Thus, even for students on medication for attention problems, self-monitoring procedures should be used. Of course, this holds serious implications for instruction in almost every general education classroom today. Specifically, how can any teacher justify not implementing a self-monitoring procedure for students on medication for attention problems when we have solid evidence that this procedure will help?

To emphasize the importance of this tactic for students with learning disabilities, allow me to share a personal example that demonstrated how critical this technique can be. As a relatively new higher education faculty member, I taught this self-monitoring technique in a methods class for special education teachers at Concord College, in Athens, West Virginia. In that

> Research has shown that almost every student with a learning disability can improve his or her attention using this procedure.

class, I had an older woman, who was the mother of a fourteen-year-old daughter who had recently been diagnosed with learning disabilities. After assigning some readings on this self-monitoring idea, the mother chose to try it with her daughter while the young girl completed her homework. The mother later shared with me that this seventh-grade girl would sometimes do homework for up to three hours per night and still not accomplish a great deal. Of course, with self-monitoring implemented, that student began to complete her homework in about ninety minutes each weekday evening, and both the mother and daughter were ecstatic, but that's not the end of the story.

Within just a few weeks, the daughter had requested that her teacher also allow her to do self-monitoring on her school tasks in class (that's when I heard about this little experiment). The teacher knew me and called to ask what self-monitoring was—imagine a student with a learning disability asking to try a particular learning method and the teacher not knowing anything about it! Needless to say, I provided some readings and actually met with that teacher to assist her in getting up to speed on this self-monitoring procedure.

Still, the importance of this technique in that young girl's life is obvious. She wanted to learn how to use a method that would help her stay on task and save time on her class work and homework.

> For students with attention problems severe enough to warrant medication, this self-monitoring procedure can dramatically enhance attention skills above the effects of medication alone.

This is the only time in my career that I've had this particular experience, and I will never forget how critically important this technique was for one young girl with a learning disability. To state again, I believe that every teacher in general and special education classes should be using some version of this technique for students with learning disabilities. Given the attention problems these students demonstrate, I can think of no technique that is more critical.

## Self-Instruction for Increasing Appropriate Behaviors

With the research continually demonstrating the success of self-monitoring procedures for increasing attention among students with learning disabilities, researchers began to apply this self-monitoring concept to behaviors other than attention. In fact, a number of researchers have recently applied the self-monitoring principles to increasing the class preparedness of students with

> Imagine a student with a learning disability asking to try a particular learning method and the teacher not knowing anything about it!

learning disabilities or even decreasing inappropriate behavior (McConnell, 1999; Snyder & Bambara, 1997). An example of this type of self-monitoring scale is presented in Teaching Tip 2.6. This scale may be easily modified to work in almost any class, and some form of self-monitoring along these lines will instill in students their responsibility for learning and for being prepared.

# THE RESPONSIBILITY STRATEGY

## What Is the Responsibility Strategy?

The "responsibility strategy" or, more appropriately, the "responsibility strategies" focus on a student's responsibilities in the classroom, as well as on the relationships to the student's teachers, classmates, and school (Bender, 2002, pp. 35–50). Whereas the self-monitoring approach described above places the responsibility for paying attention and class readiness behaviors on the student's shoulders, this strategy offers the opportunity for a teacher to elicit cooperation from students with learning disabilities by offering them serious responsibilities for the successful daily functioning of the class. This can often increase the personal responsibility that students with learning disabilities take for their learning, as well as create smoothly running classrooms.

Some students with learning disabilities derive a certain amount of attention and/or personal power from inappropriate behavior or even oppositional/defiant behavior. During the misbehavior, the attention of the class is centered on the student, and the teacher must attend in some fashion to the misbehavior. This is a powerful position for a student to be in, and some students with learning disabilities (as well as other students) enjoy this type of attention.

| Teaching Tip 2.7 |
|---|

### Ten Ways to Behave

Name _____     Class _____
Date _____      Teacher _____

Circle one of the three choices: *3 = always, 2 = most of the time, 1 = did not do.*

|  |  |  |  |
|---|---|---|---|
| 1. I worked without disturbing others | 3 | 2 | 1 |
| 2. I participated in class | 3 | 2 | 1 |
| 3. I focused on the lesson | 3 | 2 | 1 |
| 4. I asked for help when I needed it | 3 | 2 | 1 |
| 5. I helped others when I could | 3 | 2 | 1 |
| 6. I followed teacher directions | 3 | 2 | 1 |
| 7. I completed class assignments | 3 | 2 | 1 |
| 8. I turned in completed assignments | 3 | 2 | 1 |
| 9. I completed all homework | 3 | 2 | 1 |
| 10. I behaved appropriately all period | 3 | 2 | 1 |

Student Score _____

| 28-24 points: | SUPER! | 19-14 points: | Fair |
|---|---|---|---|
| 23-20 points: | Good | 13-0 points: | Make a plan to improve |

Indeed, some may find that most of their recognition in class comes from situations in which they misbehave.

One effective strategy to use with these kids is based on finding creative ways for offering attention to students who need to demonstrate their personal power in order to fill their need for attention (Bender, 2002, pp. 35–50). Using these students for an individual responsibility allows the student an opportunity to "show off" in an appropriate way, as well as take some direct responsibility for some aspect of the class. I have used the terms "responsibility strategy" or "responsibility strategies" to highlight the critical factor in this instructional tactic—the need to give kids with learning disabilities some meaningful responsibility that they wish to take and that allows them to receive attention for positive behaviors. Furthermore, such behaviors modify the student's relationship to

**Teaching Tip 2.8**

### An Illustration of the Responsibility Strategy

Dr. Bob Brooks, a former principal of a lock-door school unit in a psychiatric hospital for difficult kids, often tells of a student—we'll call him Terrance—who broke every lightbulb he could get to within the school. All lights were fair game, and Terrance really didn't care what disciplinary measures were used to punish him for breaking lightbulbs—he was going to break them anyway. This was, quite blatantly, an oppositional and attention-getting misbehavior on the part of the student.

To Dr. Brooks's credit, he reflected on Terrance's relationship to the class and the school in general, and then he took a chance; Dr. Brooks made Terrance the "Lightbulb Monitor" for the school. Each day, Terrance was encouraged to roam the halls for a brief period, visit each room, and ensure that each and every lightbulb was working properly. When lights were out, he had the responsibility of reporting the problem to the office. Of course, Terrance loved going into a room of his peers each morning—filled with his own importance—and switching on the lights several times while the teacher checked attendance. His peers saw that Terrance was given special privileges, along with his special responsibility, and that attention from his peers made a positive difference in his behavior. This responsibility strategy ended Terrance's lightbulb breaking, but perhaps the more important point is that Terrance had a responsibility—a meaningful contribution to make to the school—for perhaps the first time in his school career.

the teacher and/or others in the classroom, putting those relationships on a more positive basis, and this positive relationship is viewed today as the only solid basis for both effective classroom management and effective instruction (Marzano & Marzano, 2003; Stipek, 2006). If students with learning disabilities who are misbehaving can find ways to demonstrate their personal authority and power in productive ways, they will not need to demonstrate that power in disruptive ways. An anecdotal example, presented in Teaching Tip 2.8, can help illustrate this strategy.

## A Research-Based Responsibility Strategy

A research-based example of a responsibility tactic comes from Dr. Charles Maher (1982, 1984) of Rutgers University. Maher reported several research studies in which adolescents with horrible behavior records were used as tutors for students with mental disabilities in lower grade levels. Although the tutors in these studies demonstrated conduct-disordered behaviors rather than learning disabilities, this research does suggest how very effective this tactic can be, even for students with serious behavior problems.

> If students with learning disabilities who are misbehaving can find ways to demonstrate their personal authority and power in productive ways, they will not need to demonstrate that power in disruptive ways.

On initial reflection, Maher's application of this tactic seems frightening for many experienced educators. Imagine finding the "last-chance" students—that is, adolescent males and females in the middle and junior high years who had been identified as socially maladjusted and emotionally disturbed because of violence, aggression, and/or other severe behavioral problems—and using them as tutors! In a very real sense, there was the potential that these adolescents in middle and junior high would actually victimize the students from Grades 2 and 3 whom they were tutoring.

In fact, the opposite occurred—in the controlled study in 1982, socially maladjusted students with conduct problems who were used as tutors improved their behavior drastically, compared to another group of similar students who merely received peer counseling. The number of disciplinary problems for the tutors went down, their attendance improved, and their tutoring even assisted them academically. Furthermore, anecdotal observations suggest that the responsibility of tutoring seemed to be the deciding factor. By virtue of tutoring, these students were seen as "leaders" in some sense, and this was a novel experience for many of these students with behavior problems. Specifically, these adolescents began to "own" their tutees—to "protect" them on the playground and to play with them. In the face of these surprising findings, Maher repeated this experimental study in 1984, just to ensure that the first results were valid. The results of the second project were the same. Tutoring gave students with behavior problems a serious responsibility for others—a meaningful connection to others in the school—and that responsibility drastically improved their behavior.

When extrapolated to students with learning disabilities, one may well imagine the power of this strategy in improving behavior and setting a positive tone for learning. How often, in the past, have students with learning disabilities received attention for not completing their work on time or for being incorrect in their answers? This strategy can not only increase the responsibility that these students feel for the classroom and the school, but it also offers an opportunity for receiving praise and positive attention for students with learning disabilities for positive work (Bender, 2002, p. 38).

Of course, as in the example above, the limited academic skills of many students with learning disabilities will limit the application of this strategy. Most students with learning disabilities would not be appropriate tutors for students at the same grade level because of the limited academic skills of these students (one exception to this general guideline is classwide peer tutoring, described in a later chapter). However, using students with learning disabilities as tutors of younger children in simpler reading or language arts tasks should work quite well. Again, in the example above, the adolescents were invited to contribute something—they were given a responsibility that they thought important. For the teacher who wishes to implement a differentiated instruction classroom, having this behavioral intervention option is critically important.

### REFLECTIVE EXERCISE: YOUR DISCIPLINARY CHALLENGE

Consider your most challenging student, and think of the most recent two or three times you needed to discipline him or her. Have you invited this student to take a meaningful leadership role or responsibility in the class? Is there some responsibility that this student would undertake for the class, which would give this student bragging rights? Is a responsibility strategy right for this student?

## Who Should I Use This Strategy With?

Students with learning disabilities are often good candidates for using the responsibility tactic because these students will often demonstrate specific strengths on which a responsibility may be founded. For example, given a student with a learning disability in reading and a relative strength in math, the teacher may be able to use that student as a tutor to help weaker students in math or as a "class writer" on the dry-erase board for the math problems each day. Teachers should select the responsibility based on the strengths of the student.

> How often, in the past, have students with learning disabilities received attention for not completing their work on time or for being incorrect in their answers?

Furthermore, this strategy fits the need in a number of situations in which students with learning disabilities are angry, aggressive, or even oppositional. When a student's need for attention becomes apparent, the teacher should talk with the student about how he or she can "assist" in the class, using his or her leadership skills. The teacher may then suggest something, such as a chore in the classroom, that the student is interested in doing and that gives the student "bragging rights" in front of the other class members.

In using this strategy for students with learning disabilities, one must carefully select a task or responsibility that can be successfully completed by the student in question. These responsibilities should not "challenge" the student; teachers should not use tutoring in academic tasks that tax the tutor academically. Rather, select a task within the student's comfort level, and allow the student an opportunity to succeed and thus to receive positive attention for his or her successful contribution to the class.

## Implementing the Responsibility Strategy

When a student with a learning disability has consistently demonstrated a need for attention, the teacher should reflect on the student's opportunity for positive attention in the class, as well as the student's relationship with the teacher and others in the school. It is often effective for the teacher to mentally take several steps back and ask, "How have I invited this student to positively contribute to this class today?"

The statement above is phrased quite deliberately: Note the use of the phrase "How have I invited." Has the student been "invited" to demonstrate his or her capabilities, leadership skills, and opportunities to present a positive self to the school class? In some cases, the answer is probably that the student with the learning disability hasn't been effectively invited to make an appropriate and meaningful contribution to the class. Educators must deal with large numbers of students almost all of the time, and this may prevent any teacher—even the most effective and sensitive teachers—from giving all the attention required by some students. For this reason, a wise educator will try to find ways to involve every student with a learning disability—to make him or her feel special—by inviting the child to contribute in some appropriate fashion.

### Why Give a Behavior Problem Student Responsibility?

Most of us remember dusting the erasers, cleaning the blackboard for teachers, or doing other "teacher's helper" jobs as privileges in the classrooms

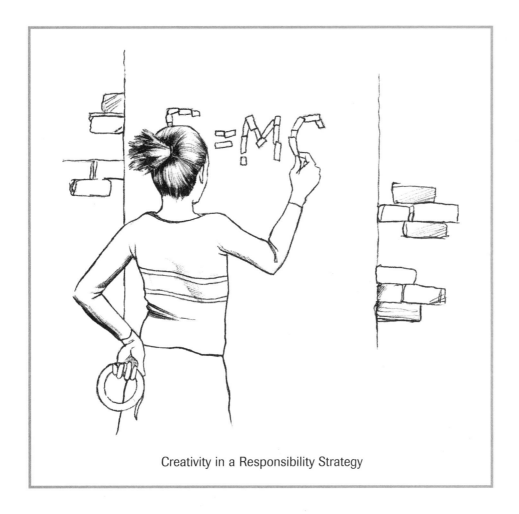

Creativity in a Responsibility Strategy

of our youth. With a moment's reflection, we can remember how special—how important and involved—those relatively boring and mundane tasks made us feel. Of course, students with learning disabilities often do not get to do these jobs because teachers frequently use these jobs as privileges or rewards, and students with learning disabilities do not earn rewards in the general education classroom as frequently as students without disabilities. In fact, when presenting this strategy around the country, I have realized that many teachers feel it may be inappropriate to "reward" misbehavior by using students with poor attention skills or behavior problems for special tasks or responsibilities. Indeed, rewarding misbehavior with a serious responsibility does seem to go against all of our behavioral training (in behavioral thought, one removes a privilege for misbehavior). Nevertheless, for some students with learning disabilities, offering an attention-generating responsibility will be just the ticket to turn negative behavior into positive behavior and to increase the sense of responsibility the student has for the class. Furthermore, by the time a teacher considers using the responsibility strategy for a student with learning disabilities, the teacher has probably already tried everything else in the intervention toolbox and has nothing to lose by trying this strategy.

> A wise educator will try to find ways to involve every student with a learning disability—to make him or her feel special—by inviting the child to contribute in some appropriate fashion.

## *Critical Aspects of the Responsibility Tasks*

In seeking an appropriate task, the teacher should consider the interests and desires of the student with the learning disability, his or her capabilities, and the needs of the classroom. The possible task options are almost endless. This is why I frequently refer to this strategy in the plural—that is, responsibility "strategies." The task that a student is assigned is relatively unimportant, and almost any necessary task (or even some unnecessary ones—e.g., lightbulb monitor) will do. However, at least two things are important.

1. The student must feel that he or she is truly given an opportunity to contribute (i.e., he or she must have impressive "bragging rights" for the opportunity to do the task).

2. He or she must feel that the task is important. The student must be made to feel like a contributing partner in a task that he or she values (Bender, 2002).

How can a teacher find the "right" responsibility for a student with a learning disability? Often the students' actions will tell you. For example, the student described earlier was fixated on lightbulbs, and the role of lightbulb monitor was perfectly appropriate for him. The teacher should try to consider a student's hobbies and interests, as well as the needs of the class or school. Does the school need pictures taken? Could the school use someone to report gang graffiti on playground walls? Could adjudicated students with learning disabilities (appropriately supervised by teachers, of course) take some responsibility for notifying teachers about verbal fights on the playground? If planned appropriately, any of these tasks could represent an effective contribution to the school and a positive responsibility.

Of course, in selecting the responsibility, teachers should consider issues such as students' confidentially, privacy, safety, and legal liability. For example, don't appoint a "bathroom" monitor (unless you want a student peeking into bathroom stalls!). Furthermore, no student's responsibility should require that he or she leave campus or get involved in physical altercations that have already begun between other students. The principal, because of required training in school law and so forth, is an excellent contact to make when considering responsibilities that involve students with learning disabilities. Also, supervision should always be available for any student completing his or her responsibility.

In addition to routine supervision, remember that students may need to be more closely supervised the first few times they try out their responsibility. In implementing tutoring as described in the example above, you should consider how and what type of training to offer tutors. How much supervision will be necessary for those tutors, and what types of reinforcement can be offered them? For example, do they get to leave the classroom a few minutes early to go to tutoring? Leaving the classroom takes place in front of the peers and indicates a great deal of trust, thus providing a great deal of reinforcement for students with learning disabilities. However, leaving the classroom also places the student in an unsupervised hallway.

> Students with learning disabilities need to earn rewards in the general education classroom as frequently as students without disabilities.

With these general suggestions and concerns in mind, the responsibility strategy can focus a student on his or her contribution to the class and to the school at large while emphasizing his or her importance as well as responsibility to the class. Students with learning disabilities often "bloom" when offered the opportunity for

> Supervision should always be available for any student completing his or her responsibility.

positive attention because their previous schooling may not have included many opportunities for attention. Thus, teachers should employ this strategy whenever possible and be as creative as necessary by actively seeking ways to involve students in their academic learning.

## WHAT'S NEXT?

Once universal design is considered in guiding one's room organization, and various strategies to facilitate personal responsibility for learning are in place for students with learning disabilities, various innovations and modifications for instructional tasks can be considered. The next chapter focuses on proven instructional techniques that can be used to foster increased differentiation in the class.

# Differentiating the Learning Process 3

## Metacognition and Scaffolded Instruction

---

**Topics Included in This Chapter:**

- ✓ Guidelines for Effective Scaffolding
- ✓ A Scaffolding Example: The Story Map
- ✓ Metacognitive Instruction
- ✓ Advance Organizers
- ✓ Graphic Organizers and Study Guides
- ✓ Reconstructive Elaborations
- ✓ Questions Associated With Pictures in Text
- ✓ Reciprocal Teaching

## THE NEED FOR STUDENT SUPPORT

Students with learning disabilities and many other learners in the classroom demonstrate a variety of academic deficits as well as deficits in planning and various other organizational problems, and, of course, the concept of differentiated instruction places strong emphasis on the diverse learning needs of the students (Tomlinson, 1999, pp. 1–60). Whereas appropriate classroom structure and universally designed assignments will support students with learning disabilities in their personal organization of schoolwork, these students will also need highly organized academic instruction and numerous academic supports for understanding the tasks assigned to them. Thus, in addition to the supportive universally designed environments described in Chapters 1 and 2, students with learning disabilities need various supports to master academic material, and this chapter focuses on two research proven approaches that provide such academic support: metacognitive instruction and scaffolded instruction (Vaughn & Linan-Thompson, 2003).

Although the theories behind these approaches developed somewhat independently, each of these approaches supports the overall emphasis of differentiating instruction based on the needs of the learner, and many would argue that these approaches are quite similar. After a brief overview of these two instructional paradigms, this chapter will focus on several specific metacognitive and scaffolded instruction techniques that will assist teachers in differentiating the instructional processes, based on the needs of the diverse learners in each class.

## Why Metacognition?

Metacognitive instruction has developed over the past 25 years and is one of the most influential concepts in the field of learning disabilities today (Vaughn & Linan-Thompson, 2003). The growing emphasis on metacognition is quite understandable given the characteristics of the students we teach. Every veteran teacher has experienced the "dog ate my homework" story from some student with a learning disability. Indeed, most of us have contemplated asking, "Why did you put your homework on the floor, where the dog could reach it?" In reality, students with learning disabilities often do the homework and then leave it on the desk or a bed where "Rover" can get to it; they may also put the paper on the desk at home, on the sofa, or even on the floor—presumably as "dog munchies." The point is they often do the work but don't put that work in their book bags to get it to school the next day. Still, that makes little difference in the long run because they frequently forget to bring their book bags to school anyway! In short, even when students with learning disabilities perform the required work, there is no assurance that their relative deficit in organizational skills will allow them to present that work to the teacher.

With these deficits in organization noted, teachers may easily understand why students with learning disabilities have so much difficulty with schoolwork. For example, consider a fifth-grade class in which the teacher makes the following assignment.

*OK, class. Since our social studies assignment involves writing our congressperson, I want you to put away your social studies books. Take out your language arts texts, and turn to page 189. On that page you will find the format for a business letter, and I want you to write a sample business letter to your congressperson, using that form. Billy will write the address for you on the chalkboard.*

This assignment involves a minimum of four different instructions—which must be followed in sequence in order to ensure success—as well as several additional critical pieces of information (including one piece of information that is not even available yet—the address on the board). Given the organizational problems noted above, why would teachers expect students with learning disabilities to successfully transition into this new task? In fact, much of the frustration that teachers feel in dealing with students with learning disabilities stems from failure to successfully transition from one activity to another, and students are often left in the dark because of the complexity of instructions offered for the transition period.

> Even when students with learning disabilities perform the required work, there is no assurance that their relative deficit in organizational skills will allow them to present that work to the teacher.

Metacognitive instruction involves providing students with the tools to assist them in improving their organization skills and completing their assignments. The term *metacognition* may loosely be defined as "thinking about one's thinking." This may include a number of different components such as the following:

- planning the steps necessary to complete a task
- ordering those steps into the correct sequence
- monitoring one's progress on those steps

In short, metacognitive instruction involves providing a structuring mechanism or support for a child to assist in completing the task—it helps students think about their assignment, plan the sequence of steps required, and monitor how they are doing on each step. Thus metacognitive strategies impact both the learning process as well as the final product of the academic effort.

In various metacognitive instructional approaches, students are trained to give themselves silent instructions using inner language for task completion while they are doing the task. Because the use of "inner language" or "silent language" is the basis of metacognition, teachers may wish to look over the original self-instructional steps to foster inner language (presented in Teaching Tip 3.1). These were first described by Meichenbaum and Goodman (1969, 1988), and understanding these steps will help in understanding the use of inner language and the concept of metacognition.

Based on research over the past several decades that is strongly supportive of metacognitive instruction, teachers today should incorporate a wide variety of these metacognitive ideas into their teaching (Ashton, 1999; Day & Elksnin, 1994; Lenz, 2006; Gregory & Chapman, 2002, p. 20; Mason, Snyder, Sukhram, & Kedem, 2006; Mastropieri & Scruggs, 1998). Furthermore, with consistent and regular practice in these techniques, students will begin to develop their own metacognitive understandings; thus, these metacognitive skills will generalize across classes. Over time, students with learning disabilities will be much better able to plan, organize, and complete complex assignments if they are trained repeatedly using metacognitive instruction (Vaughn & Linan-Thompson, 2003).

In fact, many argue that, at a time when knowledge is expanding so drastically, the major focus of education should be not mastery of factual knowledge but mastery of the processes that enable a child to process factual knowledge. In this view, the highest goal of education would be to enable every student to develop into a successful metacognitive thinker—one who carefully considers the various aspects of the available knowledge and its relationship to the assigned task and who then completes the required steps in sequence, monitoring his or her own performance. If this is a realistic goal for educating students with learning disabilities—I would argue that it is the only worthy goal—then a metacognitive instructional emphasis should be readily apparent in every classroom. A variety of metacognitive tactics are presented below.

Kids enjoy metacognitive strategies.

## SCAFFOLDED INSTRUCTION

The concept of scaffolded instruction developed more recently than metacognition—over the past fifteen years or so—and was based, in part, on metacognitive understandings. Scaffolded instruction may best be understood as a sequence of prompted content, materials, and teacher or peer support to facilitate learning (Dickson, Chard, & Simmons, 1993; Englert, Berry, & Dunsmore, 2001; Larkin, 2001; Stone, 1998). The emphasis is placed on the adult assisting the student in the learning process with individual prompting and guidance, which is tailored to the specific needs of the individual student to offer just enough support (i.e., a scaffold) for the student in a new task. The student is initially considered an apprentice in the learning effort; thus, too little support leaves the student stranded and unable to comprehend the assigned work and complete the task, whereas too much support would prohibit the student from independently mastering the task. Therefore, the level of support must be specifically tailored to the student's ever-changing understanding of the problem. Also, that support would gradually be withdrawn, allowing the student to eventually "own" the task performance. Stone (1998) provided four key features of scaffolding that sum up this process. These are presented in Teaching Tip 3.2.

**Teaching Tip 3.1**

### "Silent Language" for Self-Instruction

Imagine a teacher teaching a child with a learning disability in math how to complete a double-digit addition with regrouping problem. Specifically, imagine the several steps in that problem that must be completed in sequence to correctly solve the problem (add the digits in the 1s place. Put the first digit of that answer below the 1s column, and regroup the second digit to the top of the 10s place . . .). Instructing this student in the "silent language" task instructions represents one early form of metacognitive instruction. Here are the steps.

$$
\begin{array}{r}
35 \\
+27 \\
\hline
62
\end{array}
$$

1. The teacher completes a problem, reciting the independent step-by-step instructions for problem completion. This modeling step encourages the child to respond similarly in later steps.

2. The teacher and student complete the next problem while the student repeats the steps out loud.

3. The student completes the next problem and uses overt self-instruction by repeating the steps out loud. The student should gain confidence with the teacher immediately available to help.

4. The student completes the next problem relatively independently while whispering the step-by-step instructions softly. This is intended to approximate the last step of using "silent language" self-instruction.

5. The student completes the next problem using silent language to provide self-instructions.

SOURCE: Adapted from Meichenbaum and Goodman (1969, 1988).

This "personal attention" aspect of scaffolded instruction offers hidden benefits when scaffolding is used in differentiating instruction in the classroom. Because scaffolded instruction emphasizes individual focus on particular students, the students tend to feel more supported when this technique is utilized, and that, in turn, tends to result in enhanced relationships between students and teachers. Thus, regular use of scaffolded instruction can provide one way to strengthen pupil/teacher relationships in the differentiated class.

Although a critical component of scaffolding is the sensitivity of the adult who is supporting the student in the learning process, a variety of structured learning supports may be considered "scaffolds" on which a student may depend in the learning process. Various charts and/or graphics that assist in the learning process would be scaffolds that the student, with adult supervision initially, could use to master newly presented subject matter. One common example would be that of a "story map," as described below.

**Key Features of Scaffolding**

While there is no specific "model" for scaffolded instruction, a focus on the major emphases presented by Stone (1998) will assist in understanding the concept of scaffolding:

1. The recruitment by an adult of a child's involvement and interest in a meaningful and culturally desirable activity that is beyond the child's current understanding

2. The provision of adult support for the child's learning, based on constant observation and diagnosis of the child's understanding or skill level, together with careful calibration of the support provided to help the child accomplish the goal

3. The provision, by the adult, of a range of various types of support, including nonverbal assistance, modeling, pointing, and verbal assistance based on various questioning techniques

4. The assumption that the adult support for learning will be temporary and gradually withdrawn to foster transfer of responsibility of the task from the adult to the child

As noted throughout this text, many students with learning disabilities have difficulties organizing their thoughts during learning tasks, and this is equally true in their efforts to comprehend content material or stories. These students do not understand that, in many reading passages, there is an underlying structure, and as a result they miss the opportunity to use the story structure to enhance their comprehension of the reading passage. For this reason, a number of researchers have encouraged specific instruction in story structure for students with learning disabilities (Swanson & De La Paz, 1998), and such instruction provides a scaffold on which students may explore new stories. Specifically, most stories will include the following:

- information on the story setting and information on several primary characters
- an initiating event or problem for one of the main characters
- a sequence of actions to solve the problem
- a climax describing when and how the main character successfully deals with the problem
- a conclusion or resolution of the problem

These rather predictable components may be formulated into a story map that will assist the student with a learning disability to organize his or her thoughts. Thus, when a student with a learning disability reads a story silently in the general education classroom, he or she should simultaneously complete a story map as a scaffold on which to build understanding of that story. A sample story map is presented in Teaching Tip 3.3.

This story map activity is also very effective when completed as a "buddy" activity, and two or three students may partner together to complete the map.

Furthermore, these story maps should be reviewed in class as a post-reading activity to check for accuracy and for comprehension of the reading material. The story map can subsequently be used as a study guide for any future tests on that content. In fact, a wide variety of instructional activities can be built around the story map concept. Thus, teachers in inclusive classes can greatly enhance the likelihood of reading success for students with learning disabilities by simply using a story map as a scaffold for virtually every reading assignment in the differentiated classroom.

> Scaffolded instruction may best be understood as a sequence of prompted content, materials, and teacher or peer support to facilitate learning.

Although reading in subject content areas does not usually involve the same components as a story narrative, teachers may use this concept of a story map as a scaffold to assist students with learning disabilities while they are also reading in content areas by developing maps that are more appropriate to the specific content area. Additional examples of instructional scaffolds are presented in subsequent chapters; for example, the discussion of semantic webs in Chapter 7 represents another idea of an instructional scaffold that will assist the teacher in modifying the learning process for learners with various needs in the class.

In translating the scaffolding metaphor into instructional practice, Larkin (2001) provided a set of guidelines and instructional examples for each. These will help the novice understand the scaffolding concept.

### REFLECTIVE EXERCISE: COMPARE AND CONTRAST METACOGNITION AND SCAFFOLDED INSTRUCTION

Reflect for a moment on the similarities and differences between scaffolded instruction and metacognitive instruction. Is every metacognitive technique a "scaffold" for the learner? How do these techniques assist the learner with the process of learning?

# GRAPHIC ORGANIZERS

## The Advance Organizer

An "advance organizer" is a metacognitive technique that enables a student to comprehend the basic organization of the material to be learned prior to actually studying the material. This term was originally introduced by Ausubel and Robinson in 1969. An advance organizer may be defined as material presented "in advance of and at a higher level of generality, inclusiveness, and abstraction than the learning task itself" (Ausubel & Robinson, 1969). The presentation of this type of material allows the student to mentally organize his or her studies of the material to be learned and represents one way to "hook" or "ground" new knowledge into existing knowledge. The advance organizer was one of the predecessors to the full development of

**Teaching Tip 3.3**

### A Scaffolding Example: The Story Map

Name _____          Date _____

Story Title _____

The story setting was _____

The main character was _____

Other characters were _____

The problem began when _____

_____

Then several important things happened _____

_____

After that _____

_____

Next _____

_____

The problem was solved by _____

_____

The story ends when _____

_____

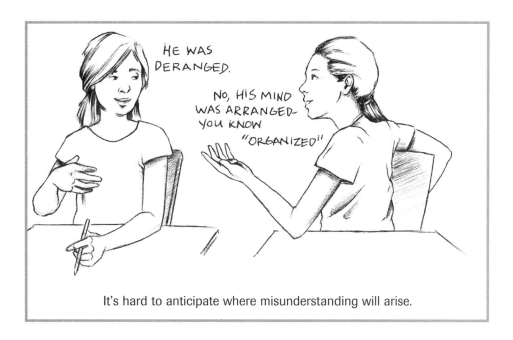

It's hard to anticipate where misunderstanding will arise.

metacognitive instruction, and much of the subsequent work on metacognition was based on the concept of advance organizers.

One example of an advance organizer was provided by Darch and Carnine (1986) and involved the use of a chart that represented some of the ideas to be described in a science instructional unit on how altitude affects climate and vegetation. A visual display was presented in which a mountain was divided into different shaded areas, which may have looked something like their Figure 3.1. Within each shaded area, a description of the types of vegetation for that area was written. At the bottom, the description stated, "Bigger trees at the bottom of the west side." The shaded area above was labeled, "Smaller trees." The area above that was described as, "No trees, just meadows." The top of the mountain was labeled, "Snow." Discussion of this type of chart prior to beginning the science unit can greatly enhance the learning of students; in fact, the chart should remain before the class for the entire unit and would therefore represent a "hook" on which to hang subsequent concepts and understandings.

Advance organizers should be provided for group projects, interactive lessons, lectures, homework assignments, class work assignments, and other content area instructional activities in almost every activity in the general education classroom (Lovitt & Horton, 1994). When class content in general education classes is structured around a set of advance organizers, students with learning disabilities are much more likely to succeed. Furthermore, for inclusive classes, the special education teacher may develop the advance organizer, which can then be used for all students in the class.

### Graphic Organizers and Study Guides

Two more recent applications of the advance organizer concept are graphic organizers and study guides. Graphic organizers and study guides represent adapted advance organizers that can focus students with learning disabilities

## Guidelines for Effective Scaffolding

- *Identify what students know.* Effective scaffolding requires that teachers are cognizant of what a student already knows (background or prior knowledge) and of the student's misconceptions (i.e., which competencies are developing and which are beyond the student's current level of functioning) (Pressley, Hogan, Wharton-McDonald, Mistretta, & Ettneberger, 1996). For example, Anna was aware that some of her students "think in terms of money." When she taught "rounding" to those students, Anna used the familiar concept of money.

- *Begin with what students can do.* Laura (not her real name), another special education teacher, was aware of individual student ability levels. When Laura began reading lessons, she gave the students with learning disabilities an opportunity to read something that could be read independently or with little teacher assistance. This enabled students to begin the reading lesson successfully.

- *Help students achieve success quickly.* Laura found that writing and penmanship tasks were laborious for some of her students with written expression disabilities. When she assisted her special education students in the general education classroom for a lesson on storytelling, Laura asked the students to dictate their ideas while she wrote them on paper. This accommodation enabled the students who had difficulty with written expression to generate ideas without worrying how to convey them on paper. Also, Laura served as an adult listener to reinforce the notion that storytelling and written expression are acts of communication and shared experience.

- *Help students to "be" like everyone else.* Miller and Fritz (1998) interviewed a successful adult with learning disabilities about his school history and found that a major theme was the individual's desire to be regarded like other students. These researchers suggested that as much as possible, teachers orient classroom tasks for students' work to be perceived as being like that of their peers. For example, Anna suggested that Mark (not his real name), a struggling student, be moved into a third-grade text like that of his peers. She informed Mark of his responsibility to work hard but also let him know that she would be there to give him the assistance he needed. Anna noted that when Mark was placed in the third-grade math book with her assistance, he was still struggling with math but holding his own. She was confident that she made the right decision to place him in a more difficult math book with assistance, because Mark felt good about using the same book as his third-grade peers.

- *Know when it's time to stop.* Anna learned from experience that continued drill and practice may not always be effective. She stated, "Overkill erases." Anna found that once her students had demonstrated mastery of a skill, continued practice may result in the students refusing to work or students producing work with numerous errors. For example, when some of Anna's students with learning disabilities were asked to complete a general education math assignment with fifty problems, she noticed that the students completed the first three rows of problems without an error. Students began making numerous errors on the final three rows. Anna found that employing systematic review and purposeful practice with a limited number of math problems was effective. She also noted that just a few written or spoken questions regarding reading or language arts assignments provided needed review without overkill.

- *Help students be independent when they have command of the activity.* Effective scaffolding means that teachers need to listen and watch for clues from their students as to when teacher assistance is, or is not, needed. Obviously, teachers do not want students to fail, but they should not allow students to become too dependent on the teacher. As special education teacher Beverly (not her real name) noted, achieving independence is different for individual students. Some students may be at identical skill levels, but emotionally they may be at different levels regarding the amount of frustration they can tolerate. Students may not be able to be "weaned" from teacher assistance at the same time. In other words, some students will need more teacher support while learning to perform a task; others will demonstrate task mastery more quickly. Like the mother bird that helps her chicks leave the nest to become independent birds, teachers need to help their students gradually move from teacher assistance to student independence as students demonstrate command of the task or activity.

SOURCE: From "Providing Support for Student Independence Through Scaffolded Instruction." by Larkin, M. J. (2001). *Teaching Exceptional Children, 34*(1), 30–35. © 2001 by The Council for Exceptional Children. Reprinted with permission.

on the task at hand both prior to and during the task (Rock, 2004). Study guides and graphic organizers differ only slightly from advance organizers in that the work on a study guide is to be completed during the study of the material rather than prior to it. Study guides may also be referred to as "participatory organizers," with the emphasis on students' participation in completing the study guide during the study itself (Dye, 2000; Rock, 2004).

Graphic organizers are graphic displays in which the structure of the graphic emphasizes the content to be mastered (Rock, 2004), and research has shown that graphic organizers are powerful learning tools that will enhance both memory and comprehension (DiCecco & Gleason, 2002; Foil & Alber, 2002; Mastropieri & Scruggs, 1998). Graphic organizers are presented today in many school curricula, and various software programs (Inspiration Software is one common example) are available to assist students in developing their own graphic organizers for content mastery. Of course, once the graphic organizer is developed it may be used to differentiate the activities in the class in a variety of ways including

- presenting labels or unlabeled graphic organizers to various class members, depending on their skill level
- having students predict the types of information that may be used to complete the graphic organizer prior to the activity
- completing the organizer as the activity in the class progresses, either individually or using a buddy system
- using the graphic organizer as a discussion tool among pairs of students in order to review the content of the daily lesson

Several theorists have provided a series of guidelines for the use of graphic organizers (Foil & Alber, 2002; Laing & Kamhi, 2002; Rock, 2004), and these are presented in Teaching Tip 3.5.

**Teaching Tip 3.5**

## Using Graphic Organizers

1. The use of graphic organizers as a study tool should be specifically taught. You should provide direct, explicit instruction on using graphic organizers. Whenever possible, indicate and discuss the structure of the organizer and how that structure represents the content independent of the actual words or labels on the organizer.

2. Structure a specific time for graphic organizers in each unit of instruction, and repeatedly refer to the organizers at various points in each lesson. Repetitive use of organizers will enhance the effectiveness of this technique as a memory aid.

3. As a differentiated lesson activity, you may increase student involvement in use of the organizers by having various groups of students develop or modify the organizers. You should stress the variety of different, yet appropriate, ways content may be structured for learning, while relating that to the various multiple intelligences and learning styles of the students in the class.

4. Scaffold the instruction in the organizer with the modeling the use of the organizer, practicing it in the large group, having students do it in pairs, and then having students implement it alone under teacher supervision.

5. Teach a brainstorming idea such as "List/label" in which a category is listed as the central theme of the organizer and other related, yet subordinate, concepts are listed around the broader label. Have groups of students work together to formulate a rational for why some concepts are subordinate to others.

6. Publish the completed graphic organizers either through class display or on school Web sites when appropriate.

Lovitt, Rudsit, Jenkins, Pious, and Benedetti (1985) provided the example of a study guide for a secondary science lesson, presented in Teaching Tip 3.6. Students were taught some science content using traditional instruction and subsequently using study guides. The results indicated that provision of a study guide for junior high school science students with learning disabilities resulted in greater gains in achievement than did traditional instruction because the students had to become involved in the lesson in order to complete the study guide. The positive results of using a study guide were demonstrated for high-achieving, normally achieving, and low-achieving students, as well as for students with learning disabilities in the experimental classes. Clearly, provision of study guides facilitates increases in achievement for all students, particularly for students with learning disabilities, and these metacognitive supports should characterize the differentiated classroom at all grade levels.

> Research has indicated that advance organizers represent one metacognitive tactic that will improve the content learning of students with learning disabilities across the age span.

One tactic for general education teachers involves development of a study guide and then using that guide as both an advance organizer and subsequently as a participatory organizer. For example, in using the mountain chart described earlier as an advance organizer, the teacher would show the chart to the students prior to beginning the unit and then ask questions about what the different shaded areas mean. In using the same chart as a participatory organizer, the teacher would reproduce the chart on a worksheet with the shaded areas unlabeled, and the students would be expected to add descriptions to those areas until their worksheets included much more information than the original visual display.

Research has demonstrated the effectiveness of using study guides for students with learning disabilities (Lovitt & Horton, 1994), as well as for other students in the class. Of course, this last point cannot be overemphasized. All students benefit from the use of study guides—not merely students with learning disabilities—which makes this instructional strategy an effective differential instructional strategy for inclusive general education classrooms. Thus, teachers should never view preparation of study guides as additional work that benefits only students with learning disabilities in the class. Rather, in either inclusive classes with co-teachers working together or in the single-teacher general education class, study guides will enhance learning for all students.

> One tactic for general education teachers involves development of a study guide and then using that guide as both an advance organizer and subsequently as a participatory organizer.

Although many study guides are based on words and reading skill, as is the previous example, study guides may also be based on charts or pictures to complete or label. Study guides in the form of visual displays may work better for

### Teaching Tip 3.6

**A Sample Study Guide**

Name: _____     Date_____

1.  Almost everything is made up of _____.

2.  A _____ is made up of _____ atoms of the same kind.

3.  The molecules for _____ is $O_2$. This_____ is made up of _____ oxygen _____.

4.  The word *kinetic* means _____.

5.  There is a _____ that all _____ are always _____. It is called the kinetic _____.

6.  Many years ago Robert Brown discovered the _____. He observed _____ grains _____ in a _____ pattern over surface of _____.

7.  Some examples of molecules moving are _____.

8.  Molecules are _____.

some students with learning disabilities than reading-based study guides. Given the wide array of learning styles demonstrated by students with learning disabilities, teachers should employ an array of study guides emphasizing both pictorial study guides, as well as language-reading-based study guides. Again, the differentiated instructional imperative would suggest that a variety of study guides should be used to vary the learning processes for all learners.

## RECONSTRUCTIVE ELABORATIONS

Mastropieri and Scruggs (1988) recommended a mnemonic strategy for content instruction that involves elaborations on the central theme to facilitate recall. Reconstructive elaborations provide more concrete information in a meaningful fashion than do the typical types of examples in text. For example, a typical history text concerning World War I may report that many soldiers died in trenches because of disease rather than combat. However, the typical pictures in those texts would show soldiers in trenches but not the living conditions in those trenches. Mastropieri and Scruggs (1998) recommended using a picture cue that shows soldiers dying in the trenches and falling among the rats that lived in the trenches because such a reconstructive elaboration is more accurate as a teaching tool and aids the memory of students with learning disabilities. A description of a reconstructive elaboration is presented in Teaching Tip 3.7.

Pictures can be a critical tool in aiding memory. In fact, a moment's reflection on Washington crossing the Delaware River during the American Revolution illustrates the power of pictures in aiding memory. Almost all Americans remember that famous story from the Revolutionary War, when Washington stood in the front of the boat to cross the river in the dead of night and lead his army in the surprise Christmas attack on the winter camp of the British in Trenton, New Jersey. Of course, historians have often pointed out two errors in that picture. First, Washington was probably not standing, exposed to blowing snow and frigid temperatures on that fateful evening; second (and somewhat more certain), the American flag on the back of the boat that was portrayed in that famous picture had not been created at the time of the battle—it was to come several years later.

Still, the potency of this image is one component of most Americans' understanding of the desperate nature of that cunning surprise attack, and that picture—errors and all—does indicate the power of imagery in learning. Thus, the use of pictures, as memory aids, is one tactic that will assist students with learning disabilities because memories associated with pictures seem to last much longer.

There are several additional issues in the use of reconstructive elaborations for students with learning disabilities. First, development of the reconstructive elaboration pictures can take some time, and although pictures are numerous in almost every textbook, most current textbooks do not include reconstructive elaborations among the pictures presented. Consequently, teachers may have to spend some time developing them. In inclusive classes, this time concern is somewhat abated because the teacher pairs can allow some flexible time for one teacher or the other to develop these reconstructive elaborations and the charts

All students benefit from the use of study guides—not merely students with learning disabilities—which makes this instructional strategy an effective differential instructional strategy for inclusive general education classrooms.

**Reconstructive Elaboration on Dwight D. Eisenhower**

*Facts to be taught.* Dwight D. Eisenhower was a general in the United States Army who later became the president of the United States. He was the supreme allied commander during the final years of World War II and planned the famous "D-Day" invasion, in which the allied armies invaded France in order to force the German and Italian forces to leave France and return to their own countries. His election to president was, in large measure, because of his successful leadership in World War II.

*Reconstructive elaboration.* (Show overhead of Eisenhower represented as the "tower" of a man—that is, taller than others in the picture—with the letters "I Tower" and "WWII" on his breast.) To remember that Dwight Eisenhower was a great general in World War II, remember the words I-Tower. That should help students remember his name. See it sounds like Eisenhower to say "I-Tower." What does the "I" mean on his chest? What picture will we think of when we think of Eisenhower? (Elicit responses.) What does the "WWII" on his chest mean? (Elicit responses.) Now close your eyes, and describe this picture to me. Who is the tallest man, or the "Tower," in this picture? (Elicit responses.) What letters are on his chest? In this example students are verbally reconstructing the picture which will greatly enhance their recall (Laing & Kamhi, 2002).

or transparencies that go with them. In single-teacher general education classes, teachers may wish to use students to develop these reconstructive elaborations (what a wonderful assessment of student knowledge this would make—see discussion of authentic assessment in Chapter 6).

Of course, once such academic supports are developed for use one year, the same reconstructive elaborations can be employed in subsequent years during the same unit. Furthermore, teachers will find that this approach to modification of content appears more frequently in textbooks published in subsequent years because the use of the reconstructive elaborations does facilitate content learning for students with learning disabilities.

> In fact, a moment's reflection on Washington crossing the Delaware River during the American Revolution illustrates the power of pictures in aiding memory.

**REFLECTIVE EXERCISE: STUDENTS' DEVELOPMENT OF RECONSTRUCTIVE ELABORATIONS**

Consider the use of reconstructive elaborations that have been developed by members of the class. How could a teacher structure a group activity that would result in development of several reconstructive elaborations by various groups of students? What types of guidelines should be provided to the groups as a starting point (teachers may wish to jot down a few of their ideas about these guidelines)? How can the students gauge the importance of the information that they intend to include in the elaboration? What types of reinforcement could be offered for the most effective reconstructive elaboration?

*(Continued)*

(Continued)

Both the multiple intelligences theory and the brain-compatible research have emphasized the importance and potency of pictures and/or video in learning (Foil & Alber, 2002; Mastropieri & Scruggs, 1998), and the use of reconstructive elaborations to create and/or describe pictures is particularly beneficial. Pictures and video can summarize a large amount of information—as did the advance organizer of the mountain regions presented previously—and in the classroom context, if a student can remember the detail of that picture or organizer, he or she will also remember much of the content (Laing & Kamhi, 2002). However, in order to maximize learning using this technique, we must consider both the quality and the use of pictures as memory aids in teaching. First, the quality of the pictorial aids involves both the accuracy of the information conveyed in the picture, as well as the importance of that information. Although textbooks, reading books, and most other reading material intended for school use include some illustrations, the quality and use of the illustrations vary widely. For example, there have been examples in the past where the "little red wagon" described in the young child's reading story was colored green in the picture accompanying the story! Clearly, the art department at the publishing house did not communicate with the reading instruction department, and such errors can be quite confusing to young readers, particularly if the plot of the story is dependent on the wagon being red.

## Teaching Tip 3.8

**Questions for Discussion on Important Pictures in Text**

1. Why is this picture important enough to discuss in class? What do you see pictured here that may represent a major concept of this unit of instruction?

2. How does this picture fit into the sequence of events discussed in this unit? Should this picture be discussed early in the unit or later? Why?

3. What details in this picture represent important aspects of the unit? How are those details illustrated by this picture?

4. What important things are not pictured here that could have been illustrated? How could those concepts have been incorporated into this picture? Who would like to draw a picture showing those additional facts?

Next, the use of the pictorial aids will determine in large measure their effectiveness in helping students with learning disabilities remember important facts. As in the case of the reconstructive elaboration presented above, teachers should talk about various pictures in text, asking questions about why the content in the picture is presented in a particular fashion or how additional content would add to the picture in the text. When teachers use the pictures presented in text as a learning tool—as a subject for class discussion—then the use of pictorial information can greatly assist students with learning disabilities in mastering important content. Teaching Tip 3.8 presents a series of questions that teachers may use in discussing pictures in texts. In fact, such a discussion of several of the most important pictures in the textbook chapter (the teacher should determine which pictures present enough critical information so as to be worthy of discussion time in class) can be an excellent instructional exercise early in an instructional unit.

# RECIPROCAL TEACHING

Reciprocal teaching represents a scaffolded instructional technique in which the teacher and the content presentation are each providing support for student learning. Eventually, the students become responsible for self-questioning through structured dialogue (Lederer, 2000; Palincsar & Brown, 1986, 1987; Vaughn & Linan-Thompson, 2003). The reciprocal teaching method focuses on the things the teacher can do to facilitate the students' planning of the task and task completion. In reciprocal teaching, students are supported by the teacher initially and use four specific techniques to explore a reading passage:

- prediction
- question generation
- summarizing
- clarifying

The teacher first models these procedures in questions for the group, and subsequently each member of the group becomes the "teacher" and leads the discussions using these same four procedures. Teaching Tip 3.9 presents a sample reciprocal teaching dialogue.

A teaching dialogue such as this is exciting for anyone who has ever attempted to involve students with learning disabilities in discussions because many students with learning disabilities are quite reluctant to answer questions in class for fear of potential embarrassment. Not only are numerous students participating in the dialogue, but the level of this small-group instructional dialogue indicates a great deal of metacognitive understanding on the part of the students. Each of the students in this dialogue was aware of the four basic procedures that are included in reciprocal teaching, and even when the students could not complete one of the goals, they were still aware of the need to complete that particular step (e.g., thinking

> Involving students with learning disabilities in a reciprocal teaching dialogue assures that every child will be involved in using the four metacognitive processes.

about what came next in the story). Reciprocal teaching is a scaffold for learning a variety of content and can easily be incorporated into almost any general education classroom. This procedure will greatly benefit students with learning disabilities, as well as many other learners in the class.

This reciprocal teaching technique has several advantages when used to differentiate instruction in the general education class. First, while it is relatively simple to differentiate by focusing on learning products (i.e., the teacher may merely require different products from various children and associate those product assignments with their learning strengths), the reciprocal teaching technique focuses on the "process" of learning. Because this technique involves a student with a learning disability on several levels (i.e., as "student" and subsequently as "discussion leader"), the process of learning is explored from several differing perspectives. Also, implementing this technique in the general education classroom tends to strengthen the student's relationships with both teachers and peers. In this technique, students with learning disabilities will be viewed as competent and capable class members, even if they do receive a bit more "coaching" from the teacher when they lead the reciprocal teaching lesson. Thus, this technique is likely to support these students' self-concept development as well as academic success.

In reciprocal teaching, the teacher and the students take turns as instructional leader. Whoever is the "teacher" assumes the role of leading a dialogue about the reading passage. In the example below, the task is a reading passage

**Teaching Tip 3.9**

## A Sample Reciprocal Teaching Dialogue

*Student 1:*   My question is, What does the aquanaut see when he goes under water?

*Student 2:*   A watch.

*Student 3:*   Flippers.

*Student 4:*   A belt.

*Student 1:*   Those are all good answers.

*Teacher:*   Nice job! I have a question too. Why does the aquanaut wear a belt? What is so special about it?

*Student 3:*   It's a heavy belt and keeps him from floating up to the top again.

*Teacher:*   Good for you.

*Student 1:*   For my summary now: This paragraph was about what aquanauts need to take when they go under the water.

*Student 5:*   And also why they need those things.

*Student 3:*   I think we need to clarify the word "gear."

*Student 6:*   That's the special things they need.

*Teacher:*   Another word for "gear" in the story might be "equipment," the equipment that makes it easier for the aquanauts to do their job.

*Student 1:*   I don't think I have a prediction to make.

*Teacher:*   Well, in the story, they tell us that there are many strange and wonderful creatures that aquanauts see as they do their work. My prediction is that they'll describe some of these creatures. What are some of the strange creatures you already know about that live in the ocean?

*Student 6:*   Octopuses.

*Student 3:*   Whales.

*Student 5:*   Sharks.

*Teacher:*   Listen and find out. Who will be our next teacher?

that the students must read silently. Using the reciprocal teaching approach, the common goals of each member of the group are predicting, question generating, summarizing, and clarifying. Each of these goals is taught separately.

First, the teacher discusses the benefits of *prediction* as a reading strategy. Prediction of what comes next in the text involves relevant background knowledge of the text and provides students with a reason to read further, that is, to confirm or refute their predictions. Therefore, this strategy involves both comprehension of material being read and comprehension monitoring of material that has already been read. The teacher may even prepare a poster or wall chart of the various aspects of prediction and keep it in front of the class to assist the student who is leading the activity on any particular day.

The second phase of reciprocal teaching is *question generation.* Question generation gives the student the opportunity to identify the type of information that may make up test questions. Also, this activity may provide an occasion to discuss the methods of study for various types of questions.

*Summarizing* is the third aspect of reciprocal teaching. This step provides an opportunity to integrate information from different sections of the text. The most important ideas of the reading sections should be jointly identified and discussed.

Finally, the fourth activity—*clarifying*—encourages students to identify the major points of the reading selection and to identify concepts that may be difficult. Identification of difficult concepts is one aspect of reading comprehension that is particularly troublesome for students with learning disabilities because these students will often read a selection and not realize that they did not understand part of the passage. Seeking clarification also allows the student to ask questions without embarrassment because the role of the student is to "question and clarify" the problem areas for other students.

Each of the four components of reciprocal teaching is taught for a single instructional period, with the teacher conducting these lessons. Initially, each strategy is explained and examples are given along with guided practice. By the fifth or sixth day, the teacher and students are using the strategies together to discuss reading material. At that point, the teacher continues to model the strategies, praises the students for using the strategies, and prompts the students to use additional strategies. Note here the "scaffolded" nature of this student support—the idea that the teacher is constantly modeling, demonstrating, and only selectively turning these responsibilities over to the students as the students' skills increase. By the end of a two-week period, the role of "teacher" is rotated and the students become the facilitators.

> Reciprocal teaching is a scaffold for learning a variety of content and can easily be incorporated into almost any general education classroom.

Research support for reciprocal teaching supports use of this teaching strategy. In fact, studies over the years indicated that reciprocal teaching is useful in helping students understand written text (Lederer, 2000; Palincsar & Brown, 1986, 1987; Vaughn & Linan-Thompson, 2003). One example of a recent research study is presented in Teaching Tip 3.10.

**Teaching Tip 3.10**

**Reciprocal Teaching Efficacy**

The study by Lederer (2000) illustrated the efficacy of reciprocal teaching for students with learning disabilities in a secondary social studies class. Lederer used six inclusive classrooms, two each in Grades 4, 5, and 6, in a comparison of the effectiveness of reciprocal teaching. The students in experimental classes were taught their social studies for a thirty-day period using reciprocal teaching, while the students in the other classes were taught in the traditional manner. Fifteen students with learning disabilities were in the experimental classes and formed the experimental group, while ten students with learning disabilities were in the control classes and formed the control group. The three dependent measures were measures of the students' ability to answer comprehension questions, generate questions, and summarize, based on a reading selection in social studies. The repeated assessments throughout the thirty-day period indicated a consistent advantage in each dependent measure for the students who received reciprocal teaching instruction. The students with learning disabilities in the reciprocal instruction group consistently outperformed the students with learning disabilities in the control group on question generation, comprehension, and summarizing the reading passages.

## CONCLUSION

These tactics represent an array of metacognitive and scaffolded instruction techniques that should be used for students with learning disabilities, as well as other students in the differentiated classroom. While implementing a differentiated instructional approach, teachers often find that these scaffolding and metacognitive techniques provide the basis for an entirely new way of teaching. Metacognitive and scaffolded learning approaches focus the teacher on presenting information in a manner that directly supports the students' academic endeavors. With these supports in place, students with learning disabilities will, in general, perform quite well in inclusive classes. Thus, the responsibility of every general education teacher is clear—we must support the learning of students with learning disabilities using an array of these metacognitive and scaffolded instruction tactics.

## WHAT'S NEXT?

In this chapter, a number of metacognitive and scaffolded instructional techniques have been described that will allow the teacher to differentiate the instruction in the classroom based on the needs of the individual students. These techniques are increasingly incorporated into the texts and curriculum materials available for instruction in today's classroom, but the critical aspect of differentiated instruction is the teacher's judgment concerning how frequently to use these techniques and when to withdraw support for a particular student during the learning process. In addition to these general instructional techniques, a series of learning strategies for use in particular types of educational tasks have been developed that are also based on metacognitive theory. These learning strategies are presented in the next chapter, and teachers should note the similarity between strategic instruction and the metacognitive techniques presented herein.

# Learning Strategy Training 4

Topics Included in This Chapter:

✓ The SCORE A Learning Strategy
✓ The FISH Learning Strategy
✓ The SELECT Learning Strategy
✓ The Learning Strategies Model
✓ Guidelines for Strategy Training
✓ The STAR Learning Strategy
✓ Developing Your Own Learning Strategies

## WHY A LEARNING STRATEGY APPROACH?

As noted in the previous chapter on metacognition, students with learning disabilities demonstrate a variety of organizational problems and can benefit from metacognitive approaches that delineate how they should proceed in accomplishing a specific task (Archer, Gleason, & Vachon, 2003; Lenz, 2006; Whitaker, Harvey, Hassel, Linden, & Tutterrow, 2006). Although mnemonic instruction can facilitate metacognitive planning, a number of researchers advocate more involved training in strategies that are specific to particular learning tasks (Day & Elksnin, 1994; Deshler, 2006; Keeler & Swanson, 2001; Marks, Laeys, Bender, & Scott, 1996; Schumaker & Deshler, 2003; Sousa, 2001; Vaughn, Gersten, & Chard, 2000) for students with learning disabilities.

For example, consider how the organizational problems of a student with a learning disability, as described previously, may play out when the student is expected to complete a complex assignment such as developing a theme or research paper. To complete this assignment, the student must, at a minimum, select a topic, identify questions/issues within that topic, research each of these (reading and taking lengthy notes), select the appropriate order in which to present these different issues, write a first draft, edit, and then complete a second draft and a final paper. These steps can be quite daunting for the average learner, and for a student with a learning disability, these steps actually prevent the student from accomplishing the task. In short, some type of strategy that spells out these various steps and the order for them is critical. Thus, *strategy training*—some use the term learning strategy instruction—for students with learning disabilities was developed, whereby specific strategies (i.e., a set of metacognitive planning and monitoring steps) are developed for specific types of instructional activities (Day & Elksnin, 1994; Whitaker et al., 2006).

## WHAT IS A LEARNING STRATEGY?

A *learning strategy* is a mnemonic device that assists a student in understanding and completing an academic task, usually by specifying a series of steps to be completed in sequential order (Archer et al., 2003; Deshler, 2006; Marks et al., 1996). Many strategies are summarized in the form of an acronym that the student is expected to memorize and subsequently apply. Although various theorists have developed a variety of strategies to assist students with learning disabilities in metacognitive planning and monitoring of the educational task (Montague, 1992; Montague & Leavell, 1994), much of the early research on strategy training was associated with Dr. Donald Deshler and his coworkers at the University of Kansas Institute for Learning Disabilities (Deshler, 2006; Ellis, 1994; Lenz, 2006; Schumaker & Deshler, 2003). This early research represents only a small percentage of the growing body of research articles supporting strategy training. This research has indicated that use of learning strategies can create dramatic increases in reading, math, and language arts performance and/or improved performance on many other educational tasks for students with learning disabilities (Lenz, 2006).

More specifically, a learning strategy may be thought of as a method of cognitively planning the performance of a learning task, completing the steps involved in the task, and monitoring completion of the task (Chalk, Hagen-Burke, & Burke, 2005; Ellis, 1994; Scheid, 1994). As one example, Teaching Tip 4.1 presents a simple learning strategy designed by Korinek and Bulls (1996) that may be used to assist a student with a learning disability in the theme paper assignment described above. By completingthe steps designated in this strategy, the student can organize his or her efforts, sequentially complete the correct tasks, and eventually complete the assignment.

The steps in this strategy form a heuristic the student memorizes to complete the task (Korinek & Bulls, 1996). This particular strategy would be used by elementary, middle school, and secondary school students with learning disabilities when a report, a research paper, or a theme paper was assigned in a subject area class. As this example demonstrates, strategy training may be differentiated from a "study skills" approach. Whereas study skills include such

**SCORE A: A Research Paper Writing Strategy**

Strategy steps include the following:

S   Select a subject

C   Create categories

O   Obtain resources

R   Read and take notes

E   Evenly organize the information

A   Apply the process writing steps

    Planning

    Drafting

    Revising

things as writing down assignments and allocating time for homework, a learning strategy encompasses a metacognitive plan for completing a specific type of school-related task, as well as structuring the inner dialogue of the student to help complete the task.

Researchers have now developed a wide array of learning strategies that address various educational tasks (Archer, et al., 2003; Day & Elksnin, 1994; Ellis, 1994; Lenz, 2006), and new strategies are being developed all the time and cover an even wider array of activities. For example, Whitaker and her colleagues (2006) developed a new strategy—the FISH strategy—to assist students in decoding words. This strategy provides a set of guidelines to focus the student on parts of the unknown word, but emphasizing the following steps.

F   Find the rime (the first vowel and the rest of the word)

I   Identify the rime (by identifying a word you know that ends like that)

S   Say the rime (the word you know without the first sound)

H   Hook the new onset (the new beginning sound) to the rime

Coupling this strategy with the concept of "hooking a fish" can serve as a useful mnemonic to assist students in memorizing this strategy. Also, given enough practice, this strategy can become the basis for word decoding for students over the years (Whitaker, et al., 2006).

Learning strategies have also been developed to provide assistance for students with learning disabilities in nontraditional academic tasks. Nelson, Smith, and Dodd (1994), as one example, provided a learning strategy—the SELECT strategy—which was designed to assist students in completing job applications. Their research proved the value of this strategy. This strategy included the following steps.

| | |
|---|---|
| S | Survey the job application |
| E | Emphasize words about previous jobs |
| L | Location cues—locate blank lines that cue you for information |
| E | Enter the information requested |
| C | Check that all information is accurate |
| T | Turn in your application |

As described in Chapter 2, the mandate of universal design suggests that teachers should use a variety of strategies and tactics to make content accessible for students with learning disabilities, and learning strategies such as those described herein can assist in that regard. Learning strategies have been developed for many tasks that students must complete, including

- test-taking skills
- word identification
- using pictures in texts
- chapter assignments in content classes
- visual imagery to improve comprehension
- self-questioning
- searching for answers in text

Some strategies are independent; others include substrategies for various steps (note the substrategies in SCORE A for the writing process itself). Some of the more common learning strategies are presented in Teaching Tip 4.2.

**REFLECTIVE EXERCISE: TIME TO MASTER A LEARNING STRATEGY**

Teachers should select one of the learning strategies presented above and consider how frequently a particular student is likely to use that particular skill during one week in his or her class. For example, the COPS strategy is intended to assist students in editing paragraphs, so teachers should consider how frequently students write paragraphs during the students' "average" week. Next, that number may be multiplied by thirty-six (the number of weeks in a given academic year) and subsequently by ten (the number of years of public schooling after students learn to write paragraphs). This calculation will help almost every teacher justify the time spent in having students master this learning strategy.

## USING LEARNING STRATEGIES

Although learning strategies can be used in various ways, Dr. Don Deshler and the other researchers associated with the University of Kansas suggest

**Teaching Tip 4.2**

### Common Learning Strategies

| RAP | A reading comprehension strategy for paragraph comprehension | COPS | An editing strategy for checking a paragraph written by the student |
|---|---|---|---|
| R | Read the paragraph | C | Capitalization |
| A | Ask questions about the content | O | Overall appearance |
| P | Paraphrase the content | P | Punctuation |
| | | S | Spelling |
| SCORER | A strategy for taking multiple-choice tests | RIDER | A visual imagery strategy |
| S | Schedule your time | R | Read the sentence |
| C | Clue words | I | Imagine a picture of it in your mind |
| O | Omit difficult questions | D | Describe how the new image differs from the old |
| R | Read carefully | | |
| E | Estimate your answer | E | Evaluate to see that the image contains everything |
| R | Review your work | | |
| | | R | Repeat as you read the next sentence |

NOTE: Learning strategies are available from a variety of sources (see Day & Elksnin, 1994; Ellis, 1994). Also, the University of Kansas Center for Research on Learning (Lawrence, KS) offers training in strategy instruction.

an eight-step model for instruction in any particular learning strategy, as presented in Teaching Tip 4.3 below. These steps are intended to provide guidance for the teacher in implementing strategic instruction, and many teachers employ variations of these instructional steps (Chalk, Hagen-Burke, & Burke, 2005). Also, for teachers who may be interested, specific strategy instruction training is provided by the University of Kansas Center for Research on Learning in Lawrence, Kansas. One major strength of this instructional model is that this is one of the few instructional models that specifically addresses the issue of transfer of learning into the general education class. For students with learning disabilities, this strategic instruction can be the single critical component that results in success in the general education class.

**Teaching Tip 4.3**

**Steps in Strategy Instruction**

1. Pretest and commitment
2. Describe the strategy
3. Model the strategy
4. Verbal rehearsal of the strategy
5. Practice with controlled materials
6. Practice with grade-appropriate materials
7. Commitment to generalize the strategy
8. Generalization and maintenance

## Step 1: Pretest and Commitment

First, a student with learning disabilities is tested to determine if he or she needs a strategy for a particular task. The results of the assessment are explained to the student, and the student is informed about the level of performance the new strategy would make possible. A decision is then made involving matching a particular strategy to the task and setting (Day & Elksnin, 1994) and determining whether the student will learn the new strategy. Students should be encouraged to "opt in" to learning the strategy; the learning strategies instructional approach stresses the need for student involvement in this decision and student commitment to the decision to learn a new strategy. This step usually takes one instructional period.

## Step 2: Describe the Strategy

During the second step, the strategy is introduced and the various components of the strategy are described to the student. This step focuses on the key elements of the strategy and how these components are used. Also, the student is told where and under what conditions a strategy may be applied. This also usually takes one class period, although the issue of appropriate applications of the strategy will be discussed throughout the course of training.

## Step 3: Model the Strategy

On the next day, the teacher models each step of the strategy while discussing the use of the strategy out loud. Thus, the teacher is modeling how a student should give himself or herself verbal instruction (quiet verbal instruction or "inner language") on using the strategy. Each aspect of the strategy is modeled, and students are encouraged to ask questions. This instructional period may include several different tasks, and the teacher may prompt students to model particular aspects of the strategy at various points.

## Step 4: Verbal Rehearsal of the Strategy

The expectation for students in this instructional model is that students must learn the strategy by rote; they must state the strategy steps very quickly before they attempt to apply the strategy. The students are also required to identify the action to be taken in each step and tell why each step is important for the strategy overall. This step is intended to facilitate independence in strategy application and can usually be completed by students with learning disabilities in one instructional period.

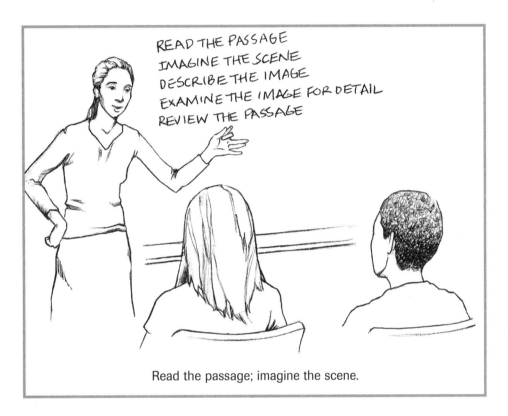

Read the passage; imagine the scene.

## Step 5: Practice With Controlled Materials

Prior to using the strategy on difficult grade-level materials, the student should master the application of the strategy on simpler materials; the assumption behind this step is that the difficulty of the material should not impair the student's ability to learn the strategy. Consequently, the strategy should be applied on "controlled materials" (controlled materials are materials at the student's academic performance level rather than at his or her grade level). If the SCORE A strategy presented in Teaching Tip 4.1 is being taught, the student would first apply that strategy in a two- or three-paragraph theme paper on material that the student had previously mastered. The student would be coached by the teacher using explicit corrective feedback. If a sixth-grade student with a learning disability was completing science work at grade level 4, he or she should be given a theme assignment at the fourth-grade level to learn the strategy. A daily record of the student's performance on both the theme and the student's complete and accurate application of the SCORE A strategy would be kept during this step. This step will be repeated over numerous instructional periods involving numerous days of instructional time (perhaps as many as one or two weeks) until the strategy is totally known and completely understood by the student on grade level 4 materials. In short, the student must master strategy application at something close to 100 percent prior to moving on. After the student has demonstrated mastery of the strategy in grade level 4 materials, he or she should move on expectations for grade level 5, perhaps a four-paragraph themed paper. Also, the student should be encouraged to chart his or her progress on mastery of the learning strategy itself.

## Step 6: Practice With Grade-Appropriate Materials

In this instructional model, the level of complexity on which the student practices is gradually increased until the materials approximate those grade-level materials with which the student works. This step also involves the fading out of various prompts and cues the student used in earlier steps. For the student described above, after mastery of the SCORE A strategy on Grade 5 themes, the student would move into expectations for a more complex paper in grade level 6. Mastery of the strategy on grade-level materials usually takes between five and ten instructional periods. Again, progress during this phase is charted to present a daily picture of the student's progress.

> The student must master strategy application at something close to 100 percent prior to moving on.

## Step 7: Commitment to Generalize the Strategy

Once the student with a learning disability has mastered the strategy on grade-level materials, the student must be encouraged to see the value of generalizing the new strategy to other similar educational tasks in the general education classroom. A commitment should then be elicited from the student to apply the strategy on all theme-writing assignments in all subject areas. This discussion with the student may take as little as a few minutes during one of the instructional periods, but this commitment to generalize is considered a critical step in the learning process.

## Step 8: Generalization and Maintenance

The generalization and maintenance step is, in many ways, the most important aspect of this model. There is little advantage in spending the number of instructional periods discussed above to teach a student the SCORE A strategy unless that student is then taught how to apply that strategy throughout his or her schooling. However, if this strategy is mastered, the student then has a skill that can enhance learning in numerous classes in the future—many of which are dependent on one's ability to successfully write extended themes or reports.

The generalization step involves three phases. The first phase is *orientation to generalization*. This is designed to make the student aware of situations in which the new skill may be tried. The student is encouraged to make adaptations of the original strategy for various types of tests. The second phase is *activation,* where the student is given specific assignments to apply the strategy in grade-appropriate materials from other general education classes. Throughout this process, the special education teacher is encouraged to work with the general education teacher in encouraging use of the strategy. The teacher then checks the output of the strategy.

Finally, a *maintenance* phase is implemented. The students who have been trained in a particular strategy should be periodically reminded to use that strategy, and the teacher should check the work output when the strategy is applied.

> The generalization and maintenance step is, in many ways, the most important aspect of this model.

**REFLECTIVE EXERCISE: INSTRUCTIONAL CROSS-FERTILIZATION AND THE REFLECTIVE TEACHER**

Reflect for a moment on the quality of the instructional strategies recommended in this eight-step instructional plan. What ideas can you identify that are presented here and have been suggested previously in this text (e.g., students taking responsibility for their learning; modeling)? Why do differentiated instructional strategies that stem from different theoretical models tend to emphasize many of the same instructional techniques?

## A STRATEGY TRAINING EXAMPLE

Although the descriptions of strategy instruction herein involve a joint effort between a special educator and a general educator, there is no reason why a single teacher—either in general education or special education—cannot apply strategy instruction. Furthermore, a number of authors have provided suggestions for implementing strategy training by any teacher who wishes to do so (Day & Elksnin, 1994; Marks et al., 1996). Consideration of the teaching tips provided by Day and Elksnin (1994) should help the teacher walk through the following application example.

With these instructional suggestions in mind, review the following strategy instruction example. RAP is a strategy for paraphrasing reading material that was presented in Teaching Tip 4.2. This was one of the first strategies developed and is applicable from the lower grades up through secondary school. The next section of the text traces the implementation of this strategy over a period of thirty-five school days to give a specific, hands-on example of strategy instruction. Again, although this example involves application of the strategy as a team effort, every teacher in the classroom today should be employing strategy instruction for students with learning disabilities, regardless of the opportunity for a team effort. The extant research on strategy instruction strongly supports that bold statement (Archer et al., 2003; Chalk et al., 2005; Day & Elksnin, 1994; Ellis, 1994; Korinek & Bulls, 1996; Vaughn et al., 2000; Whitaker et al., 2006).

Let's assume that the special education teacher, Mr. Langone, has three students with learning disabilities in an inclusive eighth-grade classroom during the first period of each day. Ms. Rooten is the general education teacher for that class, which also includes twenty-two students without disabilities. The reading level of the students with learning disabilities ranges from grade level 4 to 5, and independent of these three students, the reading level for the entire inclusive class ranges from level 5 up through level 11—in short, the typical reading variation in a general education classroom.

On the first day, after Ms. Rooten and Mr. Langone decide to use the RAP strategy for the three students with learning disabilities, Mr. Langone gives out prepared readings of five paragraphs for each student with learning disabilities at the student's grade placement. He tells the students that they are to read their paragraphs silently and then record (on a cassette recorder) what they have read. He reminds the students that they will be tested on the material the next day. Overnight, he will score the audiotapes on "story reading points" (i.e., the main idea and up to two supporting details from each paragraph are each worth 1 point if the student noted them, and the points are then totaled to get a reading score). This becomes one of the students' pretest scores.

On the second day, Mr. Langone administers an individual comprehension test, perhaps ten questions, on the passage each student previously read. The percentage of correct responses becomes the comprehension score for that student on that story. Also, on the second day, the test results are communicated to each student to demonstrate the need for a new strategy for reading comprehension. At this point, the student is asked if he or she would like to learn a new strategy to help better remember what has been read. The student should then write a long-term goal stating this commitment. Also, a management chart that records daily performance on both RAP reading points and reading comprehension is initiated for each student.

> Every teacher in the classroom today should be employing strategy instruction for students with learning disabilities.

The lesson on the next day is a description of the strategy. Using a cue card that displays the steps of the strategy, Mr. Langone will first discuss the meaning of paraphrasing and the use of this skill in various subjects. He may include both students with disabilities and students without disabilities in this segment of the instruction. He will point out the advantages of the ability to paraphrase in terms of increased comprehension. Students are then encouraged to set goals for learning the strategy, with a suggested guideline provided by the teacher. Mr. Langone will then discuss the strategy steps in order, carefully giving the students examples. First, reading is discussed, as attending to the meaning of the words. Second, several ways to find the main idea (such as looking for repetitive words in the paragraph or studying the first sentence) and details from the paragraph are provided. Next, the need to put the ideas into the student's own words is discussed. Finally, the criteria for a good paraphrase are presented to the students so that they know how their work will be graded.

The fourth day provides the opportunity for the teacher to model the strategy. Mr. Langone will read an appropriate passage of five paragraphs and implement the RAP strategy. Before starting, he will verbally remind himself of the strategy, thus modeling self-instruction in this strategy. He will then read the passage aloud and discuss the strategy with himself. "Now that I have read the first paragraph, I have to list the main idea and some details." After several ideas are specified, Mr. Langone will put these on tape, in his own words. This is done for the first several paragraphs, and students are involved in the last several paraphrasing attempts.

The next day is spent on verbal practice of the components of the strategy. Each student should be able to name the series of steps from memory and provide information on how to complete each step. With a cue card in front of the class that summarizes the steps, the students should be encouraged to state the next step of the strategy or to answer any question Mr. Langone asks. For

> The criteria for a good paraphrase are presented to the students so that they know how their work will be graded.

example, they should be able to give at least two suggestions for finding the main idea of a paragraph. The next day begins the controlled practice for the paraphrasing strategy. Each of the three students is given a five-paragraph reading at the student's independent reading level—the level at which a student has 95 percent mastery of the words (that reading level will typically be several grade levels below the grade-level placement for students with learning disabilities). First, Mr. Langone briefly reviews the steps in the strategy with the students. Then, the students are told to use the RAP strategy with each paragraph, recording one main idea and two major details for each.

The RAP reading worksheets presented in Teaching Tip 4.4 may be used for this paraphrasing exercise, and these are scored using the same criteria as the pretest. Depending on the time, the students may also take the comprehension test for that reading selection. Mr. Langone also has the option of using the class period on the next day as a comprehension test day. The comprehension test typically is a ten-question test on the reading passage. That quiz, coupled with the score on the RAP reading worksheet, can provide a very good indication of students' overall comprehension performance. Thus, the student completes a RAP reading worksheet and a comprehension test for each five- paragraph passage read, and each of these scores is placed on the student's individual progress chart.

The scoring of student work on both the paraphrase worksheet and the comprehension test for each reading selection should be used as an opportunity to provide corrective and positive feedback. Frequent feedback is a critical component of learning for students with learning disabilities, and this instructional method facilitates such feedback. To provide appropriate feedback, Mr. Langone will identify several things that each student did well and share these with the student. Also, he will review the requirements that were not met when a student did not receive credit for an answer on the RAP reading worksheet or the comprehension test. After both a RAP reading worksheet and a comprehension test are completed on a five-paragraph reading segment, the student will read another reading selection at the same grade level. This series of daily lessons is continued until the student reaches mastery level in both paraphrasing and comprehension of the material at that grade level. On average, students may be expected to reach mastery of this step in three to six practice attempts at each grade level, though some students with learning disabilities may take

**Teaching Tip 4.4**

## A RAP Worksheet

For each paragraph in the five-paragraph reading passage, the student should list the main idea and two supporting details in the space provided below.

1. Main Idea _____

    Detail 1: _____

    Detail 2: _____

2. Main Idea _____

    Detail 1: _____

    Detail 2: _____

3. Main Idea _____

    Detail 1: _____

    Detail 2: _____

4. Main Idea _____

    Detail 1: _____

    Detail 2: _____

5. Main Idea _____

    Detail 1: _____

    Detail 2: _____

longer. Thus, if a student's reading level is Grade 4, and the student is in an eighth-grade general education classroom, he or she may take up to twenty-four days to achieve mastery at grade-level work in Grades 4, 5, 6, and 7, respectively.

The next step emphasizes grade-appropriate practice for the student, and the students will, in all probability, reach this step on different days. The student will then be given grade-appropriate materials at his or her grade level and will practice until mastery is achieved. His or her final passage should be taken from a text that is normally used at his or her grade level.

> Frequent feedback is a critical component of learning for students with learning disabilities, and this instructional method facilitates such feedback.

The following step involves the post-test and student commitment to generalize the strategy. The student (we'll call him John) will complete a paraphrase task and a comprehension test for a passage that consists of five paragraphs of reading from his grade placement level. Results of these will be noted on the progress chart. Mr. Langone will discuss the entire learning procedure with John to point out the progress depicted in the chart. He will then obtain a commitment from John to generalize the strategy to other textbooks in the general education classroom. This step takes only one instructional period, but the commitment step must be done with each student individually and is critical for students with learning disabilities.

The next day, Mr. Langone begins the final step with John—generalization. John is asked to use his textbook, and Mr. Langone gathers reading material from other settings, such as the home, newspapers, magazines that interest John, and so forth. Mr. Langone will discuss with John the use of each book and material. At this stage, Ms. Rooten—the general education teacher—should become involved by meeting with John and Mr. Langone to discuss strategy application in the materials from the inclusive general education classroom. John will make cue cards for the strategy and tape these inside the front of each textbook, and other cues for using the strategy are discussed. Ms. Rooten will make an agreement with John to remind him to use the RAP strategy whenever appropriate on a reading assignment.

The next day begins the activation phase of the generalization step. Mr. Langone will present a "Report of Strategy Use" form that consists of a series of lines on which John will enter each use of the strategy from the general education classes. The form also lists the date and the type of material on which the strategy was used: textbook, newspaper, novel, or magazine. Mr. Langone will generate various assignments from these reading materials for the student to complete sometime within the next twenty-four hours. These are quickly graded by Mr. Langone or Ms. Rooten, and corrective feedback is given where necessary. The student should complete six different activities of this nature. Mr. Langone will also discuss the completion of the form for particular dates, and John will keep a record for a two-week period on utilization of the strategy.

Maintenance is the last phase of the generalization step. This consists of a series of evaluations similar to the post-test; these are generally done one week after the student completes the activation phase. At this point, John has internalized a strategy that should facilitate his reading comprehension across grade levels and for all types of reading materials. Of course, both Ms. Rooten and Mr. Langone should frequently remind John to perform the strategy on appropriate work in John's various classes.

As can be seen, the example above uses a number of methods that are the hallmark of differentiated instruction, including modeling, scaffolds for memorizing the task (e.g., RAP), use of inner language, corrective and timely feedback, and repeated guided practice. Use of effective teaching behaviors greatly enhances the efficacy of the learning strategies model of instruction. Again, the research on strategic instruction is so strongly supportive that every teacher of students with learning disabilities should be implementing this method for tasks that give particular students problems.

> The commitment step must be done with each student individually and is critical for students with learning disabilities.

Although the example above presented the ideal collaboration between a general education and a special education teacher, general education teachers who do not have a collaborative relationship with a special educator should also consider implementing this learning strategies instructional approach. Of course, this may be a bit more difficult for a single teacher to implement, yet the results of modifying the learning process through strategic instruction will greatly increase the learning level within the general education class.

## LEARNING STRATEGIES IN MATH

In addition to the learning strategies in reading, a number of learning strategies have been developed in other academic areas. In fact, almost any instructional area in the school curriculum has witnessed the development of instructional strategies to facilitate conceptual learning. To illustrate this, a number of authors have recently developed learning strategies in the area of math (Gagnon & Maccini, 2001; Maccini & Hughes, 2000). Further, there is a solid rational for implementation of learning strategies instruction in mathematics, based on the revised mathematics standards published in 2000 by the National Council of Teachers of Mathematics (NCTM, 2000). Rather than drill and practice instructional techniques, those NCTM standards emphasize the importance of students as active learners who are taught to construct meaning and understandings of mathematical principles as well as reflective problem solving. Research has shown that conceptual understanding of mathematics and procedural knowledge develop in tandem (Butler, Beckingham, & Lauscher, 2005), and learning strategies, by stipulating procedural steps in problem solving, can assist students with learning disabilities in this regard. Thus, metacognitive techniques such as a learning strategies approach are congruent with the overall emphasis in the broader field of mathematics instruction.

Several learning strategies have been presented in the literature that assist students with some of the higher order mathematics skills, such as solving word problems (see Bender, 2005, pp. 69–90; Lenz, 2006). For example, the STAR learning strategy was developed to assist students in reading and interpretation of word problems (adapted from Gagnon & Maccini, 2001; and Maccini & Hughes, 2000). The steps in the strategy assist students with learning disabilities to focus on steps required to appropriately read and interpret a math word problem. The steps are presented below.

S   Search the word problem:
        Read the problem carefully
        Ask, "What do I know, and what do I need to find?"
        Write down the facts in the problem

T   Translate the words into an equation in picture form:
        Choose a variable to solve for
        Identify the operations necessary (using cue words helps here)
        If possible, represent the problem with counters/manipulatives
        Draw a picture of the equation, include known and unknown facts

A   Answer the problem:
        Perform the necessary operations, solving for the unknowns

R   Review the solution:
        Reread the problem
        Ask, "Does the answer make sense? Why or why not?"
        Check the answer

Note that the requirement to state the knowns and unknowns in this learning strategy forces the student to consider the basic questions asked by the word problem. Also, the use of "drawing" to represent the problem algorithm makes this learning strategy particularly effective for use with students who may have a multiple intelligence strength in spatial intelligence. Implementation of this strategy should proceed along the lines discussed previously, by using the same eight-step model described herein. That would assure continual exposure of the students with learning disabilities to this learning strategy and would probably result in his or her application of this strategy throughout the remainder of their public school years in mathematics classes.

Research has shown that metacognitive strategies do enhance academic achievement in mathematics (Butler, Beckingham & Lauscher, 2005; Maccini & Hughes, 2000), so implementation of learning strategies such as the STAR strategy mentioned here in the general education math class is certainly supported by research (Bender, 2005; Maccini & Gagnon, 2006). Unfortunately, research has also shown that only a minority of teachers of mathematics use instructional accommodations that involve learning strategies in math (Maccini & Gagnon, 2006). Nevertheless, for the teacher who wishes to effectively differentiate math instruction, for students struggling in mathematics, implementation of learning strategies would seem to be a critically important first step.

## DEVELOPING YOUR OWN STRATEGIES

Although specific training in strategic instruction provides the best preparation for implementation of this instructional method (for the availability of summer institute training, you may wish to contact the Department of Special Education at the University of Kansas, Lawrence, KS), teachers can and should

**Teaching Tip 4.5**

### Developing Task Specific Strategies

1. Specify the type of task that the strategy is designed to facilitate. Identify a task that will yield a daily performance measure so that you may chart the progress of the student.

2. Describe the task in sequential order. Students should be able to use the task acronym not only as a memory tool to remember the steps but also as an organizational tool that presents the steps in the task in sequence.

3. Summarize each step. You should write a brief statement that summarizes each step in the sequence, with precise and concise instructions for the student.

4. Limit the strategy to a specific type of task. Think of examples and nonexamples that you can use to illustrate for the student when to use or not use the strategy.

5. Develop a mnemonic acronym to assist the student in memorizing the sequential steps in the strategy. Creativity will play a part here, and some license may be used. Still, you should phrase the acronym such that the most important work (usually the verb) in the step is emphasized in the acronym.

SOURCE: Summarized from Marks, Laeys, Bender, & Scott (1996).

implement strategic instruction based on the information available to them. Clearly, the use of learning strategies fulfills the universal design mandate since these strategies greatly assist students in making curricular content accessible for students with learning disabilities. Furthermore, rather than merely apply strategies that are presented in this chapter or other available literature, many teachers have begun to develop specific learning strategies for use in their own classrooms (Marks et al., 1996). The steps suggested by Marks et al. (1996) and presented in Teaching Tip 4.5 should help you in developing strategies specific to the needs of your students.

As one example, one veteran teacher in a special education classroom noted that several of her students needed assistance in interpreting information from pictures in their reading material, and she developed the AIDE strategy, presented in Teaching Tip 4.6. Every veteran teacher realizes that much of the information presented in pictures and picture captions in various texts may not be presented in the text sections of the chapter. However, this information may very well appear on the end of chapter test. Thus, students with learning disabilities should be taught a specific strategy to glean information from pictures and picture captions in text.

The teacher printed the AIDE strategy on a task card that was presented to the students each day. Also presented each day were three picture cards that each student had to interpret. Students were told to use the AIDE strategy with each picture and were then presented with a ten-question comprehension test on the three pictures. A multiple baseline research project demonstrated that this procedure worked quite well in assisting students with disabilities to focus

**Teaching Tip 4.6**

### The AIDE Strategy for Picture Interpretation

| | | |
|---|---|---|
| A | Action | Look for the action in the picture |
| I | Idea | Guess the main idea of the picture |
| D | Details | Study each picture detail |
| E | Explanation | Read the explanation with the picture |

SOURCE: Adapted from Marks, Laeys, Bender, & Scott (1996).

on the information contained in pictures. Furthermore, this illustrates differentiated instruction, based on a teacher noting a specific need on the part of one or more of the students and addressing that with a strategic instructional approach.

## CONCLUSION

The use of strategic instruction for students with learning disabilities is as strongly supported by research as any available instructional technique (Chalk et al., 2005; Deshler, 2006, Lenz, 2006; Vaughn et al., 2000). Furthermore, the research has likewise demonstrated that this technique (like many others described in this book) works quite well for a large number of other students in the general education classroom also. As a response to this powerful research, I can truthfully suggest that every teacher in general education should employ some type of strategic instruction for his or her students with learning disabilities.

## WHAT'S NEXT?

The last several chapters have provided a solid set of differentiated instructional ideas that can enhance learning in any classroom in almost any subject area. With these ideas as the background, the next chapter will present suggestions for modification of the instructional process via modification of instructional groupings. Specifically, several options for peer tutoring will be explored.

# Peer Tutoring in the Inclusive Classroom 5

## Differentiated Instruction and Increasing Instructional Time

Students with learning disabilities often make significant demands on the teacher's time. Because of their noted problems with attention skills, these students need examples explained many more times than nondisabled learners and generally seem to require assistance more than other students. They also need to be reminded to return to task, or they are disciplined for unruly behavior more frequently. In the differentiated classroom, the teacher must address all of these needs for students with disabilities. For this reason, it is not uncommon for teachers to feel overwhelmed when three or four students with learning disabilities are in their general education classroom. Teachers often feel that there is simply not enough time to do effective instruction for many students with learning disabilities. Furthermore, when considering differentiating the instruction based on the needs of learners with learning disabilities, teachers may simply feel there are not enough hours in the day to accomplish these many instructional tasks.

For these reasons, numerous researchers and practitioners have recommended peer tutoring as one innovative instructional procedure that increases instructional time for students with learning disabilities while reducing the time that the teacher has to spend with each student (Fulk & King, 2001; Greenwood, 1991; Greenwood, Tapia, Abbott, & Walten, 2003; Maheady, Harper, & Sacca, 1988; Mortweet et al., 1999; Saenz, Fuchs, & Fuchs, 2005). In short, students can and do learn from each other—in many cases, students learn better from each other than they do when instructed by a teacher. Furthermore, with appropriate instructional scaffolds (e.g., in the form of a set of instructions for modeling a learning task), students can teach other students and still benefit from the teacher's expertise. For this reason, the wise general education teacher will take advantage of the peer tutoring option for increasing instructional time. Thus, peer tutoring, in some form, is one critical instructional skill for the differentiated classroom that every teacher should have as an option in the general education class.

One emphasis in universal design involves making the curriculum accessible, and certainly the grouping patterns used for differentiation can enhance accessibility. In using peer tutoring, students receive individual attention in their instruction, without the teacher having to provide all of that time to each child (Greenwood et al., 2003). Tutoring typically involves help with academic work and an immediate check of the work, and thus results in providing effective instruction for students with learning disabilities. In this sense, peer tutoring can be regarded as one strategy that facilitates a more universal, comprehensive curriculum in the differentiated class.

Peer tutoring works!

# INITIATING A PEER TUTORING SYSTEM

## REFLECTIVE ACTIVITY: PREDICTING THE ISSUES IN INITIATING A PEER TUTORING SYSTEM

As a reflective activity, jot down a series of notes on the decisions involved in initiating a peer tutoring system in your class. What types of things will have to be considered in advance? After listing a series of issues and concerns, compare your notes with the issues noted below.

Tutoring systems are relatively easy to initiate (Burks, 2004; Fuchs et al., 2001; Fulk & King, 2001), although certain tutoring systems require more time than others. Also, there are several specific decisions to make before you start. These are summarized in Teaching Tip 5.1.

**Teaching Tip 5.1**

### Decisions in Preparation of a Tutoring System

I. What can a tutor do in the classroom?

What types of tasks would save the most time?

What types of tasks require major training time?

Are self-checking materials used a great deal?

Can tutors assist in setting up equipment?

How frequently is such equipment used?

Can tutors monitor academic tasks in the class, such as listening to a child read?

What guidelines should a tutor receive concerning when to request the teacher's assistance?

II. Who should be used as a tutor?

Who is available? With a little public relations work, are other tutors available?

Given the teacher's particular teaching style and methods of behavioral management, will sharing authority with a tutor be a problem? How does this affect the selection of tutors?

III. Can the necessary training for tutors be provided?

What types of tasks should tutors be trained for? What is a good time for tutor training?

Can someone else conduct the training (perhaps a school principal, if the tutoring system involves the entire school)?

IV. Has a good communication method been identified?

Does the teacher have time for effective communication about student progress?

## What a Peer Tutor Can Do

The first consideration in initiating a tutoring system is delineating the specific tasks for the student tutor to accomplish. It may be helpful to think of the various tasks in terms of different levels, depending on the degree of complexity of the tutoring assignment and the instructional skills a person should have before attempting to teach a particular task to a student with learning disabilities. For example, with very little preparation, almost any peer tutor can enter the inclusive class and begin to assist in checking a student's objective answers on a worksheet, particularly if an answer sheet is provided. However, if the teacher wants a student to assist with reading comprehension questioning exercises or lead a pre-reading discussion using an advance organizer for a story, some training may be necessary. Clearly, the types of tasks required from a tutor will affect the training the tutor requires, and considering these tasks as different tutoring levels should assist in the decisions about what particular peer tutors can do.

> The first consideration in initiating a tutoring system is delineating the specific tasks for the student tutor to accomplish.

The teacher must take the final responsibility for deciding what the peer tutors do in the class. Teachers may consider the types of activities typically done that do not require complex instruction, and peer tutors can begin those tasks immediately. The list of simple peer tutoring tasks may include the following:

- checking student worksheets
- rechecking the self-checking worksheets students complete
- listening to oral reading and correcting oral reading errors
- assisting with dictionary skills
- monitoring group art projects

Each of these activities (and many others) can be accomplished with very little training for the tutor. For our purposes in this text, these tasks will be considered Level 1 tasks because these require very little (if any) preparation on the part of the tutor.

However, certain activities require more training. These activities may include assisting a student with comprehension of a math problem, using an advanced organizer to assist in reading comprehension, or offering reinforcement for completed work. Because these skills are more complex, teachers will want the tutor to learn how to accomplish them prior to using the tutor to instruct other students. Still, training in these skills can be as simple as having the new peer tutor observe while the teacher works with a student on one of these tasks, and in most cases, very little out-of-class instructional time will be necessary in training tutors for these tasks. This type of task is referred to as a Level 2 task; some training is necessary, which is generally conducted during "in-class" time and involves modeling the tutoring for the tutor and discussing it with him or her.

Next, certain tasks may require some training outside of class, and these may be considered Level 3 tasks. Examples would include implementation of a learning strategies curriculum or assisting students in completing self-management behavioral charts on their own performance. The specific training associated with these tasks is described throughout the remainder of this chapter.

Finally, there are certain types of instructional tasks that only the teacher should perform. These are referred to as Level 4 tasks and are some of the more difficult decision-making tasks involved in teaching. These tasks, if done incorrectly, may have a very negative impact on the student's development, and for this reason, these tasks should be completed only by the teacher. These Level 4 tasks would include such things as providing initial instruction on a new type of math problem, punishing students for misbehavior, or planning the next set of instructional activities for the students.

Clearly, when contemplating a tutoring system, teachers must consider the level of task the tutor will perform; teachers must then make time for the appropriate training for the peer tutors. For Level 3 tasks in particular, training can be critical to the success of the peer tutoring efforts, and nothing positive will be gained if the teacher begins to use peer tutors for complex tasks for which the tutors have received no training.

## Who Should Be a Peer Tutor?

Tutors may be obtained from any number of sources, including the teacher's class, the school, or other schools on the same campus. As one example, many teachers obtain peer tutors by inquiring in the scheduling office about having two or three study hall students who may wish to serve as tutors assigned to the class. The guidance counselor can often identify several students who would be willing to serve as a tutor for a semester. These students would then begin to assist with Level 1 tasks immediately, and, with a few training observations, they may also begin to assist in Level 2 tasks.

Research has also demonstrated the effectiveness of having students with learning disabilities tutor other students with or without disabilities (Burks, 2004; Fulk & King, 2001). Thus, in either a general education class or in a special education class, one potential supply of peer tutors is in the class. Using this resource pool of potential tutors, the teacher's initial exploration with tutoring may be as simple as an individual, single assignment tutoring experience—that is, using one student to assist another student on a single assignment in class. Many teachers feel more comfortable beginning in this limited fashion and then expanding their tutoring program to more students and more complex assignments. Of course, this can easily grow into an exercise for the entire class, and later in this chapter we will describe several plans for using the entire class in tutoring.

With these potential tutoring sources noted, tutoring seems to become more feasible for almost any classroom today. Thus, if you wish to differentiate the instruction in your classroom, and some type of tutoring system is not in place, you should consider starting one. The simplest method is to use students in the class to tutor others. Although using students with learning disabilities as tutors has been supported by research, this type of tutoring system requires more active monitoring of the tutor-tutee interactions (Burks, 2004; Fulk & King, 2001; Greenwood et al., 2003). Still, with very little training, students with learning disabilities can assist others in the class, and this holds many benefits for students with learning disabilities in areas such as self-concept enhancement and improved peer interactions. Obviously, although almost any student can successfully manage Level 1 tasks prior to assigning a peer tutor to Level 2 or Level 3 tasks, teachers should train the tutors to ensure that the student knows the material and the instructional tutoring method in the proposed lesson completely.

> Some tasks, if done incorrectly, may have a very negative impact on the student's development, and for this reason, these tasks should be completed only by the teacher.

Teachers should also consider the gender of the tutor-tutee pairs. At certain ages (generally Grades 1 through 5—the early years through the puberty years), children of opposite sexes do not mix a great deal socially, and teachers may want to use only male tutors with male students and female tutors with female students. Beyond that age, gender should still be considered (i.e., be cognizant of who is dating or friends with whom), but it is quite permissible to use students of a different gender as tutors if the teacher feels that the pairing will be beneficial. Furthermore, the teacher will need to consider the social acceptance of each student in the proposed tutoring pair. Teachers should pair students together who have some history of working together, if at all possible. Tutors selected on this basis can begin to assist in Level 1 tasks immediately. However, one word of caution is in order. The teacher will have to maintain complete control over the tutoring system and may have to discipline the tutors discretely if they begin to misbehave in the tutoring situation or to overstep the responsibilities of tutoring.

One critical concern in tutoring programs that must be emphasized for tutors in every level of tutoring is the requirement for confidentiality. Tutors must understand that they should never discuss a student's work outside the context of the class, nor is it ever appropriate to poke fun at students for mistakes on work during a tutoring session. Some teachers develop a "tutoring contract" that the tutors are requested to sign prior to participating in the tutoring. That contract should include the expectations of the tutoring, the length of the tutoring commitment (the second author of this chapter used a one grading period commitment in the tutoring contract), and a privacy/confidentiality provision.

If students are unwilling to sign and abide by this contract, other tutors should be found.

### Training the Tutors

As noted previously, the task level assigned to tutors has a direct bearing on the types of training that must be provided. Level 1 tasks can be assigned to any tutor on the first day of tutoring, whereas Level 3 tasks may require complicated training. For implementing a peer tutoring option, there are at least three training choices. First, one observation combined with a critical review/debriefing session may be enough of a training process for many peer tutors in Level 2 tasks. This generally involves merely having the student observe the teacher while tutoring another child once or perhaps twice. On each occasion, the teacher should debrief the tutor to ensure that he or she understands the role. Delquadri, Greenwood, Whorton, Carta, and Hall (1986) recommended this type of training.

A more involved level of training for Level 3 tasks actually involves some out-of-class time. For a tutor to be of benefit in conducting an advanced organizer lesson for a reading assignment, as one example, the tutor may be required merely to watch for several days as the teacher works through an advance organizer prior to having students read the assigned material. The teacher can then discuss the concept of the advance organizer with the tutor after class, answering any questions concerning the use of such an organizer as a pre-reading activity. Finally, the teacher may wish to role-play with the prospective tutor, having the peer tutor "teach" using an advance organizer. Afterward, the teacher would debrief the student and critique his or her performance. The advantage of this type of training is that the peer tutor would be able to conduct more involved lessons than tutors with less training.

> One critical concern in tutoring programs that must be emphasized for tutors in every level of tutoring is the requirement for confidentiality.

The highest level of tutor training involves extended extra-class training. For example, for a tutor to understand the purpose of a learning strategies instructional method, the teacher may require the tutor to read certain materials on learning strategies prior to conducting observations of teaching sessions or role-play activities. Also, extra-class time may be needed to go over these materials with the peer tutor before he or she is considered ready to observe a learning strategies lesson in your class. Much of the research on tutoring has used models of tutor training that require extra-class training time during the initial stages (Fuchs et al., 2001). For example, Beirne-Smith (1991) used a more involved tutor training to prepare tutors to teach math to students with learning disabilities. She had two instructional sessions of forty-five minutes each, during which tutors were trained in two different instructional methods. Clearly, the level of task you want tutors to perform will determine the type and extent of necessary training, with Level 2 tasks and Level 3 tasks requiring much more training.

Finally, if extensive training of tutors for Level 3 tasks is necessary, you should prepare a set of detailed written instructions for the tutors to follow to ensure that their instructional presentation is standardized. This type of lesson format may be an appropriate choice for you in preparing the instructional session for your peer tutors to conduct. There are numerous examples in the literature of scripted lessons for tutors. Teaching Tip 5.2 presents a set of instructions for tutors that Beirne-Smith (1991) used in tutor training.

## Communication With the Tutor

If the tutors are merely conducting Level 1 tasks, there is very little need for structured communication concerning student progress because the tutees' progress is typically represented in the form of some corrected worksheet or score sheet on some activity. These tutors merely do the types of activities identified by the teacher, and these suggestions are generally made while class is in progress. However, not all work results in a worksheet, and thus, for some peer tutoring activities, teachers should construct the tutoring lessons specifically to require a permanent product (i.e., a written record) of the student's performance on the task, such as collection of the worksheet the tutor has graded.

This allows the teacher to monitor the student's progress and plan the student's instruction appropriately.

> The task level assigned to tutors has a direct bearing on the types of training that must be provided.

However, in situations where the tutor is trained to conduct instructional Level 2 and Level 3 tasks (or in inclusive classes where two or more teachers may direct the tutor), additional and more structured communication about the student's progress may be necessary. For example, many teachers assign a particular time slot to the tutor each day for conducting an instructional assignment with a student (e.g., during the first fifteen minutes of the period each day, the tutor may be expected to work with Billy on spelling exercises). Clearly, some form of daily communication between the peer tutor and the teachers regarding Billy's performance is necessary. One option is to require a brief written summary each day—usually a single paragraph—that summarizes the lesson and notes the number and types of errors made during the day. This would be turned in to the teacher in addition to copies of the student's worksheets.

As a final option for Level 2 and Level 3 tutoring tasks, many researchers recommend some type of daily performance chart (Greenwood et al., 2003;

## Teaching Tip 5.2

### Instructional Session Plan for Tutor Training

In the Beirne-Smith (1991) study, students with learning disabilities received tutoring in addition facts from older students without learning disabilities. Training in math facts was based on twenty sets of three "related" math facts in which the first addend in each set was held constant and the second addend was increased by 1 (e.g., $2 + 4 = 6$; $2 + 5 = 7$; $2 + 6 = 8$). For each set, a file folder was prepared showing the math facts without the answer on the front and the math facts with the answer on the back. With materials prepared in that fashion, the following task instructions were provided.

The tutor should display the file with answers, point to second addends and sums, and follow the steps below.

1. Rule stating (e.g., "Each time the addend increases by 1 the sum increases by 1. Say it with me.")

2. Demonstration (e.g., "My turn, $2 + 4 = 6$; $2 + 5 = 7$; $2 + 6 = 8$.")

3. Unison responding (e.g., "Say it with me: $2 + 4 = \dots$")

4. Individual turns ("Say it by yourself.")

5. Testing ("Say it again," while showing the file without answers.)

This type of task card, prepared for the instructional situations in which you expect your tutor to function (Level 2 or Level 3), will facilitate effective instruction.

SOURCE: Adapted from Beirne-Smith (1991).

Mortweet et al., 1999). Charting students' performance is often very helpful, and for many kids, the chart itself begins to serve as a reinforcer for successful performance. For this reason, almost every peer tutoring research demonstration has emphasized the use of charted performance measures for each tutoring session each day. In any case, it should be stressed to all concerned that the teacher is responsible for the instruction in his or her class and needs to be fully informed of student progress, and some communication format will need to be in place to fully inform teachers of their students' progress.

## Putting the Tutoring System Together

The four major concerns discussed earlier will be the basis of success or failure of your tutoring program: who will do the tutoring, tasks of the tutors, tutor training, and communication with the tutor. Of course these issues are all interrelated, and once the teacher decides on these factors, the peer tutoring strategy is ready. The steps in initiating a tutoring system are presented in Teaching Tip 5.3.

These steps are based on a tutoring system in which other students from the school (i.e., not in the teacher's class) are to be used as tutors. This tutoring system is a bit more complex to initiate; thus, if teachers can accomplish this, they will easily be able to initiate a peer tutoring system by using tutors from their own class. Also, most of these recommendations are generally appropriate during the initiation of each type of tutoring system.

First, permissions should be obtained from the administrators, including the school principal and, perhaps, the director of special education in your district. Teachers may wish to share some research articles or reviews of the literature (cited throughout this chapter) on the effectiveness of using peer tutoring for students with disabilities.

In particular, one fear concerning peer tutoring is the possibility of wasting the time of the tutors, and this concern must be addressed. Not only will other teachers express this fear, but many parents of the tutors may also share this concern. Of course, the research on peer tutoring will lay this fear to rest. The research demonstrates that a tutoring program is usually quite beneficial for all persons involved; specifically, both the tutors and tutees learn better and develop better attitudes toward academic work, and those results have been demonstrated repeatedly over the years (Beirne-Smith, 1991; Fulk & King, 2001).

Second, teachers should involve the school guidance counselor to discuss the students who may become tutors. For example, this person may be able to identify any students with potential behavior problems among the pool of potential tutors. Likewise, the guidance counselor will be able to identify students who may make very effective tutors. If your school has an "Honors Club" or similar organizations, teachers should select potential tutors from those organizations by going to a meeting and asking for volunteers.

Third, teachers should identify more tutors than they can initially use. This will provide a pool of prospective tutors. Then the teacher should meet with the prospective tutors themselves, explain the proposed tutoring job and

**Teaching Tip 5.3**

## Checklist for Initiating a Tutoring System

### Permissions

___ Obtain permission from school administrators.

___ Obtain permission from each prospective tutor's parents.

### Tutor selection

___ Identify time slots when tutors are needed.

___ Request that the guidance counselor suggest some tutors.

___ Request recommendations and support from other teachers.

### Meeting with tutors

___ Discuss your needs from tutors.

___ Outline the prospective duties and privileges of tutors.

___ Elicit a commitment from tutors for one grading period.

___ Verify each student's parental permission.

### Begin tutoring system

___ Have student observe in each task for which he or she will be used.

___ Observe the tutor while he or she conducts a tutoring session.

___ Allow tutors to conduct the sessions themselves.

### Initiation of tutor training

___ Identify which Level 2 or Level 3 tasks you wish to have tutors conduct.

___ Identify the tutors whom you think capable of conducting these tasks.

___ Identify method of training (reading, modeling, videotapes).

___ Begin in-class training after the tutor completes tasks.

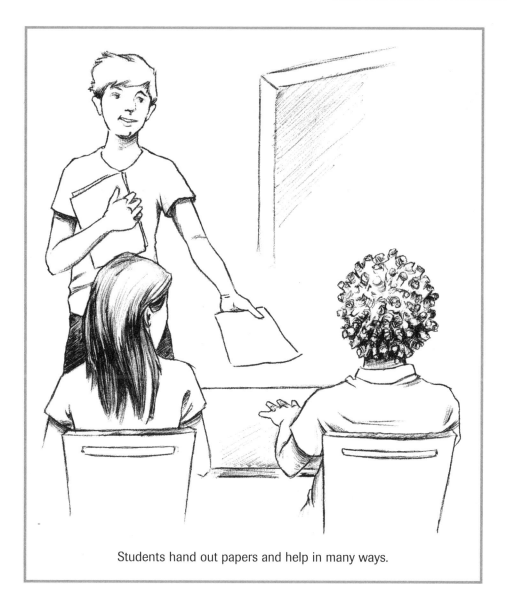

Students hand out papers and help in many ways.

responsibilities, and elicit their cooperation. After hearing about the program, some tutors may choose not to participate, and this is fine if teachers have initially selected more than enough. Tutors should sign an agreement to act as tutors for at least one grading period, and every student tutor should have the option of leaving the tutoring program at that time. At this point, the teacher would then send a parental permission letter home to the parents of the tutors, explaining the system, the time involvement of the tutors, and the advantages of tutoring. For tutoring applications that are not reciprocal in nature (such as the tutoring described thus far in this chapter), teachers should use students as tutors only after parental permission has been obtained.

Fourth, begin the tutoring responsibilities with Level 1 tasks on the first day of tutoring. Generally, all students in schools can check a paper when an answer key is provided. These Level 1 tasks from the first week of the tutoring program let the teacher observe the tutors and their relationships with the students with learning disabilities in your class. At this point, the teacher will have the option of using some tutors exclusively for Level 1 tasks and selecting other tutors for more involved training for Level 2 and Level 3 tasks. These decisions may be made through observation of the tutors in their early tutoring experiences. On rare occasions, teachers may have to counsel some student tutors to withdraw from the tutoring program, explaining that not everyone has the personality to be a teacher or tutor. However, this should be a fairly rare occurrence.

Finally, after the teacher determines which students to use for more complex tasks, the teacher may approach them and inquire about a year-long commitment; there is little reason to provide extensive tutor training for tutors who may choose to leave the tutoring experience after only one grading period. After several tutors indicate a desire to continue over a longer time period, a more extensive training session may be designed to prepare those tutors for monitoring of comprehension through the use of advanced organizers and other complex instructional strategies. As discussed previously, teachers may use some combination of modeling the lesson format, required readings, and scripted lessons as the basis for the training.

> There is little reason to provide extensive tutor training for tutors who may choose to leave the tutoring experience after only one grading period.

## CLASSWIDE PEER TUTORING (CWPT)

Peer tutoring is one of the most effective tactics available to assist students with learning disabilities in the differentiated classroom and can increase the quality and amount of instruction that students with learning disabilities receive. Furthermore, research has been strongly supportive of peer tutoring in terms of positive results for both tutors and tutees. For these reasons, tutoring has received increasing research attention during the past decade, and several more involved forms of tutoring have been developed that involve the entire general education classroom. The first of these newly developed systems is classwide peer tutoring (CWPT), which was developed in the 1980s by Charles Greenwood and his coworkers (Greenwood et al., 2003; Mortweet, Utley, Walker, Dawson, Delquadri, Reddy, & Greenwood, 1999; Utley, Mortweet, & Greenwood, 1997). The program has been used successfully as an integration strategy for children with a range of disabilities in addition to high-risk students and students with learning disabilities, and it works very well in inclusive classrooms. Furthermore, CWPT may be used in many content subjects such as reading, vocabulary, spelling, and mathematics; this versatility suggests that CWPT should be considered as one strategy for every inclusive classroom (Burks, 2004; Greenwood et al., 2003).

CWPT is reciprocal in nature, and unlike the peer tutoring options discussed previously, every student will serve as both tutor and tutee. Again, this makes this tutoring approach particularly appropriate in inclusive classes. During the CWPT sessions, all students are paired with a partner, and each student pair is assigned to one of two competing teams. One student, serving initially as the tutor, will use preselected materials and call out problems to the tutee. Halfway through each tutoring session—after approximately ten minutes—the teacher signals the students to change roles; the tutors then become tutees and vice versa.

The tutees earn points for their team by correctly responding to specific tasks when presented to them by the tutor (Utley et al., 1997), and the team with the most points wins. The winning team can be determined daily or weekly and is based on each team's total points. Another strength of this program is that the tutor and tutee roles are highly structured to ensure that tutees receive questions

### Teaching Tip 5.4

**CWPT Spelling Lesson**

Burks (2004) recently implemented a classwide peer tutoring project to enhance spelling among three students with learning disabilities in elementary school. Using a baseline and intervention design, the target behavior was identified as spelling accuracy on weekly spelling tests. During baseline, each of the three students participated in traditional spelling lessons, but during a 7 week intervention, peer tutoring was implemented once per week for 20 minutes. During the tutoring, students worked in pairs. One student would call out words to his or her partner for 10 minutes, and when the tutee wrote a word, the tutor would check it for accuracy. If a word was spelled incorrectly, the tutee was required to write the word 2 times correctly. Each pair received 2 points for each word spelled correctly and 1 point for corrected words. After ten minutes, the pair was reversed with the tutor becoming the tutee, with the other student (the original tutee) calling out words for the next 10 minutes. Spelling words were changed each week. Results of this tutoring experience indicated that all of the target students improved their word accuracy in spelling, and the intervention condition spelling scores were much higher than the baseline scores.

or problems rapidly and in a consistent format. This results in increased time-on-task for the tutees and makes this strategy particularly effective as a differentiated instruction strategy for students with learning disabilities. Furthermore, all students are trained during this process to become effective tutors, and the structure of the tutoring sessions ensures consistency of instruction across pairs of students (Arreaga-Moyer, 1998; Greenwood et al., 2003; Mortweet et al., 1999). A more detailed example of a CWPT spelling lesson is presented in Teaching Tip 5.4.

### REFLECTIVE EXERCISE: CONTEMPLATING CWPT

Establishing a CWPT system may seem to be quite a chore but teachers who have established this system have indicated that after the initial work, they were quite relieved to be teaching in this fashion. Consider how you may undertake this type of tutoring system in an oral reading daily exercise. Initially, you would specify an appropriate oral reading level for each class member and select some reading comprehension passages. What would be the next step in implementing the CWPT system? Is this a strategy you could implement in your teaching situation?

## The Tutor's Role in CWPT

Although CWPT gives the teacher the option to have all of the students in the general education classroom involved in tutoring at the same time, the teacher's role is still critical. Prior to initiating CWPT, the teacher organizes the content of the course material into daily and weekly lessons and then formats the materials to be used by the students. Instruction is planned individually, and each student is assigned spelling, reading, math, or language arts work at his or her instructional level. Needless to say, this may take some time because many of the students will have different instructional needs, but this organization of the curricula content also allows the teacher to specifically differentiate the instruction based on the needs and learning styles of the particular learners.

Once the material is organized, training for the tutoring occurs simultaneously for all tutor-tutee pairs involving the entire class at the same time (Arreaga-Mayer, 1998; Mortweet et al., 1999), and this is a major advantage of this method in general education classrooms. This procedure will free the teacher to supervise and monitor all students' responses during the tutoring sessions.

Students should be trained in the use of CWPT through modeling and practice from the teacher, as described previously for Level 3 tutoring tasks. The teacher starts by explaining how the "game" (i.e., the tutoring) works, including a discussion of winning teams, points, and tutoring. Students are introduced to both worksheets and scoring sheets for various types of activities. Emphasis should be placed on the concept of good sportsmanship during the tutoring sessions. The teacher then demonstrates by having a student perform the schoolwork as the tutee/student while the teacher acts as the tutor. The awarding of points is demonstrated, as is the appropriate error correction procedure. The teacher then selects two additional students to model tutoring procedures in front of the class while the other students watch, and the teacher provides feedback. After a few demonstrations, the teacher has all students practice the tutoring procedure (Arreaga-Mayer, 1998), and actual CWPT may begin the next day.

> Instruction is planned individually, and each student is assigned spelling, reading, math, or language arts work at his or her instructional level.

After the training phase, during the actual CWPT procedure, the teacher's role is that of monitoring the tutoring sessions. The teacher will evaluate the quality of tutoring, correcting tutoring procedures, as necessary, and may award bonus points to tutors for demonstrating correct teaching behaviors. In this monitoring role (rather than the traditional lecture or discussion leader role), the teacher is free to respond immediately as students request assistance. Again, this results in increased instructional time and attention provided for students with learning disabilities in general education classes because the teacher can respond more freely, and one half of the students in the class are also providing instruction. Furthermore, because of this careful monitoring on the part of the teacher, CWPT is a system that engages students with the subject matter at higher levels. Students doing CWPT usually spend 75 percent to 95 percent of the session engaged in the learning task, and that on-task time is quite high for students with learning disabilities in any educational endeavor (Utley et al., 1997).

CWPT has been proven beneficial in a variety of subject areas for both elementary and high school levels. For example, at the elementary level, CWPT is designed to supplement traditional instruction and to replace seatwork, lecture, and oral reading group activities. At the secondary level, CWPT is often focused on practice, skill building, and review of subject matter. Building- and system-level CWPT procedures also are available for supporting the implementation of this tutoring system schoolwide (Burks, 2004; Mortweet et al., 1999; Utley et al., 1997).

## Advantages of CWPT

A number of advantages of CWPT make this system particularly effective in inclusive general education classrooms. First, CWPT can be used in conjunction with teacher-made instructional materials or with commercial curriculum materials, and thus one does not have to purchase specific materials to use CWPT. Next, CWPT enlists extensive help and influence of the classroom peer group in the teaching process, and depending on the age of the students involved, this can be a powerful instructional method. Students can and often do learn a great deal from each other, and teachers in today's classrooms must learn to take advantage of the power of students learning from other students through tutoring.

Next, the reward system of individual students in CWPT depends not just on their own performance but also on the performance of other members on the team. This offers the advantage of strengthening the social interaction possibilities for students with learning disabilities. Changing the tutor-tutee pairs weekly and changing the roles within daily sessions keeps the students motivated and provides for a variety of social interactions that may not occur in more traditionally taught classrooms. Each student is also provided the opportunity to learn teaching skills needed in the teacher's role (Burks, 2004; Mortweet et al., 1999; Utley et al., 1997).

Several studies demonstrate the positive outcomes for students with learning disabilities and other disabilities using CWPT (Greenwood et al., 2003; Utley et al., 1997). Mortweet and colleagues (1999) investigated the academic effects of CWPT for students with mild disabilities and their typical peers in two inclusive classroom

> Students doing CWPT usually spend 75 percent to 95 percent of the session engaged in the learning task, and that on-task time is quite high for students with learning disabilities in any educational endeavor.

settings. Twenty-five students without diagnosed disabilities and two students with mild mental retardation were enrolled in each classroom. Data were collected on the two students with mild mental retardation and two typical peers from each classroom. The four students with mild mental retardation were included in the general education classrooms for spelling, a social activity period, and a lunch period in accordance with their individualized education programs. A withdrawal of treatment design was employed to compare the effects of teacher-led instruction with CWPT on spelling test performance. Each target student's rate of academic engagement was then observed once during each teacher-led instruction and CWPT condition.

Spelling instruction in both classrooms consisted of twenty minutes of teacher-specified lessons using a grade-level spelling book. During the teacher-led instruction in one classroom, the teacher used small groups of two to three students and individual seat assignments for spelling instruction. The teacher in the other classroom mainly used whole-class lectures and picture flash cards of the spelling words for spelling lessons during the teacher-led instruction phase. Dependent measures included performance on weekly spelling tests and direct observations of academic engagement. The results of this study demonstrated that CWPT was more effective than teacher-led instruction for both increasing spelling accuracy and increasing levels of on-task time for students with disabilities.

> Changing the tutor-tutee pairs weekly and changing the roles within daily sessions keeps the students motivated and provides for a variety of social interactions that may not occur in more traditionally taught classrooms.

The studies to date have demonstrated the effectiveness of CWPT in the areas of reading, spelling, vocabulary, and math (Burks, 2004; Mortweet et al., 1999). Several used single-subject and experimental control group designs that included students with learning disabilities, behavior disorders, or mild mental retardation, and all of these studies have shown positive outcomes. Furthermore, CWPT has been reported to be effective for secondary students with mild disabilities and students with disabilities in inclusive settings. Clearly, this tutoring strategy should be employed in many general education classes for students with learning disabilities.

## PEER-ASSISTED LEARNING STRATEGIES (PALS)

Peer-assisted learning strategies (PALS) is another highly structured peer tutoring system, which was developed in the early 1990s to provide general education teachers an effective, feasible, and acceptable intervention for the entire class (Fuchs et al., 2001; Fulk & King, 2001; Saenz, Fuchs, & Fuchs, 2005; Utley et al., 1997). Fuchs, Fuchs, Hamlett, Phillips, and Bentz (1995) observed that general education teachers using this system made less adaptation in their classroom instructions to address the special needs of students with learning disabilities. This was the case even after teachers had been provided frequent information on the progress or lack of progress of individual students. To address the need for general educators to provide differentiated instruction in the inclusive classes, these authors recommended that general educators use curriculum-based measurement within the context of classwide peer tutoring structures to differentiate class instruction for students with learning disabilities (Utley et al., 1997). Curriculum-based measurement involves frequent measures of student performance embedded within the daily instructional tasks. Thus, in doing curriculum-based measurement, students typically complete work for a grade each day and chart that performance to generate a highly sensitive indicator of their daily learning progress.

PALS is built around a classwide tutoring concept, but it includes a number of different instructional approaches that are linked to computerized curriculum-based measurement. For example, math in PALS provides teachers with group and individual progress reports on a student's learning of specific math skills using classwide curriculum-based measurement (Fuchs et al., 2001). This enables the teacher to provide instruction to the group as well as address the needs of specific students. A PALS tutoring session is described in Teaching Tip 5.5.

Research on the effectiveness of PALS provides convincing support for its superiority compared to conventional general education instruction in reading and math (Fuchs et al., 2001; Fulk & King, 2001; Mathes, Fuchs, Fuchs, & Henley, 1994; Utley et al., 1997). The results of these studies indicated that all students with and without learning disabilities made measurably greater progress on test scores in the same amount of time. Teachers and students both

### Teaching Tip 5.5

**A PALS Tutoring Lesson**

The three parts to PALS are *partner reading*, *paragraph shrinking*, and *prediction relay*.

In a reading lesson using PALS, each student reads aloud for ten minutes. The higher performing student reads the lesson first. The lower performing student rereads the same material. Whenever a reading error occurs, the tutor says, "Stop. You missed that word. Can you figure it out?" The reader either figures out the word within four seconds or the tutor says the word. Then the reader says the word. Then the tutor says, "Good job. Read the sentence again." Students earn 1 point for each correctly read sentence (if a word-reading correction is required, 1 point is awarded after the sentence is read correctly) and 10 points for the retell. After both students read, the lower performing student retells for two minutes the sequence of what occurred in the text (Fuchs, Fuchs, & Kazdan, 1999).

In paragraph shrinking (i.e., paragraph summarization), the tutors guide the identification of the main idea by asking readers to identify who or what the paragraph is mainly about and the most important thing about the who or what. The reader is required to put these two pieces of information together in ten or fewer words. When the tutor determines that a paragraph summary error has occurred, he or she says, "That's not quite right. Skim the paragraph and try again." The reader skims the paragraph and tries to answer the missed question. The tutor decides whether to give points or give the answer. For each summary, students earn 1 point for correctly identifying the who or what, 1 point for correctly stating the most important thing, and 1 point for using ten or fewer words. Students continue to monitor and correct reading errors, but points are no longer awarded on a sentence-by-sentence basis. After five minutes, the students switch roles (Fuchs et al., 1999).

In prediction relay, the reader makes a prediction about what will be learned on the next half page. The reader reads the half page aloud while the tutor identifies and corrects reading errors, (dis)confirms the prediction, and summarizes the main idea of the half page. When the tutor judges that a prediction is not realistic, he or she says, "I don't agree. Think of a better prediction." Otherwise, the word reading and paragraph summary correction procedures are used. The student receives 1 point for each viable prediction, 1 point for reading each half page, 1 point for accurately (dis)confirming each prediction, and 1 point for each component (i.e., the who or what and what mainly happened in 10 or fewer words) of each summary. After five minutes, the students switch roles (Fuchs et al., 1999).

Research on the effectiveness of PALS provides convincing support for its superiority compared to conventional general education instruction in reading and math.

reported high levels of satisfaction with PALS instruction (Fuchs et al., 2001; Mathes et al., 1994; Saenz, Fuchs, & Fuchs, 2005; Utley et al., 1997).

## CONCLUSION

Regardless of the tutoring approach one selects, peer tutoring is one of the most effective tactics available to assist students with learning disabilities in the differentiated classroom. Using these methods, teachers can differentiate instruction and address the instructional needs of many students, including students with disabilities in the general education class. Research has been strongly supportive of each of the peer tutoring methodologies described above; both tutors and tutees learn more and are engaged more in tutoring situations than in traditional classroom instruction.

These peer tutoring systems will generally save the teacher time in the class and can therefore greatly enhance the opportunities for implementing various differentiated instructional strategies. This system also makes the academic goals much more attainable for students with learning and other disabilities in the general education class, and thus peer tutoring can be considered as one aspect of universal design for the curriculum. Finally, peer tutoring changes the process of learning and tends to emphasize relationships between students, which grow as a result of the tutoring process. For these reasons, the differentiated class should be characterized by variations in instructional groupings and various peer tutoring plans.

## WHAT'S NEXT?

In the next chapter, the focus will be placed on the final of the three major elements of differentiated instruction—differentiation of evaluation of the products produced by the students.

# Response to Intervention **6**

## Performance Monitoring for Differentiating Instruction

---

**Topics Included in This Chapter:**

✓ Curriculum-Based Assessment
✓ Precision Teaching
✓ Performance Assessment
✓ Portfolio Assessment

---

## RESPONSE TO INTERVENTION: MONITORING STUDENT PERFORMANCE

The recent reauthorization of the Individual with Disabilities Education Act of 2004 has focused teachers on the issue of how students respond to interventions. Further, this legislation has bolstered the emphasis on universal design of assessments, as well as performance monitoring for students with learning disabilities in the general education classroom (Bender & Shores, 2007, pp. 1–32; Fuchs & Fuchs, 2006; Gersten & Dimino, 2006; Marston, 2005). In that legislation, the issue of determining eligibility for learning disabilities services was addressed by allowing schools to use measures of student performance on well-designed, scientifically based interventions as one option for determining the existence of a learning disability. This logic suggests that if students are exposed to a series of well-designed instructional interventions, and their performance does not improve, one may conclude there is some disability in learning. Moreover, this emphasis on performance monitoring for students with learning disabilities parallels a similarly increased emphasis on frequent performance monitoring for all students (Deno, 2003; Salend, 2005; Stiggins & Chappuis, 2006). Clearly, with the emphasis on response to intervention, and the increased emphasis on monitoring of student performance on all educational endeavors, teachers must become fluent in these newly developing assessment/performance monitoring tactics.

In understanding Response to Intervention (RTI), teachers should understand the relationship between this and previous innovations in assessment over the last several decades. RTI has its roots in a variety of innovation practices such as curriculum-based assessment, criterion-referenced testing, precision teaching, and more general performance monitoring initiatives (Deno, 2003). These assessment practices represent an increasing emphasis on using assessment practices as tools for learning; Stiggins and Chappuis (2006) for example, emphasize the importance of assessment *for* learning rather than assessment of learning. In this emphasis, assessment is seen as a tool to enable the teacher and student, working in concert, to strengthen the student's learning. Both assessment and instruction are not seen as separated endeavors, but rather as techniques to move students into greater understanding. With that emphasis in mind, the recent innovations in assessment are presented below, beginning with general performance monitoring.

## Performance Monitoring Systems

As noted in previous chapters, students with learning disabilities in the general education classroom will require much more support for their learning efforts than will other children, and one of the most effective supports teachers can offer is an effective system for monitoring student performance (Deno, 2003; Fuchs & Fuchs, 2006; Fuchs et al., 2000; Gregory & Chapman, 2002, pp. 37–56; Jones, 2001a; Mathes, Fuchs, Roberts, & Fuchs, 1998). Thus, in the differentiated classroom, teachers will typically initiate a performance monitoring system to support students academically, and this may include monitoring response to intervention, performance assessment measures, portfolios, or curriculum-based assessment procedures. This monitoring of daily performance will frequently result in charts of performance data on specific objectives from the child's individualized education program. Most students with learning disabilities respond quite favorably to seeing their academic progress charted, and this can become, for many students with learning disabilities, a very effective motivational tool. Many students will strive to post a "better" score today than yesterday; in fact, this phenomenon is frequently commented on when I require a daily databased performance chart as a class project in my graduate special education methods class.

Within the past twenty-five years, a number of tactics have been developed for portraying a student's progress over time in charted form, and to offer the most effective supports for students with learning disabilities, teachers must delineate a system of charting progress for most students with learning disabilities in the inclusive class. Because the behavioral model of learning—which has been so influential in special education—emphasized accurate measurement, many performance monitoring systems are founded on it, and teachers who are moving toward a more differentiated class frequently adopt this innovation.

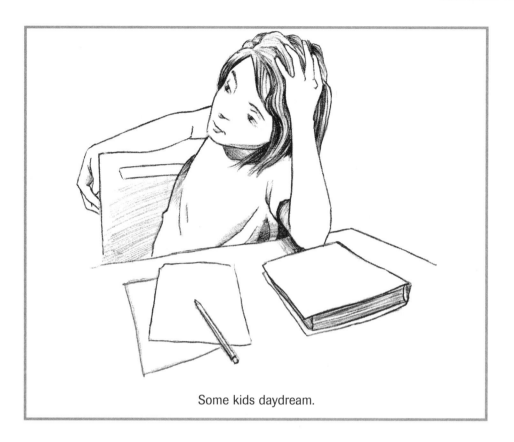

Some kids daydream.

## Curriculum-Based Measurement

Curriculum-based measurement has evolved over recent decades as one performance monitoring system that allows teachers to focus specifically on highly discrete skills in the curriculum, and to differentiate their instruction to emphasize the specific skills a child has not mastered (Deno, 2003; Fuchs & Deno, 1994; Fuchs, Fuchs, Hamlett, Phillips, & Bentz, 1994; Jones, 2001b; Wesson, 1991). Whereas traditional assessment often emphasized measurement of cognitive ability deficits (e.g., auditory perception, visual memory, or other disabilities that may hamper learning) or occasional measures of academic performance on a limited number of test questions, the newer emphasis involved direct assessment of academic skills within the curriculum. Thus, researchers in the field use the terms "curriculum-based assessment" or "curriculum-based measurement" (Jones, 2001b).

Scholars agree that through repeatedly measuring a child's progress on a particular set of academic skills, we obtain information that is highly useful for planning the next instructional tasks for that child (Fuchs et al., 2000; Jones, 2001a; Mathes et al., 1998; White, 1986). For this reason, assessment based directly on the skills in the child's curriculum, measured on a repeated and frequent basis, seems to be the option of choice for differentiating instruction for students with learning disabilities.

Scholars disagree on the frequency with which a child's behavior should be assessed in curriculum-based assessment models. For example, some theorists argue that a teacher-made assessment administered weekly may be sufficient (Fuchs & Fuchs, 2005), whereas others feel that student progress should be assessed every day (White, 1986). Despite these differences of opinion, the components of curriculum-based assessment are fairly widely accepted. These include the following:

- that assessment for educational planning should be based only on the skills listed in the child's curriculum
- that assessment should be repeated regularly and frequently throughout the year
- that these repeated assessments should be used as the basis for educational decision making for the child with a learning disability

The last factor has proven to be a strong advantage in favor of curriculum-based assessment. As one example, most adults today can recall having a "trial test" on spelling words every Wednesday in elementary school, and that trial test was an attempt to prepare us for the "final test" on the same words on Friday. This is a good instructional technique because it allows the students to note their areas of deficiency on Wednesday, well in advance of the final, graded assessment on Friday. Also, on Thursday, the most effective elementary teachers would plan a spelling lesson that included an emphasis on the difficult words that were identified on the Wednesday test. In this example, educational activities were planned based on recent data concerning the actual academic performance of the students. When teachers extend this example to the logical conclusion, they may find that they are grading daily homework or class work on the spelling words and not conducting a final test on Friday at all! Thus, rather than generating a grade on one—relatively artificial—test of performance on Friday, the student's daily performance on the spelling exercises would serve as the basis for the spelling grade.

> Scholars agree that through repeatedly measuring a child's progress on a particular set of academic skills, rather than on noncurricular abilities, we obtain information that is much more useful for planning the next instructional tasks for that child.

Another example may be helpful. Imagine a teacher in the third-grade basic skills class who introduces two-digit multiplication on a Monday. After teaching for two weeks through examples on the dry-erase board, seatwork, and homework, she tests her students on the second Friday. To her surprise, she determines that half her class has not mastered this skill. Furthermore (although she may not realize it), several members of the class had mastered that new skill by the second day of the two-week lesson and did not really need to spend any additional time on that skill. Thus, their participation over the past two weeks has been wasted time. Clearly, this is not effective instruction for many students in that class.

Suppose, however, that the same teacher had used the daily worksheets as a continuing assessment and required that each student chart his or her performance after each day's lesson. After only one or two days, she would have discovered that some students had already mastered this skill, whereas other students whose daily work indicated problems with comprehension of this task would then be instructed on a one-on-one basis until they mastered the work. Obviously, repeated assessment, even when it is as informal as worksheets done in class, can be a very effective tool for instructional planning in the differentiated class. Furthermore, the more frequent the assessment (a daily basis assessment seems to be the general consensus), the more responsive the instruction can be. Finally, if the assessment data are summarized in some readily interpretable form, such as a chart of performance, this information is even more useful. Imagine the teacher in the example above having to look through all of the worksheets for each child to determine that child's progress, and compare that with the teacher looking at a simple chart of daily performance for each student; the latter summary of the data saves a great deal of time. Clearly this assessment practice represents the best possible example of assessment for instruction (Stiggins & Mappois, 2006).

Theorists in curriculum-based assessment generally do not accept a distinction between "assessment" on one hand and "instruction" on the other. In fact, by basing instructional decisions on repeated measures of academic work, the traditional separation between "testing" and "teaching" becomes blurred. Furthermore, with comprehensive curriculum-based assessment data, it is possible to envision a day when more traditional assessments of innate abilities or unit tests of academic comprehension become obsolete (Fuchs et al., 2000; Jones, 2001b).

Although that possibility has not yet been realized, this concept of basing instructional decisions on repeated measures of academic skills is the cornerstone of curriculum-based measurement. This concept represents one of the most powerful instructional strategies for students with learning disabilities, as well as for many other students in the differentiated class.

> Obviously, repeated assessment, even when it is as informal as worksheets done in class, can be a very effective tool for instructional planning in the differentiated class.

## Criterion-Referenced Testing

Criterion-referenced testing (CRT) served as one basis for the development of curriculum-based measurement (Jones, 2001b). Most assessments compare a student's performance with the performance of a group of students on whom the assessment was normed. The scores and information for that norm group are usually published in the test's manual, and that group serves as the basis to generate the commonly accepted scores on the test—the grade-equivalent or norm-based scores. In contrast to this "norm group" comparison score, the purpose of the criterion-referenced test is to compare a student's performance to a specific set of academic skills that are appropriate for the student's age and grade level (Monda-Amoya & Reed, 1993). Thus, a criterion-referenced test is an assessment that lists sequenced behavioral skills in a particular area and compares a student's performance to the optimal performance on the listed objectives. For example, consider the sequenced skills involved in whole-number addition. A test including the specific types of problems associated with each individual skill in this area would involve some problems such as those presented in Teaching Tip 6.1.

With a criterion-referenced assessment along these lines in hand, it is relatively easy to determine the specific skills on which a student with a learning disability has problems. If a student with a learning disability completed the first two rows of math problems at 80 or 100 percent accuracy and then achieved only 20 percent accuracy on the third row, the teacher could be fairly certain that the student was having a difficulty understanding the

**Teaching Tip 6.1**

## Criterion-Referenced Test in Whole-Number Addition

1.
| 5 | 7 | 4 | 2 | 8 | |
|---|---|---|---|---|---|
| + 2 | + 2 | + 4 | + 6 | + 2 | Percentage Score _____ |

2.
| 6 | 3 | 8 | 2 | 9 | |
|---|---|---|---|---|---|
| + 8 | + 9 | + 4 | + 4 | + 2 | Percentage Score _____ |

3.
| 35 | 47 | 54 | 25 | 83 | |
|---|---|---|---|---|---|
| + 42 | + 32 | + 24 | + 13 | + 22 | Percentage Score _____ |

4.
| 27 | 27 | 37 | 28 | 69 | |
|---|---|---|---|---|---|
| + 46 | + 25 | + 34 | + 13 | + 22 | Percentage Score _____ |

5.
| 64 | 87 | 98 | 79 | 78 | |
|---|---|---|---|---|---|
| + 36 | + 35 | + 24 | + 14 | + 22 | Percentage Score _____ |

6.
| 73 | 87 | 98 | 76 | 81 | |
|---|---|---|---|---|---|
| + 36 | + 35 | + 21 | + 13 | + 22 | Percentage Score _____ |

**Teaching Tip 6.2**

### Objectives for the Whole-Number Addition Problems on This CRT

1. When presented with a series of five whole-number single-digit addition problems involving math facts that sum to less than 10, the student will complete the problems with 100 percent accuracy.

2. When presented with a series of five whole-number single-digit addition problems involving math facts that sum to 10 or more, with regrouping in the 1s place, the student will complete the problems with 100 percent accuracy.

3. When presented with a series of five whole-number double-digit addition problems involving no regrouping, the student will complete the problems with 100 percent accuracy.

4. When presented with a series of five whole-number double-digit addition problems involving regrouping in the 1s place, the student will complete the problems with 100 percent accuracy.

5. When presented with a series of five whole-number double-digit addition problems involving regrouping in the 1s place and the 10s place, the student will complete the problems with 100 percent accuracy.

6. When presented with a series of five whole-number double-digit addition problems involving regrouping in the 1s place, the 10s place, or both, the student will complete the problems with 100 percent accuracy.

concept of regrouping or place value because that is the difference between the problems completed successfully and those that were not completed successfully. In other words, the student would need specific work on place value and regrouping.

The sequenced objectives associated with each type of problem on a CRT are typically printed in the test manual. For informal CRTs that are developed by the teacher, objectives could be written and attached to the individualized education program for the student. A list of objectives for the whole-number addition CRT is presented in Teaching Tip 6.2.

Of course, use of a CRT on one occasion during the school year does not constitute curriculum-based measurement. Clearly, although CRT assessment is preferable to assessment of intelligence or other ability deficits discussed previously, the last two components of curriculum-based assessment from the list above cannot be addressed if the CRT is administered only once during a school year. Curriculum-based measurement requires frequently repeated CRTs to allow for instructional decisions based directly on student performance (Jones, 2001b), and this strategy is one of the most powerful teaching strategies that can be used for students with learning disabilities.

> The sequenced objectives associated with each type of problem on a CRT are typically printed in the test manual.

**REFLECTIVE EXERCISE: WHERE CAN YOU DO CURRICULUM-BASED ASSESSMENT?**

If you wished to find a motivating tool for a student with a learning disability, curriculum-based assessment (CBM) may be the tool you are looking for (Deno, 2003). Are there students in your class for whom you cannot seem to find an effective motivation? You may wish to initiate a CBM project and offer the entire class some reinforcement on days when the individual student's performance increases in comparison with the day before. Would this be an option in your class?

# PRECISION TEACHING

Precision teaching is a method for closely monitoring the academic performance of students that originated in the behavioral school of psychology (Lindsley, 1971; Vail & Huntington, 1993; Wesson, 1991; White, 1986). Of course, behavioral psychology emphasized readily observable behaviors, measured precisely, and antecedents or consequences that tended to increase or decrease these behaviors. When applying these behavioral principles to education, Lindsley (1971) enumerated five principles as having a direct bearing on educational success. Each of these principles, presented in Teaching Tip 6.3, relates directly to monitoring the individual performance of students on learning tasks, and for this reason, precision teaching provided one cornerstone for the current movement toward curriculum-based assessment.

Given the obvious emphasis on monitoring individual achievement in these principles, theorists developed a focus on charting specific behaviors of a student. First, the behavior was pinpointed by stating an appropriate behavioral objective. Behavioral objectives traditionally stipulated three things: the task the student would perform, the conditions under which the student would perform the task, and the criteria used to evaluate the performance.

An example of a behavioral objective would be as follows:

When presented with twenty double-digit addition problems that do not involve regrouping, the student will complete the problems with 90 percent accuracy.

This is a relatively standard behavioral objective, and the three components are evident. With this type of objective in hand, the teacher's job becomes relatively easy. The student must be instructed in this skill and repeatedly assessed until he or she meets the criteria stipulated in the objective. Performance may be charted daily on a simple graph such as that presented in Teaching Tip 6.4, and for most students with learning disabilities, the chart itself will serve as a motivator and reinforcer. Furthermore, when the student reaches mastery for three consecutive days, he or she is ready to move on to the next skill in the academic sequence—in this case, double-digit addition with regrouping.

However, teachers quickly realized that the problems of some students were not related to their accuracy but rather to their speed in completing problems in class. Needless to say, this is true of many students with learning disabilities, making the precision teaching innovation a critical instructional option for these

Teaching Tip 6.3

**Five Principles of Precision Teaching**

1. *The learner knows best.* This principle suggests that if the child is progressing, the teaching method is appropriate, whereas if the child is not progressing, some other procedure must be tried. In short, only the learner's actual progress is a valid measure of success or failure of a particular instructional method.

2. *Focus is on directly observable behavior.* Lindsley (1971) demanded that teachers focus on behavior that is observable to glean a clear, unambiguous picture of progress.

3. *Frequency is the measure of behavior.* Because of the dissatisfactions with tabulation of correct responses as a measure of success, the focus in precision teaching is frequency or rate of the response (how many correct responses per minute the child demonstrates).

4. *Use of a standard chart for measuring success.* Charting has numerous advantages over other methods of measuring success, and charts of pupil progress are a must for the precision teacher.

5. *Description of environmental conditions.* A teacher must understand the effect of the environment on the child's behavior and be able to construct the appropriate antecedent and consequent conditions that shape behavior. Consequently, knowing what the child can do (prerequisite behaviors) facilitates the decision making for the present instructional sequence. For a more complete description of these five principles, see Lindsley (1971) and White (1986).

students. Clearly, for some students with learning disabilities, the problem is to get them to work both correctly and quickly, and this is the one of the few instructional methods to address that critical concern. For this reason, behavioral objectives today often specify a certain rate (i.e., speed) of behavior as follows:

- When presented with a page of double-digit addition problems that do not require regrouping, the student will successfully complete an average of twenty problems during each two-minute period.
- With this type of objective in hand, students and teachers were prepared to concentrate their focus on the speed of the work as well as the accuracy.

## A Sample of Precision Teaching

Teaching Tip 6.4 presents a behavioral chart of Benito's performance on the objective above. The dots represent correct problems, and the "x"s indicate the number of errors for each day. For example, Benito answered seventeen problems correctly and had two errors on Tuesday, September 22. You will also note a dashed line on the "20" line. This represents the "aim line," or the goal expressed in the objective. For most students with learning disabilities, reaching the aim line for three days becomes a very rewarding experience. The dashed

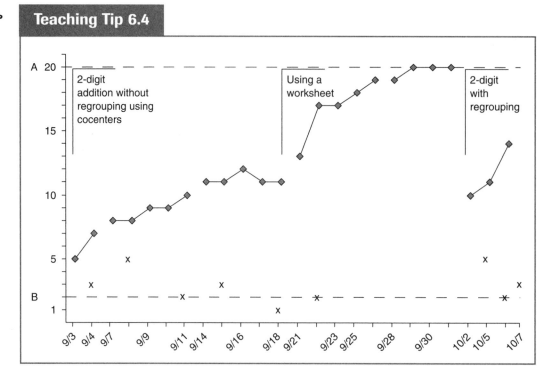

**Teaching Tip 6.4**

line on the "2" line is called the "record floor." This indicates the length of the timed exercise, as described in the objective. In addition to the terms "record floor" and "aim line," precision teaching, as initially recommended, involved the use of many additional terms—that is, a language of precision in teaching—as well as a particular type of chart for charting of performance data. Although most teachers have left these nuances behind, the concept of data charted on a daily basis as the decision-making tool was one cornerstone of precision teaching that has endured and forms one basis for the current initiatives in curriculum-based performance monitoring.

> For some students with learning disabilities, the problem is to get them to work both correctly and quickly, and this is the one of the few instructional methods to address that critical concern.

In reviewing the chart, you will notice that during the week of September 14 through September 18, Benito did not continue to make progress. Whenever three days of "flat data" are recorded, the teacher and the student must make some type of change because the data have demonstrated that the instructional exercises are not showing any results. This type of decision making is highly sensitive to the instructional needs of the student with learning disabilities, and this precision in instructional decision making was one goal of precision teaching theorists.

Notice the "phase change" lines at the top of the chart. These indicate that instruction was adjusted, either because the warm-up activities were not effective or because Benito reached the aim. For example, during the week of September 14 through 18, the instructional activity involved the use of counters to complete the addition problems. On each of these days, Benito spent five to ten minutes working a page of problems using counters to represent each of the digits in the 1s column and each of the digits in the 10s column. After a warm-up session,

Benito would indicate that he was ready for the timing. The teacher would hand Benito a worksheet of math problems and begin a two-minute timing. After the time period ended, Benito would use a self-check answer sheet to check his answers and count the number of correct answers.

The chart shows that, on September 18, the teacher and Benito jointly decided that the warm-up activity was not helping Benito improve his work. Consequently, the phase change line on September 21 indicated that a new warm-up activity was in use: completion of problems on a worksheet without using counters. Apparently, this activity worked out well because Benito began to show

> This type of decision making is highly sensitive to the instructional needs of the student with learning disabilities.

progress and reached aim for three days at the end of the next week. The next phase change line (October 5) indicates that Benito moved on to the next math skill in the sequence—double-digit addition with regrouping in the 1s place.

## Initiation of a Precision Teaching Project

Many teachers have students with learning disabilities in their classes who never seem to complete the assigned work. For those students, a precision teaching performance monitoring tactic may be exactly what is needed because this is one of the few instructional strategies that directly address the speed with which children with learning disabilities complete their work. When initiating a precision teaching instructional project, certain steps should be followed.

First, you will need to delineate a series of sequential behavioral objectives for the project. The objective should be stated as a "rate-based behavior" and specify a length of time or rate of behavior.

### REFLECTIVE EXERCISE: DEVELOPING RATE-BASED OBJECTIVES

Teachers may wish to take the objectives in Teaching Tip 6.2 and make each a rate-based objective. All that the teachers need to add is the phrase "in a one-minute period" to the end of each objective. How could these objectives be turned into two-minute objectives, and does that change the number of required successes in the objective?

Second, you should discuss the objectives with the student with the learning disability and make every effort to get the student to "buy into" the objective. The relationship that the teacher has with the student will be critical at this point, and this effort to get the student to take responsibility for learning reflects the emphasis on personal responsibility for learning, as discussed in Chapter 2.

Next, teachers will need to establish a goal—called an aim line—for the student with the learning disability. Although precision teaching theorists have recommended different procedures for setting the aim, the simplest method is to have the student's performance timed for three days and then use that information for an educated "guess" at an appropriate aim. Note that the aim line should reflect a performance for each individual student, and aims for one student should not be automatically used for other students.

*(Continued)*

(Continued)

> Finally, the teacher will want to select a three- to five-minute instructional warm-up activity directly related to the objectives. For example, flash cards may be good exercise for math facts. Likewise, "word window" exercises that reveal only one syllable of multisyllabic spelling words may be appropriate for a spelling or language arts exercise.
>
> Note that, unlike many of the other differentiated instructional tactics described in this text, precision teaching is really somewhat eclectic in that no particular teaching method is recommended. The teacher is free to choose any instructional tactic as a warm-up activity that may work for the student with the learning disability. In this sense, precision teaching must be considered an instructional monitoring technique rather than a single instructional teaching strategy itself.

> A precision teaching performance monitoring tactic may be exactly what is needed because this is one of the few instructional strategies that directly address the speed with which children with learning disabilities complete their work.

It is quite possible to develop a precision teaching monitoring system for almost any instructional strategy; even metacognitive techniques such as reciprocal teaching exercises could be structured to conclude with an objective comprehension test on each day for each student, and those data could be charted. This performance monitoring aspect of precision teaching makes this strategy much more reactive to the individual needs of students with learning disabilities and gives the teacher the necessary information to make very frequent instructional decisions for students with learning disabilities in the inclusive class.

Precision teaching performance monitoring may also be used for the entire inclusive class. In essence, using precision teaching typically involves using a worksheet and counting students' correct problems in a given amount of time. Students with and without learning disabilities in the general education class can be taught to do this work and subsequently to chart their own performance from day to day. Thus, inclusive teachers, working two teachers per class, may wish to use precision teaching with the entire group. However, even in the general education class, when a special education teacher is not present, precision teaching will assist in saving time for the teacher because students will, over time, take much more responsibility for their own work.

Another option is to do all of the timed work during the last fifteen minutes of the inclusive class period. For example, Benito may have the addition worksheet, a worksheet on identification of subjects and predicates, and a worksheet on punctuation. Other students would likewise have several timed worksheets to complete, and the length of their various timings would probably vary. After checking to see that each student had the correct worksheets, the teacher would start a bell-tone tape that rang a bell at one-minute intervals and merely leave it running. When Benito finishes a two-minute timing, he could use the next couple of minutes to check his work and put his score on the math chart. When the next bell rings, he would begin his language arts worksheet for a one-minute timing. Other students would be completing other worksheets specifically designated for the two-, four-, or ten-minute timed exercises.

## Advantages of Precision Teaching

The advantages of this system over traditional group instruction are numerous. First, this instructional monitoring procedure makes instruction highly sensitive to the needs of students with learning disabilities, as shown in various research efforts (White, 1986). Specifically, some aspect of instruction for the student must change if three days' data are "flat" because "flat data" on a chart represent no progress. Teachers may change the warm-up activity, identify a particular prerequisite behavior the student did not have, or provide tangible reinforcement for correct responses above a certain level. The point is that something must change if the data reveal that the current instructional tactics are not working. Obviously, if the student attains aim for three consecutive days, he or she should move to the next skill in the sequence.

Second, each student is instructed as an individual, as mandated by special education law. Furthermore, when using precision teaching, there is a demonstrated and direct relationship between the particular objectives on a student's Individualized Education Program (IEP) and the daily work in class for each student with a learning disability. Surprisingly, such a relationship is not always apparent in much instruction in special education and/or inclusive classes. Also, this relationship between the objectives and the actual worksheets done in class can easily be communicated to parents and to the student with the learning disability by using the chart; that is, the chart serves to make the educational attainment very "real."

> Note that, unlike many of the other differentiated instructional tactics described in this text, precision teaching is really somewhat eclectic in that no particular teaching method is recommended.

Third, when a student's progress is graphically portrayed, the students tend to "own" more responsibility for achieving the goals set forth in their educational program. Achieving aim—in and of itself—becomes reinforcing for most students with learning disabilities.

Fourth, instructional decisions may be made on a daily basis, which minimizes the wasted time associated with two- or three-week unit tests. In that sense, the precision teaching approach does become an "assessment FOR learning" as described by Stiggins and Chappuis (2006). Finally, communication with other teachers is facilitated by showing progress using the data charts. In fact, charted data can become one of the most effective communication mechanisms for teacher-to-teacher communication. With these advantages in mind, application of precision teaching will increase for students with learning disabilities. Precision teacher materials are currently available from a company called Sopris West in Longmont, Colorado (these are referred to as their "Basic Skills" curriculum).

> When using precision teaching, there is a demonstrated and direct relationship between the particular objectives on a student's Individualized Education Program (IEP) and the daily work in class for each student with a learning disability.

# RESPONSE TO INTERVENTION

The performance monitoring systems described above evolved over time, and each has significantly impacted the most recent emphasis in special education for students with learning disabilities—Response to Intervention (RTI) (Bender & Shores, 2007; Deno, 2003). In fact, RTI is founded solidly on research literature on performance monitoring in the general education classroom, and most of the recent supportive research involves the area of reading instruction in the general education class (Fuchs & Fuchs, 2006). Of course, 80 percent of students with learning disabilities have noted difficulty in reading, and this often results in poor academic performance in many reading-dependent subject areas. Clearly, given the recent changes in the law, every special education and general education teacher must have a firm grasp of RTI procedures and be capable of implementing RTI in his or her classes (Baskette, Ulmer, & Bender, 2006; Marston, Muyskens, Lau, & Canter, 2003; Mastropieri & Scruggs, 2005; NCJLD, 2005; O'Connor, 2003). Finally, RTI provides perhaps the strongest basis for differentiation of instruction, since closely monitoring the progress of struggling students allows the teacher and the student to jointly and specifically focus instruction on the exact curricular skills that challenge the child. Thus, RTI may be viewed as frequent assessment *for* learning rather than assessment *of* learning (Stiggins & Chappuis, 2006).

While RTI involves many of the procedures described in the precision teaching section above, it is also more involved. Specifically, whereas the previous precision teaching example involved one intervention, the proponents of RTI recommend a minimum of two separate interventions in order to protect the child. For example, if a child does not respond to one educational intervention,

> Every general education teacher must have a firm grasp of RTI procedures and be capable of implementing RTI procedures.

it may mean that the child requires a different emphasis in his or her instruction, and that child should not immediately be classified as learning disabled. However, if a child continues to not respond to two or more separate educational interventions, which are scientifically based, one can then conclude that the child has a learning disability (Bender & Shores, 2007; Fuchs & Fuchs, 2006; Fuchs, Fuchs, & Compton, 2004).

Thus, proponents of RTI recommend a minimum of two separate education interventions, and most recommend three interventions for documenting how a child responds to intervention. Further, each intervention or "tier" involves increasing intensity of instruction as well as careful monitoring of the child's performance (Mastropieri & Scruggs, 2005; NCJLD, 2005; Vaughn, Linan-Thompson, & Hickman, 2003). Some have suggested that the three tiers may be considered primary, secondary, and tertiary interventions, with the first tier focused population wide, the second tier focused on more intensive smaller group work, and the third tier individually focused (Mellard, Byrd, Johnson, Tollefson, & Boesche, 2004). Thus, the first tier, or the first intervention, would take place in the general education classroom and would be the responsibility of the general education teacher. Further, monitoring a child's progress closely documents how that child is performing, and can greatly enhance a teacher's ability to provide differentiated instruction for that child. Here is an example.

## Reading of New Words in the First Grade

Dustin is in the first grade and has not been doing well. The teacher, Ms. Carpenter, noticed during the first couple of weeks of school that Dustin was struggling in reading, and doesn't seem to be learning new vocabulary words as quickly as he should. When Ms. Thompson checked Dustin's reading screening score from the previous year, she verified that Dustin was in the lower 25 percent of kindergarten students. Ms. Carpenter began to suspect that Dustin might have a learning disability, so she initiated a tier one intervention in reading to ascertain how Dustin responds to intervention.

In undertaking this intervention, Ms. Carpenter was differentiating the instruction for Dustin, since she would, from that point on, be monitoring his performance more closely than some other class members. Her responsibility under the law was to implement a scientifically proven curriculum, with fidelity to the instructional procedures delineated in that curriculum, and to monitor Dustin's performance closely (Bender & Shores, 2007; Fuchs & Fuchs, 2005; Marston, 2005). Ms. Carpenter had been using a basal reader instructional curriculum that had been scientifically validated, and each lesson in that curriculum focused on phonemic skills and word attack skills. Thus, her intervention was sound, and related directly to the academic problem experienced by Dustin—learning new vocabulary terms. In this case, she did not have to implement a "new" intervention. Therefore, in this case, she chose to continue that instruction and couple that with increased performance monitoring of Dustin's performance. Specifically, Ms. Carpenter monitored Dustin's progress in recognition of new vocabulary terms in isolation on a weekly basis for the next eight weeks, as recommended in the literature on RTI (Fuchs & Fuchs, 2005). She also developed a chart as a performance monitoring tool to graphically display Dustin's individual progress.

The data in Teaching Tip 6.5 represent weekly progress monitoring for Dustin in his ability to read first-grade vocabulary words. In order to generate these data, Dustin was presented with a list of vocabulary terms at the first-grade reading level and asked to read those terms at the end of each week for one grading period. Ms. Carpenter counted the number of words read correctly from that list of first-grade words in one minute. For grade level 1, Dustin would normally be expected to read 15 to 19 words correctly in one minute, and any student who could not read 15 words correctly in one minute would be judged to have a significant reading difficulty.

As shown by the data, Dustin was not progressing in the first tier of the RTI process. In short, Dustin should have responded to that intervention, but the data show that he did not. However, two questions must be addressed in order to assure that the child is not incorrectly placed in special education.

1. Did the child have the opportunity to learn from a scientifically validated program?

2. Did the teacher teach the program as recommended by the instructor's manual?

These questions must be addressed in the RTI process in order to assure that children are not inappropriately placed in special education (Bender & Shores, 2007). The use of scientifically validated curriculum should be the goal of every teacher for every student. Also, the second question—was the curriculum used appropriately—deals directly with the child's opportunity to respond

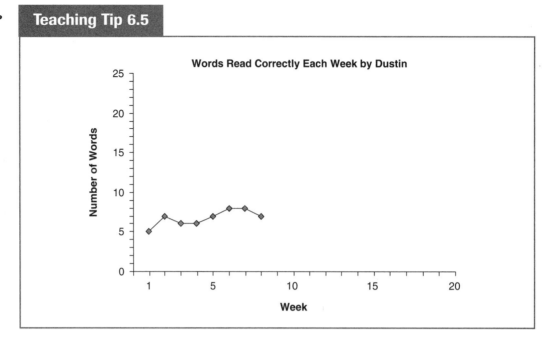

**Teaching Tip 6.5**

favorably to the intervention. This second issue is commonly referred to by the term "treatment fidelity" or "instructional fidelity."

Fortunately, these issues can be dealt with rather easily by having an outside observer come into the classroom and observe a lesson delivered by Ms. Carpenter that includes Dustin (Bender & Shores, 2007; Mellard et al., 2004). Bender and Shores (2007) presented a simple observational form that teachers could utilize for this purpose, but in reality, any observational notes that address the two questions above would suffice, as long as they are signed and dated by the observer.

Perhaps at this point, it would be beneficial to explicitly state several of the guidelines mentioned above in this example of a tier one intervention. Teaching Tip 6.6 below presents guidelines for teachers in consideration of how to implement a tier one intervention (Bender & Shores, 2007).

Once the child has not responded favorably to a tier one intervention, the RTI process requires children to be provided a more intensive intervention, typically referred to as a tier two intervention (Fuchs & Fuchs, 2006; Marston, 2005; Vaughn, 2003; Vaughn et al., 2003; Vellutino et al., 1996). The tier two interventions involve a more intensive instructional program for an additional period of several weeks. Bender and Shores (2007) recommend that the planning and preparation of the tier two intervention, even though it precedes placement in special education, should involve the special education teacher as a support for the general education teacher. Others may likewise become involved in planning and implementing this more intensive intervention, including principals, reading specialists, or school psychologists. According to Bender and Shores (2007), while consultation for selection of the tier one intervention may be considered optional, consultation regarding the second tier intervention should be considered mandatory. Further, the second tier

**Teaching Tip 6.6**

### Guidelines for Tier One Interventions

1. When a teacher suspects a problem, he or she must obtain an appropriate score on a general screening measure (typically in either reading or math), or administer such a measure to get a general picture of the child's academic ability in comparison with other children.

2. When the screening score indicates an academic score in the bottom 20 percent to 25 percent of the population, a tier one intervention must be initiated (Fuchs & Fuchs, 2005). Tier one interventions are undertaken in the general education classroom and are the responsibility of the general education teacher.

3. Tier one interventions may involve educational curricula and procedures that the teacher has implemented for the entire class or for a subgroup of students within the class.

4. Tier one interventions may be implemented by the general education teacher without consultation, as these are a function of the general education classroom.

5. During the reading instructional lesson for the student, the reading teacher, or school administrator, should observe the teacher teach reading, and should prepare a set of notes from that observation attesting to the implementation of the reading curriculum in a manner commensurate with the recommended teaching procedures.

6. Because tier one interventions are a function of the general education classroom, these interventions are available to all students. Thus, implementation of tier one interventions do not require specific notification of parents, though teachers would typically be expected to communicate with all parents regarding general progress of their children.

7. Tier one interventions should result in a minimum of six data points or six assessments of academic progress, which allow the teacher to determine how the student responded to intervention a minimum of six times over a specified time period, which may be from six to ten weeks. This should involve assessments at least once a week.

intervention should directly target the specific skill deficit identified for Dustin. In this case, that program should involve various phonemic-based reading activities that would be expected to prepare Dustin for improved oral reading of words in isolation.

To return to our example, Ms. Carpenter would consult with the special education teacher and perhaps the reading teacher in the school. In that consultation, she finds that the reading teacher may be able to add Dustin to a reading group for some intensive small-group instruction for 30 to 45 minutes daily for a period of several weeks. Thus, this would provide a wonderful opportunity for a tier two intervention, since a scientifically validated curriculum is utilized in that reading class, and Dustin would receive intensive small-group instruction.

As shown in the precision teacher literature described previously, daily progress monitoring is truly the "best practice" in education today, since it allows a teacher to be highly responsive to the progress or lack of progress shown by the student. Further, the literature on curriculum-based measurement documents that very frequent monitoring of pupil progress results in enhanced instruction (Deno, 2003). Finally, many scientifically validated curricula that are currently on the market present the option for daily monitoring of pupil progress. Thus, Bender and Shores (2007) recommend daily progress monitoring in the tier two intervention.

For the tier two intervention, based on discussions with the reading teacher, Ms. Carpenter chose to let Dustin participate with that reading teacher who was using the Reading Mastery Reading Program, a direct instruction reading program that has been scientifically validated in a repeated series of studies. Thus, Dustin received intensive reading instruction for 35 minutes each day in a small group, and his progress was monitored during this intervention. Ms. Carpenter and the reading teacher decided to chart Dustin's progress for part of the next grading period in that intensive reading instruction. Teaching Tip 6.7 presents a chart of daily performance of Dustin's progress in reading first-grade words in a one-minute time period for his second tier intervention.

Again, the instruction provided for Dustin during the tier two intervention should be monitored for instructional fidelity (Bender & Shores, 2007). Again, the school administrator, the special educator, or school psychologists should be used to observe the reading instruction for Dustin in tier two and make some notes as to the appropriateness of the instruction provided and the scientific validation of the curriculum utilized. Ideally, the person doing this observation

**Teaching Tip 6.7**

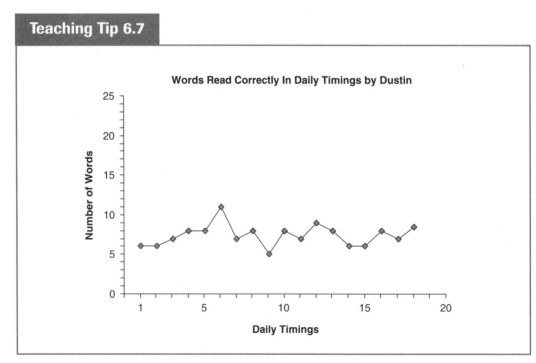

**Words Read Correctly In Daily Timings by Dustin**

should not be the same person who conducted the validation of instruction observation for tier one, because it is desirable for a third educator to carefully observe not only the instruction presented, but Dustin's response to that instruction on a first-hand basis. In fact, in the RTI procedure these individuals will eventually be meeting with Dustin's parents and may be discussing the possibility of a special education placement for Dustin. Thus, these observations can provide several instructional personnel some opportunity to get to know Dustin's work first hand.

While some may be concerned with the extra time these observations on instruction may take during the RTI process, we should all realize that in implementing RTI, other types of assessment are no longer needed. When implementing the RTI process as the main eligibility mechanism for documenting a learning disability, it is quite likely that these other individuals such as the special education teacher or the school psychologist will not spend nearly as much time testing Dustin as they would have under previous eligibility procedures. Therefore, these individuals will have more time for conducting these observations of Dustin's instruction, as well as noting how Dustin responds to that instruction.

The data in Teaching Tip 6.7 demonstrate that even in an intensive phonemically based reading program, Dustin's performance did not improve. At this point, two distinct interventions have been implemented and progress has been carefully monitored in each. Further, each has shown that Dustin did not respond positively to these scientifically based instructional interventions. Teaching Tip 6.8 presents guidelines for conducting tier two interventions.

At that point, the entire special education eligibility team should meet and consider Dustin's further education, and Dustin should be deemed to have demonstrated a learning disability. A third tier intervention based on an individualized educational program would then be implemented by the special education teacher (Mellard et al., 2004).

The legislation allowing RTI is quite recent and as a result, RTI procedures are still being developed. Bender and Shores (2007) presented a simple RTI summary document, which can serve as the basis for effective RTIs. A completed sample of that document is presented in Teaching Tip 6.9.

As this discussion demonstrates, the use of RTI as an eligibility procedure for students suspected of having a learning disability is quite new, and many questions are as yet unanswered on implementation of RTI (Baskette et al., 2006). However, it is certain that general education and special education teachers will be heavily involved in the implementation of RTI, and many teachers will require training in this performance monitoring approach. However, teachers will quickly realize that RTI procedures represent the "best practice" instructional techniques today, and thus preparation in RTI is likely to enhance instruction in many classrooms. Moreover, RTI clearly fits well with the differentiation of instruction paradigm since RTI allows teachers to precisely pinpoint academic problems and differentiate their instruction to remediate them.

**Teaching Tip 6.8**

### Tier Two Implementation Guidelines

1. When the tier one intervention is deemed unsuccessful, the special and general education teachers should briefly discuss the student's problem and select an intensive curriculum that addresses his specific reading problem. Other teachers might be involved if placements in a specialized reading program are considered, for example. These individuals should likewise make a determination as to who should implement this intensive instruction and how often.

2. Tier two interventions that are undertaken in the general education classroom would be the responsibility of the general education teacher, and/or his or her co-teacher or inclusion teacher. Interventions that involve the child's placement into another class must involve parental notification, parental permission, and hopefully parental participation in this meeting.

3. Tier two interventions must be intensive interventions, involving a teacher and a small group of students in the instructional process. These interventions should, thus, be offered each day or a minimum of four days per week.

4. During the tier two reading instructional lesson, the reading teacher or school administrator should observe the reading lesson and, again, prepare a set of notes from that observation attesting to the implementation of the tier two reading curriculum in a manner commensurate with the recommended teaching procedures.

5. Implementation of tier two interventions should involve specific notification of parents, since intensive instruction, which is not typically offered to all children, is being implemented for the student suspected of having a learning disability.

6. As noted above, prior to a tier two intervention, the general education teacher should briefly consult with some other educator with particular expertise in the type of problem demonstrated by the student. This may be a special education teacher, school psychologist, a reading teacher, a curriculum coordinator for reading, or other specialist, but prior to implementing tier two interventions, some specialist must become involved.

7. Tier two interventions should result in a minimum of twenty data points or twenty assessments of academic progress, which allow the teacher to determine how the student responded to intervention a minimum of twenty times over a specified time period. The intervention itself may last from twenty days to up to ten weeks. This should involve assessments at least twice a week.

## ASSESSMENT INNOVATIONS

Because of the importance of performance monitoring for students with learning disabilities, a number of innovative assessment approaches have been developed over the past decade, including performance assessment and portfolio assessment (Bryant, 1999; Deno, 2003; Gregory & Chapman, 2002, pp. 37–56). Although a complete exploration of these innovative concepts is beyond the scope of this text, some examples are provided (see Teaching Tips 6.9a and 6.9b).

**Teaching Tip 6.9a**

*Summary of Response to Intervention*

Pupil <u>Dustin Prowner</u>                    Date <u>10/25/06</u>

Initiating Teacher's Name <u>Jane Carpenter</u>

School Address <u>Beaverdam Elementary</u>

Pupil's Grade <u>1</u>          Pupil's Homeroom Teacher <u>Jane Carpenter</u>

*Teacher's Statement of Academic Problem:*
I noticed Dustin had extreme difficulty reading independently. This difficulty was noticed on CRCT (Criteron Referred Critical Skills Test) where his score in April of last year was only at the kindergarten level. The scaled score was 83 showing a reading deficit in vocabulary in April of last year.

J. Carpenter

*Description of Tier One Intervention:*
In the first grade, Dustin had been using the open court reading series, which is a scientifically validated reading program. I charted his mastery of new words once a week for the first 8 weeks of school (see chart 6.5 attached) and he is learning only an average of 1 new vocabulary term per week.

J. Carpenter

*Observation of General Instruction and Tier One Intervention:*
As principal, I observed Ms. Carpenter in her reading instruction on 9/18/06, noting particularly that she followed the lesson plan in the teacher manual on that day. She called on Dustin twice during those vocabulary practice activities and Dustin answered the first question correctly. He did not respond to the second.

Ms. Tammy Wiley
Principal

*Tier One Intervention Summary:*
As shown in chart 6.5, Dustin can only recognize a very limited number of words. He seems to try to sound out various terms but still is not increasing his vocabulary recognition, often missing even the initial consonant sounds.

J. Carpenter

*Post Tier One Meeting Notes:*

Ms. Carpenter, Ms. Wiley, and I met to discuss an intensive intervention in reading for Dustin Prowner on 10/30/06. As a reading teacher, I can work with Dustin in the Direct Instruction SRA reading program for 20 minutes each day at 8:30 am. Dustin will join a reading group of 4 other students and I will chart his word recognition skills each day.

Ms. Renee Jones

*Observation of Instruction and Tier Two Intervention:*

I observed Ms. Jones at work with Dustin and several other students on 11/22/06, in using the SRA reading materials. Dustin participated in the sessions and responded correctly each time he was called upon. Ms. Jones was optimistic about his progress.

Ms. Wiley

*Tier Two Intervention Summary:*

The daily data in chart 6.7 indicated that this intervention is not working for Dustin. At this point, futher individual interventions are required. The team recommends placement of Dustin into the special education program for learning disabilities, with his primary service in Ms. Carpenter's class and one period a day in the resource room for individual learning instruction.

Ms. Wiley

## Performance Assessment

Performance assessment—which may also be referred to as authentic assessment—is based on the concept that students should produce actual products that are similar to products that would be produced in the "real world," and evaluation of the students' understanding should be based on those products or their performance in producing those products. Authentic tasks require that the student perform tasks in as realistic a fashion as possible, based on the context of the real world (McTighe & Emberger, 2006). Below are several examples that have been used in various schools.

Clearly, these projects involve sophisticated understanding of the concepts that are typically taught in history, English, or science, but these concepts are applied in a real-world context. This aspect of performance assessment tends to make this instructional innovation into a rich teaching/learning experience, during which students actually experience the application of their growing knowledge in these fields. For this reason, many teachers become quite loyal to this teaching/assessment paradigm and consider it much more "fun" than traditional instruction.

| Knowledge of Late Middle Ages | Students may be required to plan, conduct, develop costumes for, and then perform, a "King's Dinner." They must develop and dress in period costume, eat with the utensils used at that point (i.e., only a knife), speak some approximation of "Olde English," serve the school administrators the dinner with appropriate waitpersons, and so on. |
|---|---|
| Theme Writing | Students may be required to develop a campus newspaper, including news stories, various weekly columns, and so on, and produce an edition each week for the semester. |
| Studies of Ecosystems | Students may be required to sample water from several local creeks and rivers, testing for turbidity, microscopic life, and so on. |

Kids enjoy acting out their learning.

Of course, not all performance assessment projects involve extensive class-wide projects such as those described above. Less involved projects for individual students may be used for daily or weekly tasks. These may include the following:

- write a song or poem of a particular period
- draw a picture of a historical scene

- develop a model from toothpicks and glue
- illustrate a story
- teach a fifteen-minute period of class
- develop a multimedia report

As these projects suggest, the list of performance assessment projects is virtually endless, and the only limit is the creative imagination of the teacher. However, brainstorming various projects is merely the first step in performance assessment; teachers must also plan carefully what constitutes a finished performance and how those authentic assessments may be evaluated. Typically, in evaluating projects of this nature, a rubric (i.e., a specified set of evaluation criteria) is developed prior to the instructional exercise, and students are encouraged to compare their performance or product with the rubric continually throughout the work. Rubrics may be as extensive as necessary but should stipulate the specific components of the performance assessment project, as well as the relative grading "weight" of each component. In that fashion, students quickly realize what aspects of the project to emphasize.

## REFLECTIVE EXERCISE: WRITING THE RUBRICS

One differentiated instructional exercise that can be based on a performance assessment model is involvement of the students in the initial planning of the performance-based product and in the writing of the grading rubric for that project. Could students in your class participate constructively in such an exercise, and would that lead to higher involvement with their learning if they helped to develop the project idea and the grading standards for it?

## Portfolio Assessment

Another assessment innovation that has been incorporated into differentiated classes is the use of portfolios (Gregory & Chapman, 2002, pp. 50–54). A portfolio is a compilation of selected work by the student, which demonstrates the academic growth of the student over time and provides evidence of student accomplishment on particular skills. Portfolios encourage student ownership of the responsibility for the work and make the teacher and the student joint collaborators in the student's academic progress.

The portfolio should include work that the teacher and the student believe reflects the student's accomplishments most accurately. Students may include work that they are particularly proud of, that represents the most difficult task, or that represents a work in progress. Also, the portfolio should include an index prepared by the student as well as a reflective written document concerning why the student believes that this work represents his or her most important efforts. The index may be developed as an ongoing project with the portfolio, but the reflective essay should be completed prior to the end of the grading period.

Finally, the portfolio should include work from a student over a period of time and may include work from the first of the year as a comparison for work from the end of the year. All of these materials should be gathered and placed in some type of container (many teachers use an actual portfolio—hence the name—whereas others use small boxes). For both development and evaluation of the portfolio, a rubric should be developed with detailed indications of the level and scope of the work to be included within the portfolio, as well as the grading criteria to be used.

## ASSESSMENT MODIFICATIONS FOR THE DIFFERENTIATED CLASS

With the data generated by criterion-referenced assessments, curriculum-based measures, precision teaching projects, response to intervention projects, or authentic assessment, teachers will be well prepared to individually describe, in considerable detail, the exact functioning of the students in their class. Such detailed assessment data provide a rich basis for making instructional decisions about how to foster increased understanding, and in that sense, those assessment paradigms provide one vehicle for differentiation of assessment.

However, in many instances, teachers are called upon to implement group-administered assessments, and these assessments can be daunting challenges to many students with learning disabilities. For this reason, teachers may need to consider other differentiated assessment strategies, as well as ways to modify more traditional tests in order to accommodate the needs of students with learning disabilities, and there are a variety of modifications that can be considered (Chapman & King, 2005; pp 167–177; Forsten, Goodman, Grant, Hollas, & Whyte, 2006, pp. 58–69; Salend, 2005).

For example, in the differentiated class where students are exposed to different learning activities based on their learning strengths, teachers may wish to consider differentiating the assessment strategies for those students along the same lines. Imagine a classroom in Grade 6 that is focusing a unit of instruction on the settlement of the "Wild West." If one group of students, who each demonstrate a visual/spatial learning strength, have participated in an art project to draw a group picture of a frontier fort, the teacher may assess those students by having them each draw a version of that fort, label the buildings, and explain the construction materials used. Those students would, via their drawings, demonstrate the understanding of those forts. In fact, while Hollywood always depicts "Indian" forts as wooden palisade constructions, many historic forts on the plains were earthworks, since trees and lumber were very hard to find in that region. The students' drawings would, presumably, show that understanding, and such an assessment would be more representative of their knowledge than would their performance on a traditional paper and pencil test.

In addition to these individualized assessment practices, teachers will be called upon to modify group administered assessments, and should be prepared with an array of strategies that will allow for accommodation for students with learning disabilities. The sample strategies below will assist in that regard (Chapman & King, 2005; pp 167–177; Salend, 2005), and of course, rather than merely selecting one group of these tactics, teachers should individually tailor their accommodations to the particular needs of each student.

*Omit complex multiple choice questions:* These questions provide an "answer set" and the actual answer selections involve combinations of the answer set; (e.g., a. answer 1 and 2; b. answer 1 and 3; c. answer 3 only). These are very difficult for many students with LDs, and the same information can be obtained via traditional multiple choice formats.

*Use technology:* Judicious use of grammar checks, spell checkers, or calculators will assist many students with LDs.

*Extend the testing time:* Extending time may be necessary to obtain a clear picture of how well students with LDs understand the information.

*Allow alternative response mode or location:* Paper and pencil tests are scary events for some students, and providing the same test verbally may obtain a better picture of the child's performance. On essay questions, some students perform much better when the writing expectation is eliminated, and allowing those students to audio tape their essay answers can enhance their performance. Also, allowing students to take tests with a paraprofessional or special educator teaching in another room will sometimes help relax the student, resulting in a more accurate picture of performance.

*Present fewer items:* Presenting fewer items can alleviate test anxiety for many students; also, teachers should consider presenting only half of the items on a test at a time.

*Provide individual directions:* Students with LDs often are challenged to understand directions, and providing individual directions can provide students an opportunity to respond more completely. Also, teachers should consider (for some children) having the child repeat the directions back to the teacher prior to beginning the assessment.

*Offer extra credit:* Extra credit (in some cases, the mere opportunity to earn extra credit) can alleviate test anxiety and result in a more accurate measure of the child's understanding. One or two questions at the end of the test allow students to "show their comprehension" more. Also, allowing the students some choice in which questions to answer has the same effect.

## CONCLUSION

Students with learning disabilities require considerably more structure in their lessons than many other students, and monitoring students' academic performance on a daily basis can assist in providing much of the needed structure for differentiating instruction. The RTI process, in particular, will drastically impact the general education class, as one or more of the initial tiers of instruction are presumed to take place in the general education setting. While routine performance monitoring represents the most effective basis for instruction for all students, when eligibility determinations are made based on how a child responds to intervention, the issue of monitoring his or her response to that intervention assumes increased importance. Further, the RTI procedure, as well as other performance monitoring procedures described herein, will enable the student with the learning disability to see his or her performance in relation to previous efforts and to celebrate his or her growth toward the specific objectives on the IEP. For many students with learning disabilities, charting their performance is one of the most effective motivational tools teachers can employ and will enhance the student's self-concept and his or her relationship to the teacher.

This chapter has reviewed several strategies that are founded on this need for performance monitoring, including curriculum-based assessment, criterion-referenced testing, precision teaching, response to intervention, performance assessment, and portfolio assessment. Although there is considerable overlap between some of these strategies, application of any of these monitoring systems will increase the academic growth of students with learning disabilities in the inclusive class. Thus, one or more of these strategies should be incorporated into the IEP for almost every student with a learning disability.

## WHAT'S NEXT?

With a variety of differentiated instructional tools covered in the first six chapters, the next chapter focuses on the single most frequently noted disability among students with learning disabilities—a problem in reading. Many of the instructional and assessment innovations described previously will be discussed in the context of various reading skills, and an emphasis will be placed on practical strategies that can be incorporated into almost every general education classroom.

# Differentiation in Reading and Literacy Instruction 7

Approximately 80 percent of students diagnosed with a learning disability have some difficulty in reading, and these difficulties are most apparent in the general education classroom, where the child may be expected to perform the same work at the same reading level as his or her classmates. Although students with learning disabilities present a wide array of academic deficits, no deficit is as prevalent within the population of students with learning disabilities as deficits in reading. Furthermore—although math deficits, writing problems, and/or language deficits can certainly be debilitating—a deficit in reading is even more critical simply because this deficit will prevent learning in every other area (Kameenui, Carnine, Dixon, Simmons, & Coyne, 2002, pp. 1–40). For this reason, this chapter will present differentiated instructional strategies for teaching reading in the inclusive general education class. Because of the critical importance of reading for these children, every teacher, regardless of the grade level or instructional responsibility, should have access to differentiated instructional strategies for reading instruction.

Fortunately, research in the area of reading among students with learning disabilities has exploded within the past decade, with major advances in several related areas, including brain functioning during reading, literacy instruction, phonological research, and reading intervention tactics (Chard & Dickson, 1999; Joseph, Noble, & Eden, 2001; Lyon & Moats, 1997). This chapter will briefly explore these areas to describe an array of specific instructional tactics that have been shown to be effective for students with learning disabilities in the general education setting.

## WHAT IS LITERACY INSTRUCTION?

In 2000, the National Reading Panel summarized research in the area of reading and focused teachers across the nation on five areas of reading instruction (NRP, 2000). These five areas include phonemic awareness, phonics, vocabulary, reading fluency, and text comprehension. Each of these areas has received much research attention over the decades (Hammill, 2004), but with the publication of this important report in 2000, research in these five areas has increased. The report of the National Reading Panel also defined a "language of literacy," which involves integration of instruction for speaking, writing, and reading skills from the earliest years of childhood, throughout the public school years. The timing of the release of this report, immediately prior to passage of the No Child Left Behind legislation of 2001, assured that this report on reading instruction would receive even more attention than might be expected.

Within this context, literacy instruction is a fairly new concept and incorporates more than merely the basal reading instruction. Literacy approaches focus not only on the phoneme-based instruction that students with learning disabilities need (Bos, Mather, Silver-Pacuilla, & Narr, 2000; NRP, 2000; Patzer & Pettegrew, 1996; Smith, Baker, & Oudeans, 2001; Vaughn, 2006) but also on the students' ability to speak, write, and listen effectively and to use these literacy skills in their daily work in a variety of school settings (Winn & Otis-Wilborn, 1999). The emphasis on a literacy approach is on the interrelationship between reading, writing, and language, and tactics such as storytelling that involve several of these areas are favored (i.e., using a language-based process to teach reading [Craig, Hull, Haggart, & Crowder, 2001; Santoro, Coyne, & Simmons, 2006]; teachers will note that many of the strategies discussed in this chapter are effective for instruction in both reading and language arts). Furthermore, there is a growing emphasis on assisting struggling readers to improve their literacy rather than focusing on remediation of specific reading deficits (Dayton-Sakari, 1997).

To make this concept of "literacy instruction" more concrete, we should review the various components of literacy. Smith et al. (2001) delineated

Students remember what they describe for the class.

several components of early literacy instruction that they felt constitute an effective literacy program. These include the following:

- allocation of time for daily, highly focused literacy instruction
- consistent routines for teaching the big ideas of literacy
- explicit instruction for new letter names and sounds
- daily "scaffolded" or assisted practice with auditory phoneme detection, segmenting, and blending
- immediate corrective feedback
- daily application of new knowledge at the phoneme and letter-sound levels across multiple and varied literacy contexts
- daily reviews

Of course, these components include some of the basic differentiated instruction concepts that have been presented previously in this text. For example, note the emphasis on scaffolded instruction and the focus on immediate corrective feedback. Thus, the "literacy" emphasis really is quite broad and encompasses a variety of ideas from other instructional paradigms; in point of fact, almost all instructional tactics for the differentiated classroom do. With these literacy components in mind, one may formulate a solid understanding of what literacy instruction involves, and these components will provide something of a guideline to the topics discussed from this point on in the chapter.

## Research on Literacy Instruction

Research on early literacy instruction for students with learning disabilities has been summarized in a variety of sources (Bos et al., 2000; Hammill, 2004; Kameenui et al., 2002, pp. 53–78; Patzer & Pettegrew, 1996; Smith et al., 2001). For example, the research has supported a strong phoneme-based instructional approach for students with learning disabilities and/or reading disabilities (Kameenui et al., 2002). Next, an emphasis on oral reading fluency is also recommended because students are often called on to read orally in class across the grade levels (NRP, 2000). Next, early instruction in reading should be quite robust; that is, instruction should be undertaken with sufficient intensity to assist students in reaching their early reading goals. Research has also shown that, for young readers who lag behind others in kindergarten and first grade, phonological instruction is even more important in their early literacy instruction. The good news from the research is that phonological awareness is a "teachable" skill, and adequate instruction in that area will enhance the reading of students—even older students—who display subsequent reading disabilities (Hammill, 2004; Kameenui et al., 2002; Smith et al., 2001).

## A Literacy Checklist

Literacy instructional tactics have been offered by a number of authors in the literature and generally reflect the entire array of reading skills ranging from early phonemic awareness to higher order reading comprehension (Bos et al., 2000; NRP, 2000; Smith et al., 2001; Winn & Otis-Wilborn, 1999). As one example, Winn and Otis-Wilborn (1999) suggested the use of individually developed checklists for monitoring the literacy of students with learning disabilities in the inclusive classroom. A sample of such a literacy checklist is presented in Teaching Tip 7.1. As you can see, this informal literacy checklist encompasses a wider variety of literacy skills than would a traditional reading instructional lesson, and this "broader view" is the perspective supported by proponents of literacy instruction. Of course, teachers should vary the reading skills on the checklist for each student with a learning disability to reflect specifically those literacy skills that are relevant for that particular student.

# PHONOLOGICAL AWARENESS AND INSTRUCTION

One aspect of early literacy instruction that is heavily emphasized is phonological awareness (Kameenui et al., 2002). In fact, within the past decade, research has documented that phonological awareness is both a critical component of many subsequent language arts and literacy skills (Bos et al., 2000; Chard & Dickson, 1999; NRP, 2000), as well as a primary deficit area for many students with learning disabilities (Kameenui et al., 2002). Based on recent research, a general consensus has emerged that students with learning disabilities demonstrate an early inability to manipulate phonemes, and this inability is the primary cause of subsequent learning disabilities in a wide variety of areas (NRP, 2000; Vaughn, 2006). For this reason, it is critical that every general education teacher in the

## Teaching Tip 7.1

### A Literacy Checklist

Student Name _____ Date _____ Student's Grade _____

Student's Approximate Reading Level _____

Type of reading activity (circle one below).

oral reading  group/choral reading  studying text  individual reading with teacher

Title and approximate grade level of reading material_____

### *Reading Behaviors Noted*

| | Never | Infrequently | Frequently | Always | Not observed |
|---|---|---|---|---|---|
| 1. Attempts to decode unknown words | ___ | ___ | ___ | ___ | ___ |
| 2. Sounds out onsets | ___ | ___ | ___ | ___ | ___ |
| 3. Sounds out rimes | ___ | ___ | ___ | ___ | ___ |
| 4. Blends onsets/rimes | ___ | ___ | ___ | ___ | ___ |
| 5. Reads this material fluently | ___ | ___ | ___ | ___ | ___ |
| 6. Uses context clues | ___ | ___ | ___ | ___ | ___ |
| 7. Predicts plot/content | ___ | ___ | ___ | ___ | ___ |
| 8. Notes sequence of events | ___ | ___ | ___ | ___ | ___ |
| 9. Checks predictions | ___ | ___ | ___ | ___ | ___ |
| 10. Summarizes text | ___ | ___ | ___ | ___ | ___ |

Comments and Notes on Observed Reading Behaviors _____

lower grades understand the concept of phonological awareness and have access to several phonological awareness instructional strategies.

At the outset, we should note several important definitions, as stipulated by the National Reading Panel (2000). First, phonemic instruction is different from phonics instruction in that phonemic instruction involves only the sounds of phonemes without any reference to printed letters. In phonemic instruction, the emphasis is on a child's ability to detect and manipulate individual meaningful sounds in our language (Chard & Dickson, 1999). Of course, phonics instruction emphasizes the relationships between the printed letters and their associated sounds. Finally, the National Reading Panel also differentiated between phonemic awareness and phonological awareness (NRP, 2000). Phonological awareness is a much broader concept than phonemic awareness, since phonemic awareness involves individual discrete sounds, whereas phonological awareness may also involve sounds of combinations of phonemes, syllabication, segmenting words, or even segmenting or manipulation of word phrases.

With these distinctions noted, it is apparent that phonics instruction is something that many teachers are currently familiar and will not be addressed in this context. However, in order to grasp these newer literacy concepts, the discussion provided below highlights phonemic instruction and phonological instruction.

## Phonemic Awareness Instruction

Phonemic awareness involves a student's ability to detect and manipulate phonemes, and many students with learning disabilities demonstrate significant problems at this level of reading skill (Kameenui et al., 2002, pp. 58; Santoro, et al., 2006). Furthermore, there is a hierarchy of phonemic skills that students must master in order to become effective readers. For example, most theorists suggest that detecting similar sounds (rhyming) is a phonemic skill that precedes detecting different initial sounds (i.e., the difference between the first sound in "cat" vs. "hat"). This continuum of phonemic skills varies somewhat from one researcher to another, but the following sequence of skills represents this general concept.

| | |
|---|---|
| Detecting rhyming sounds | Various rhyming exercises may be used |
| Isolating initial sounds | What is the first sound in *ball*? |
| Isolating middle/ending sounds | What is the last sound in *house*? |
| Blending sounds into words | What word do you have if you put these sounds together? (ho-may-ker) |
| Segmenting or dividing sounds within words | What do the parts of this word sound like if you divide it up? (banana) |
| Changing/manipulating sounds | What would cat sound like if you put an "ha" sound in front? |

Of course, after a student can manipulate sounds in this fashion, the student must be trained in the alphabetic principle (sometimes referred to as the alphabetic code)—the idea that the forty-four different phonemes in the English language may be represented by twenty-six letters or combinations of those twenty-six letters (Sousa, 2001). This instruction in the alphabetic code is referred to as phonics and involves a process of mapping speech sounds to written or printed letters. Thus, phonics instruction proceeds only after a student has mastered phonemic awareness and phonemic manipulation (Kameenui et al., 2002, pp. 58–65). Furthermore, students must learn letter sounds and these phonemic manipulation skills to a very high level of automaticity to learn to read fluently.

With this distinction between phonics and phonemic instruction noted, it is immediately apparent that merely teaching students "letter sounds" may not be enough for students with learning disabilities because those students may not be able to discriminate between the various letter sounds anyway. Thus, phonemic activities in phonological awareness skills are necessary for many students with learning disabilities (Kameenui et al., 2002, pp. 50–65; Smith, 1998). Typically, phonemic instruction would precede instruction in phonics itself and may begin as early as prekindergarten. However, for students who have not mastered phonemic awareness and manipulation skills, even as late as elementary grades and middle school, this instruction must precede higher level instruction in reading (Kameenui et al., 2002, pp. 50–65; NRP, 2000).

Phonemic instruction can involve a wide variety of instructional activities such as rhyming word activities, hunting for sound-alike word activities, or sound blending. To give teachers a better sense of how phonological skills may be taught, here are two examples that would be appropriate for the inclusive class. A series of sample instructional activities that emphasize sounds and sound-blending activities are presented in Teaching Tip 7.2. Note that these activities involve no presentation of letters at all; rather these activities stress the sounds in the language.

## Phonological Instruction

In contrast to phonemic instruction, phonological instruction is much broader and involves sounds of phonemes, syllables, words, and even word phrases. This emphasis is more inclusive than merely phonemic instruction, and the National Reading Panel encouraged teachers to focus directly on phonological instruction in teaching reading. In fact, research has shown that instruction in phonological skills can greatly enhance a student's capacity to read (Kameenui, et al., 2002; NRP, 2000; Simos et al., 2002; Smith, 1998). For example, Simos and his colleagues (2002) provided an interesting recent report on the impact of phonological instruction on the brain. In a brain imaging study, these researchers used functional neuroimaging brain scans obtained prior to and after students with severe reading disabilities had been exposed to an intensive phonologically based reading intervention. These brain scans are designed to show how the brain "activates" during the act of reading. The eight target students all read in the lower 20 percent of the population, and six of those eight students read in the bottom 3 percent of the population. After an initial brain scan while these students engaged in the act of reading, the students each received intensive reading instruction for two hours per day, five days a week, for only eight weeks. Prior to the intervention, their brain scans showed a pattern of brain region activation that has long been associated with poor word recognition. However, scans taken just eight weeks later after the intensive phonologically based reading intervention showed that these brain activation patterns had changed drastically, and that the brain functioning of these poor readers was more reflective of the brain activation pattern of normal readers. Thus, this study provides hard evidence that intensive phonological based reading interventions actually change brain patterns among poor readers and make their brains perform more similarly to successful readers.

Kameenui and his coworkers (2002, pp. 68) recommended a series of instructional scaffolds, presented below and designed to support students in learning phonological recognition skills. Note the similarity between these activities and the metacognitive/scaffolded approach described in a previous chapter.

### Teaching Tip 7.2

**Sample Phonological Activities and Lesson Plans**

**Guess the Word Game Lesson**

*Objective*: Students will be able to blend and identify a word that is stretched out into component sounds.

*Materials needed:* Picture cards of objects that students are likely to recognize, such as sun, bell, fan, flag, snake, tree, book, cup, clock, and plane.

*Activity:* Place a small number of picture cards before children. Tell them you are going to say a word using "snail talk"——a slow way of saying words (e.g., fffff lllll aaaaa ggggg). They have to look at the pictures and guess what the snail is saying. It is important to have the children guess the answer in their head so that everyone gets an opportunity to try it before hearing other answers. Alternate between having one child identify the word and having all children say the word aloud in chorus to keep the children engaged.

**Segmentation Lesson**

*Objective:* Students will be able to segment various parts of oral language.

*Materials needed*: List of brief phrases or poems children would know (e.g., "I scream. You scream. We all scream for ice cream").

*Activities:*

(a) Early instruction involves teaching the children to segment sentences into individual words. Have the children clap their hands with each individual word.

(b) As children advance, teach them to segment words into syllables. You may wish to start with children's names (Al-ex-an-der; Ra-chel).

(c) When children have learned to remove the first phoneme from a word, teach them to segment short words into individual phonemes (s-u-n: s-t-o-p).

SOURCE: Adapted from "Phonological Awareness: Instructional and Assessment Guidelines" by Chard, D. J., & Dickson, S. V. (1999). *Intervention in School and Clinic, 34,* 261–270. © 1999 by PRO-ED, Inc. Adapted with permission.

| | |
|---|---|
| Scaffold 1—Model | The teacher says the sounds in a word while touching each letter: "My turn to sound out this word. When I touch a letter, I'll say its sound. I'll keep saying the sound until I touch the next letter." |
| Scaffold 2—Overt sound out | The teacher touches under each letter while students say each sound: "Your turn to sound out this word. When I touch a letter, you say its sound. Keep saying the sound until I touch the next letter." |

| Scaffold 3—Internal sound out | The teacher touches under each letter while students say each sound in their head: "You are going to read this word without saying the sounds out loud. As I point to the letters, sound out this word to yourself." |
|---|---|
| Scaffold 4—Whole-word reading | The teacher points to the word and students sound it out independently: "You are going to read this word the fast way. When I point to a word, sound it out to yourself. When I signal, say the word the fast way." |

## REFLECTIVE EXERCISE: LITERACY INSTRUCTION VERSUS READING INSTRUCTION

Pretend that you are explaining the concept of literacy instruction to a parent. Describe how this approach may differ from traditional phonics-based basal reading approaches in terms of the scope of the instructional activities, as well as the emphasis on reading as related to other skill areas.

# DIBELS: MEASURING EARLY LITERACY

With the drastic expansion of research on early literacy, a number of newly developed assessment techniques have emerged. Perhaps the most important and frequently used of these is the Dynamic Indicators of Basic Early Literacy Skills (DIBELS). This individualized assessment is designed as a quick measure of a student's early literacy in a variety of areas such as phonemic, phonetic, and phonological skills, as well as oral reading fluency.

Research has shown that if students in kindergarten through Grade 3 reach certain benchmarks at certain points in their early reading experience (e.g., ability to recognize initial sounds in words by the second month of kindergarten), those students will be likely to progress throughout their elementary years with little difficulty in reading. Further, the opposite is also generally true—that students who experience early reading difficulties are likely to develop longer term reading difficulties. For example, Lipka, Lesaux, and Siegel (2006), in a longitudinal study, recently demonstrated that some 75 percent of the students who had significant reading disabilities in Grade 4 were identified as early as kindergarten as students who would be likely to develop reading problems. Thus, DIBELS was designed to assess students in grades kindergarten through 3 only in relation to the appropriate benchmarks, and so there are different measures in the various grades. The specific measures obtained include: initial sound fluency, phoneme segmentation fluency, nonsense word fluency, and oral reading fluency.

DIBELS was developed by Roland Good and Ruth Kaminski (2002) and has received broad acceptance nationwide. In particular, many school districts require that their general education teachers implement this informal and easy-to-administer assessment in order to identify children who are struggling in reading. In the context of the response to intervention initiative, which was described in the last chapter, an assessment such as DIBELS can provide an excellent repeated measure of how well a child is responding to instruction. Also, frequent progress monitoring using an instrument such as DIBELS can provide teachers with the exact knowledge they need to differentiate instruction in their classes, since some students will need phonemic instruction on the earliest literacy skills whereas others need instruction in some of the higher level skills. In that context, many more general education teachers will become involved in implementation of this assessment measure for early literacy in the near future. For more information on DIBELS, you should refer to the Web site established by the authors: (www.dibels.org).

# WORD ATTACK AND WORD RECOGNITION

Once phonemic and phonics skills are established for a child, the student will need to focus on vocabulary building, which involves a focus of developing automatic sight word recognition and word attack skills. While various activities may be utilized, the various tactics presented below represent effective instructional techniques that can be implemented on an individual or small group basis.

## Word Bank Instruction

Many teachers use a word bank, in which five to ten unknown sight words are enclosed and used for an instructional activity of some type each day. Generally, the teacher begins by having the student read a word list, which may be either a list of sight words or a list of vocabulary words from a subject content text. The teacher marks the errors and stops the child when ten words have been misread. A mark is made under the last word attempted, and that line is dated; the page is filed and will be used again as an informal assessment measure. The ten unknown words are written on cardboard (or light paper stock) and become the student's word bank. The cards can then be placed in a word can. Although any type of personal container will do, I used the cardboard "potato chip cans" and had the junior high students in my class decorate their individual word cans. Although many teachers use word bank activities for teaching sight words, I had junior high–age students use word bank activities to learn subject content words from their subject area classes. This is a great activity in which the special education teacher can support the content of the inclusive class.

Daily word bank activities may include having the student write each word several times and read them to the teacher. On other days, the students may look up their words, use them in sentences, use them in a story, or locate them in a story. The critical aspect of the word bank tactic is that the student must use each word in the word bank each day for one task or another. After about two weeks, the student will be able to read these words with very little problem.

At that point, the student is told to take the words home and share them with his or her parents. The word list is used again, and another ten words are selected for the word bank. For higher level students learning content area words, you may change words in the word bank as the units of instruction change in the inclusive class.

At the end of the year, the student will have learned a large number of new words, and the teacher will be able to show to the parents the word list, which indicates specifically the vocabulary level of the student at the first of the year and the succeeding mastery of various groups of words throughout the year. Parents generally respond quite favorably to specific evidence of academic growth, such as that represented by this word list. Teaching Tip 7.3 presents additional word bank activities that may be completed using these words. Also, precision teaching provides one of the best methods for monitoring progress on sight word recognition for word bank activities. Such a project is presented in Teaching Tip 7.4.

## Syllabication

The ability to divide a multisyllabic word into syllables enhances a student's ability to read unknown words in at least two ways. First, syllables are easier to read than longer words for many students with learning disabilities. Next, syllabication allows for the subsequent phonetic decoding of each syllable. Because syllabication makes the use of phonics possible, an inability to divide words into syllables can greatly hamper a student's reading efforts. For this reason, teachers across the grade levels should stress syllabication skills.

### Teaching Tip 7.3

**Activities for Word Bank Words**

1. Look for words that have the same spelling.

2. Look for words that rhyme.

3. Look for words that may mean the same thing (i.e., synonyms).

4. Write words on cards and play a "dominoes" game by matching the first two or the last two letters of each word.

5. Categorize words by their type: nouns, pronouns, verbs, and so on.

6. Have students write stories together using all of their words.

A number of syllabication rules are generally applicable and may be taught as general guidelines for reading even in higher grades in the content area classes. Although no single set of rules is comprehensive enough to cover every situation in English, several of the most common rules for syllabication are presented in Teaching Tip 7.5.

### Teaching Tip 7.4

**Precision Teaching Project on Sight Word Recognition**

This tip describes a precision teaching project used to monitor sight word recognition for a student with a learning disability. This type of project works well, regardless of the specific types of activities the child uses each day to study his or her words from the word bank. First, as described above, the teacher should identify only those words the student does not know. Approximately ten words should go in the word bank. To get an accurate count on reading rate for the ten words in the word can, the teacher must prepare a reading sheet that lists those ten words in random order, with each word listed at least ten times. This should provide enough words for the child to be able to continue reading through a one-minute or two-minute period. After the child's word bank activity for the day is finished, the teacher and the child sit together, and at the beginning of the timing period, the child begins to read the words. During this timed reading activity, the child reads as many words as possible in the allotted time. Words read correctly and errors made are counted and charted; the teacher should mark corrections and errors on another sheet.

After the student reaches his or her goal, the teacher should change the words in the word bank. If a word has proven to be particularly hard, it may be kept, along with nine new words. Of course, each change of words should be indicated as a phase change line on the precision teaching chart, as described in Chapter 6.

### Teaching Tip 7.5

**Common Syllabication Rules**

1.  When two consonants come between two vowels, as in hammer and slumber, divide the word between the two consonants: *ham/mer*, *slum/ber*.

2.  When a single consonant comes between the two vowels, divide the word after the first vowel: *be/gan*.

3.  When a word ends in a consonant followed by le, as in table, the final syllable is made up of the consonant and the le: *ta/ble*.

4.  Generally, multiletter suffixes are syllables by themselves: *head/ed*, *load/ing*.

Syllabication skills are generally taught using these general rules, and students with learning disabilities can usually master these rules once specific and explicit instruction is provided. Teachers should make a chart of these rules and place it permanently in the classroom. In fact, one may think of these rules as a metacognitive strategy that enables a student to recognize the likely positions of syllables in words. Instruction would proceed, as described in Chapter 4, by eliciting cooperation and modeling the rule application with known words, application to unknown words, and daily checks of progress. The creative teacher may even identify an acronym to represent each of these rules.

## Structural Analysis

For students with learning disabilities beyond Grade 3, the use of structural analysis of words is recommended. Structural analysis involves direct instruction in the ability to recognize prefixes, suffixes, and root words. For example, the word "playing" looks considerably longer and more complicated to many third graders than the more common word "play." Indeed, for some students with learning disabilities, such a multisyllabic word may seem quite intimidating. However, identification of the suffix syllable "-ing" will aid those students in recognition of the word.

Teaching the most common prefixes and suffixes will thus assist in the overall reading performance for most students with learning disabilities, and most

### Teaching Tip 7.6

**A Visual Scan Worksheet for Locating Prefixes/Suffixes**

Directions: You should look at each word, identify the prefix or suffix, and circle it.

| | | | |
|---|---|---|---|
| fighting | write | coming | subtopic |
| women | using | taken | learned |
| home | restless | prohibit | habit |
| insight | beside | before | sightless |
| desks | chair | table | insight |

This listing could also include more advanced suffixes and prefixes. Also, a worksheet such as this would be appropriate for use on a timed precision teaching task to document mastery of suffixes and prefixes.

general education teachers spend some time on word structure. Various strategies may be used to which prefixes and suffixes are taught. Teaching Tip 7.6 presents a worksheet that uses a visual scanning technique to identify prefixes and suffixes. Teachers may use this model with other lists of words and develop a series of worksheets stressing structural analysis. Completion of this type of worksheet on a daily basis would result in a total number of correct answers and errors that could then be plotted on a precision teaching chart for evaluation of the student's performance.

## A Structural Analysis Learning Strategy

As discussed in Chapter 4, the University of Kansas researchers have produced a number of learning strategies to assist students with learning disabilities with performing various tasks. The DISSECT strategy (Bryant, Ugel, Thompson, & Hamff, 1999; Ellis, 1994; Lenz, Schumaker, Deshler, & Beals, 1984) was developed to enable secondary students to identify the meaning of unknown words in text. This strategy would be presented to the students in the same fashion as discussed in Chapter 4, including presentation of the strategy, modeling, teaching of known words, application of the strategy to unknown words, and generalization of the strategy. For students with learning disabilities who have difficulty with structural analysis, this tactic would be applicable in almost every general education class. Teaching Tip 7.7 presents the steps in the DISSECT strategy.

### Teaching Tip 7.7

**The DISSECT Learning Strategy**

D   Discover the word's context. Reread the sentence before and after the word. Look at the pictures.

I   Isolate the prefix. Look for common prefixes the student already knows.

S   Separate the suffix.

S   Say the stem. See if the stem is recognizable in isolation (without prefix or suffix).

E   Examine the stem. If the stem is not immediately recognizable, the student may have to sound it out or at least sound out the pronounceable parts.

C   Check with someone. If the student has some idea of the word, he or she should check that out.

T   Try the dictionary. If a student has no one to ask, or if that person doesn't know, the dictionary should be referred to.

SOURCE: Adapted from Ellis (1994) and Bryant, Ugel, Thompson, and Hamff (1999). See also Lenz and Hughes (1990) and Lenz, Schumaker, Deshler, and Beals (1984).

NOTE: Training in this and other learning strategies instruction is available through the University of Kansas, Lawrence (phone: 913-864-4780 for information).

# VOCABULARY: COMPREHENDING WORDS

Whereas the techniques reviewed earlier concentrated basically on recognition of words, the following techniques address the issue of vocabulary or word comprehension in text. There are numerous methods that address word comprehension. Some of these are useful for lower level readers in the earlier grades, whereas other techniques may be used in higher grade levels in subject content areas.

## A Semantic Webbing Strategy

Many students with learning disabilities have difficulty in vocabulary as well as difficulty in detecting the relationships between the concepts in their reading assignments, and those relationships often represent the basis of higher order understandings. Both the student's vocabulary, as well as the student's sense of relationships between concepts, may be strengthened by using a semantic web for most reading assignments (this same tactic is sometimes referred to as semantic maps) (see Bos et al., 2000; Bryant et al., 1999).

A semantic web may be considered a scaffold for student learning and address the process of learning new content. Typically, the web presents a word or a phrase, written in a central circle on the dry-erase board or worksheet, and the activity involves having the students and the teacher together determine what other words relate to the central word, as presented in Teaching Tip 7.8. Those additional terms and concepts are written on the board in separate circles and placed in proximity to each other as dictated by the underlying relationships between them. The emphasis is on meaningful relationships, and some teachers in developing the semantic web write in each circle not only the related term but also an abbreviated rationale describing the relationship between the new term and the central term in the web.

In Teaching Tip 7.8, the term "creeks" is related to "rivers" and thereby to the central term "water sources," but because creeks rarely flow directly into the ocean, there is no relationship depicted directly from "creek" to "ocean." As this example illustrates, the semantic web is one literacy instructional concept that can be used across the grade levels and in a variety of topical areas. For students with learning disabilities, each reading assignment may be the opportunity to develop a semantic web, and for students of differing ability levels, the teacher may differentiate the instruction by supplying some of the terms for the web placed in their appropriate positions.

Further, in a differentiated lesson as discussed in Chapter 1, one of the differentiated groups may be assigned the task of creating a semantic web for later use by others in the class. In multiple intelligences terms, the students with strong spatial intelligence would be good choices for this differentiated group activity.

 **Teaching Tip 7.8**

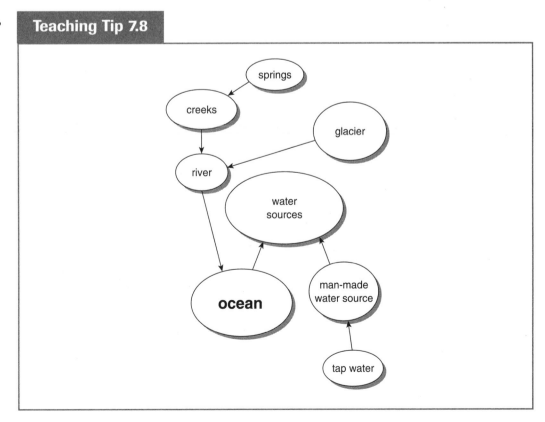

## A Cloze Procedure

A cloze procedure is a structured fill-in-the-blank activity that emphasizes word comprehension and use of context clues. This tactic may be used across the grade levels and in a variety of subject areas. Teaching Tip 7.9 presents an example of a cloze procedure.

In using a cloze procedure, the semantic and syntactic clues embedded within the reading passage serve as an aid in the student's selection of the correct content term, which would then be used to fill in the blank. For many students with learning disabilities, this can be a very effective reading technique. Inclusive class teachers can form a cloze procedure reading activity from almost any reading section by selecting every seventh content word (i.e., omitting words such as "a," "and," and "the" from the count of words) and deleting these content terms. In contrast, teachers may merely select a reading passage and choose random content words to replace with a blank line. Not only does this force the students to read the words, but this tactic also forces students with learning disabilities to attend to the content of the reading passage to interpret the context clues. Of course, prior to use with students, the newly prepared reading selection should be checked to ensure that the blanks may be completed by use of the available clues.

As an alternative, this cloze procedure activity can easily be differentiated to vary the task difficulty for students with learning disabilities by providing a word list from which the correct terms may be selected. These terms would then be matched to the particular blanks in the reading selection to demonstrate the student's comprehension. This represents a differentiation accomplished by variations of both the learning product and content difficulty.

As a final step, teachers may wish to adapt a series of cloze procedure reading activities into a daily precision teaching instructional project. For students with learning disabilities, reading a prepared reading selection of this nature every day would quickly yield information on their progress in building the vocabulary for that unit of instruction. Again, the daily scores for correct and incorrect answers should be charted to demonstrate progress. This activity is particularly appropriate for use in the late elementary and higher grades to teach vocabulary particular to the subject area. Historically, this cloze procedure has been used to assess passage comprehension, though "comprehension of words in text" may be a more accurate description of this particular skill.

**Teaching Tip 7.9**

### A Cloze Procedure for Reading Instruction

I remember visiting my grandparents on their farm way out in the _____.
They raised corn and oats, and the farm was also a noisy home to many animals. Each morning, before I got out of _____. I could hear the _____ crow at first light. Shortly after those morning noises, I would hear the _____ mooing, as my grandfather began milking them. Making the farm even noisier, the dog always seemed to be _____. Mornings were noisy times at Grandfather's _____.

### REFLECTIVE EXERCISE: THE CLOZE PROCEDURE AS THE DEFINITIVE COMPREHENSION EXERCISE

Reflect on the various ways educators measure reading comprehension (e.g., read a passage and then answer written questions; read a passage and then point to a picture that it describes). For many researchers, the cloze procedure is the most effective way to measure comprehension, simply because the comprehension exercise is embedded within the reading itself and is not exclusively a postreading activity. This makes the cloze procedure more similar to actual reading comprehension. Can you think of other ways to measure comprehension that are more directly tied to the written text?

# READING FLUENCY

## Teaching for Fluency

In delineating the various areas within reading, the National Reading Panel indicated that reading fluency is a critically important reading skill. Reading fluency allows students to access meaning in text, and research has shown strong relationships between reading fluency and reading comprehension. Therefore, teachers and researchers alike are attending more to reading fluency among students with LDs as well as all others in the class. As noted above, the DIBELS (Good & Kaminski, 2002) included a measure of reading fluency as one of the higher level reading skills assessed, and a variety of assessments and reading curricula are now available that address the issue of reading fluency.

The National Reading Panel (2000) identified several broad reading strategies that facilitate fluent reading including repeatedly reading the same passage and using reading models (e.g., audiotapes that are verbally reading the same passage, while the target student reads along). More specifically that report encouraged the following reading techniques for fluency building:

- Repeated reading—having the student read the same passage multiple times. (While there is some debate concerning how often a student should read the same passage, having a student repeat a passage three or four times is usually sufficient. Each time the student should receive some feedback—e.g., discussion of difficult vocabulary terms, or a model reader—as described below.)
- Student-adult reading—reading one-on-one with an adult who provides a model of fluent reading, helps with word recognition, and provides feedback.
- Choral reading—reading aloud simultaneously in a group.
- Tape-assisted reading—reading aloud simultaneously or as an echo with an audiotaped passage. (Typically tape-assisted reading involves an audiotaped model that presents between 80 and 100 words per minute—which is taken to be optimal reading fluency at most grade levels.)

- Partner reading—reading aloud with a more fluent partner or a partner of equal reading ability who provides a model of fluent reading, helps with word recognition and provides feedback.
- Reader's theater—rehearsing and performing before an audience a dialogue-rich script.

Because of the increased emphasis on reading fluency, a variety of reading fluency curricula have been published recently. Perhaps the most frequently used of the recently developed curricula for enhancing reading fluency is *Read Naturally* (Ihnot, Mastoff, Gavin, & Hendrickson, 2001). The *Read Naturally* curriculum promotes oral reading fluency in Grades 1 through 8, and is based on proven fluency building strategies such as repeated reading, reading with a fluent model, and frequent progress monitoring. In this program, students are exposed to brief reading selections that they select, at a grade level appropriate for them. They first write a "prediction" about what the reading selection might be about given the title. Next the students read those selections alone while timing himself or herself (in terms of the number of words read correctly per minute). The student then graphs his or her reading fluency score. The next step involves reading the same passage with a "reading model," which may be an audiotape, CD, or computer voice reading the passage. This reading model provides a "scaffold" for the reading process during the early readings of a particular passage. Students are also encouraged to set goals concerning their reading fluency in terms of reading rate, again in terms of the number of words read correctly per minute. This goal setting and frequent progress monitoring allows students to see even minute improvements in their oral reading fluency.

One can readily note the similarities between the activities in *Read Naturally* and those activities recommended as best-practice by the National Reading Panel (2000). Having a reading model, repeated readings, and prediction were all highly effective reading strategies recommend by the NRP, and incorporation of these tactics into our differentiated reading activities will enhance reading fluency among our students.

Moreover, research has documented that intensive interventions that explicitly concentrate on reading fluency problems can alleviate those reading problems for many children (Denton, Fletcher, Anthony, & Francis, 2006; Mastropieri, Leinart, & Scruggs, 1999; Vaughn, 2006; Vaughn, Linan-Thompson, & Hickman, 2003). For example, Denton and her coworkers (2006) implemented an intensive reading intervention for students who had not reached the benchmark indicators in reading fluency during the first three years of school. That study involved 27 students who displayed persistent reading problems in decoding and fluency. After an eight-week exposure to daily one-hour lessons in the *Read Naturally* instructional program, the students demonstrated a significant increase in reading fluency. This and similar research suggest that instruction in reading fluency, based on repeated readings and model fluency reading with teachers or peers, is a very effective reading strategy and should be built into every differentiated classroom. Mastropieri and her colleagues (1999) provided some additional suggestions for implementing the repeated readings tactic, as presented in Teaching Tip 7.10.

**Teaching Tip 7.10**

### Ten Steps for Implementing a Repeated Reading Tactic

1. The teacher should explain to the student how reading practice will help the student read more fluently; this will typically lead to less embarrassment in inclusive classes for many students with learning disabilities and/or reading problems. Most students with learning disabilities will be highly motivated to use this tactic if it is presented in this fashion.

2. The teacher and each student with a learning disability should select an appropriate reading rate goal, and each goal should be stated in terms of words read correctly per minute.

3. Based on the reading instructional level for each individual student (i.e., the reading level at which the student accurately reads a minimum of 85 percent of the words correctly), the teacher and the student should select reading passages for use in the repeated reading tactic.

4. The teacher should calculate the reading rates for each student (a review of the precision teaching tactic described in Chapter 6 will help here).

5. The teacher should also teach each student how to calculate, record, and interpret his or her own reading rates.

6. Tell the students to choose a story that interests them and practice reading the story or reading selection alone (or with a buddy, if you wish to use the buddy system) three times.

7. Students should be encouraged to ask for help in pronouncing words when needed during the first three readings or practice readings. This will assist them in learning the new terms.

8. After practicing three times, the student should read the story again, as fast as possible, while using a stopwatch or clock with a second hand to time himself or herself.

9. After the final reading, the student should record the time on a graph.

10. The student should be encouraged to compare that performance with the reading rate goal set earlier and also with previous performance.

## Reading Practices to Avoid

When moving into differentiation, teachers will be actively seeking a wide variety of activities that can be incorporated into the differentiated class for the various groups of students during small-group instruction. While a wider array of tactics and strategies is certainly consistent with the goal of differentiation, we should note that two common reading fluency practices have been actively discouraged by the NRP: individual oral reading in class and silent reading.

While many teachers traditionally had students read aloud before the whole class, this practice has always been embarrassing for readers who have difficulty with the text at hand; of course, that would include many students with learning disabilities. However, teachers are encouraged to use choral reading in the class, and having a few (perhaps four or five) students read a passage together diminishes embarrassment for those who might have difficulty with the passage, but still allows teachers to individually "tune in" to the readers they wish to hear for diagnostic purposes. In short, with only four or five readers in the class chorally reading a passage, a teacher can still hear individual readers and make diagnostic notes concerning their reading—thus choral reading allows the teacher to accomplish the same task as individual oral reading, but prevents the embarrassment associated with the latter practice.

In addition to discouraging individual oral reading in front of the class, the National Reading Panel (2000) indicated that various silent reading programs do not have strong research support. Programs such as Sustained Silent Reading (SSR) or Drop Everything and Read (DEAR) are not strongly supported by research. Rather than continue to engage in these programs in the differentiated class, the NRP report recommended that teachers encourage students to read silently at home, but that for in-class reading, some reading model and some feedback be provided for the reading activity. As teachers plan which differentiated reading activities to employ, they should remember these general guidelines.

# READING COMPREHENSION STRATEGIES

A number of instructional tactics for enhancing reading comprehension have been described previously in this chapter and in this text. However, a number of additional tactics are described below that are particularly effective for reading instruction in the elementary and middle grades, both for increasing reading fluency or reading comprehension (Bryant et al., 1999; Denton et al., 2006; Mastropieri et al., 1999; NRP, 2000; Swanson & De La Paz, 1998).

Reading in content areas is quite different from reading stories in the elementary grades. Content area readings from textbooks are likely to be more highly related across days than are the stories in the basal reading series in the elementary classroom. Chapters of reading material in content areas tend to be related in a sequential way in almost every subject (e.g., studies of the Revolution precede studies of the Federalist period, and studies of invertebrates precede studies of vertebrates). Thus, students need to understand the differences in these reading assignments, as well as the relationships across chapters in content area reading. The strategies presented below will facilitate reading comprehension in both elementary reading and reading in content areas.

## A Prediction/Summarization Tactic

Students with learning disabilities approach a reading task differently than normal readers, in that they neither predict what is likely to come next in a reading selection nor summarize their reading to monitor and enhance their comprehension (Bryant et al., 1999). In short, many students with learning disabilities, particularly in oral reading activities, merely "say the words" without truly understanding that they should be deriving understanding from the text. Thus, strategies that assist students with learning disabilities to mentally get involved and interact with their reading material will assist these readers (NRP, 2000). Specifically, strategies should encourage students to do the following:

- predict what the reading passage is likely to contain
- summarize the passage to monitor comprehension

These two strategies are likely to result in higher levels of comprehension; in fact, both prediction and summarizing were emphasized in the reciprocal teaching strategy described in Chapter 3. When assigning a reading selection to students with learning disabilities, teachers should emphasize prediction and summarization by using a worksheet that the student must complete during the reading process. A sample prediction/summarization worksheet is presented in Teaching Tip 7.11, and you can easily adapt this prediction/summarization worksheet for a wide variety of reading tasks across the grade levels. This tactic will assist students with learning disabilities to become more involved in the reading content.

### REFLECTIVE EXERCISE: TIME TO READ

As critical a skill as reading is, many teachers may view the repeated reading strategy described above as too expensive in terms of the student's time. How can any teacher in any busy classroom find the time to monitor a student reading the same text three or four times as a repeated reading activity? A moment's reflection can dissipate that concern. First, no activity in school is as important as a student learning to read, and strategies in this field must supersede all other instruction. Next, using a buddy system or peer tutoring as described previously gives teachers a way to implement this repeated reading strategy while not having to spend all of their time with one student. Teachers should reflect on the importance of this idea and jot down a few ideas for implementing this strategy as they move toward a more differentiated classroom.

## A Text Lookback Tactic

One idea that will assist older students with learning disabilities in their reading summarization in content area reading is instruction in "text lookbacks" (Swanson & De La Paz, 1998). In using a text lookback tactic, teachers should directly teach the skills involved in looking back over a text chapter or assigned reading to find specific information. When partnered with a set of specific comprehension questions, the ability to look back in the text to find answers to the questions will greatly assist students with learning disabilities in comprehension of the assigned reading material.

Some general education teachers may assume that telling students with learning disabilities to "look back over the chapter and find the answer" is sufficient for those students. However, the fact is that there are a number of

## A Prediction/Summarization Tactic

Before Reading

What is the story title?

What content predictions can I make based on that?

Are there pictures that suggest the topic?

What do I want to learn about that topic?

During Reading

What is the main idea or problem?

How was the problem managed?

After Reading

Was the problem successfully dealt with?

What is the main story or lesson?

What did I learn?

different skills involved in looking back through a chapter for specific information, and many students with learning disabilities in the middle and upper
grades do not know how to search for answers to questions in the textbook. At
a minimum, these text lookback skills would involve the following:

1. remembering when certain information was covered—early or late in
   the chapter

2. using headings to find the right section of text

3. reading topic sentences under the appropriate heading

4. identifying a specific paragraph where the answer might be

5. finding the answer in that chapter or continuing the search

Swanson and De La Paz (1998) encouraged teachers to directly model this
text lookback strategy for their students while verbally rehearsing the skills.
These authors suggested the dialogue presented in Teaching Tip 7.12 as a
model instructional lesson for teaching text lookback skills to students with
learning disabilities.

## The Verbal Retelling Tactic

Many strategies for increasing comprehension today emphasize the
students' telling or retelling what they have read (Craig et al., 2001; Ward-
Lonergan, Liles, & Anderson, 1999; NRP, 2000). In fact, verbally retelling the
information from a story, a reading passage, or even a lecture in a subject content area has been shown to increase comprehension among students with
learning disabilities in the middle and upper grades (Ward-Lonergan et al.,
1999). Verbally retelling the main information helps a student focus on the
important aspects of the information presented and thus represents one
method by which a student may summarize the information in the text. For this
reason, middle and upper grade teachers in the general education classroom
should frequently require students to retell information that has just been read
or otherwise presented in class. When a selection is read, either silently or orally
in the class, the teacher may invite students to retell the important aspects of
the reading selection by saying something like the following:

Now we're going to work together to retell the information we just read.
You may refer to your books as you need to. I'd like for someone to tell me the
names of the persons we just read about, and then I'll call on someone else to
tell me the first thing that happened.

With this type of "team" approach, it will be easier to get students with
learning disabilities to participate in retelling a part of the reading passage.
Also, teachers can strengthen this activity by having another student summarize the main points of the passage on the dry-erase board in outline form.
Subsequent to the retelling, teachers may call on yet another student with a
learning disability to review that outline for the class and add to it as necessary.

**Teaching a Text Lookback Strategy**

Teaching students how to look for answers to questions in text can be very beneficial for students with learning disabilities. The use of modeling in which the teacher looks for information in text while he or she "thinks aloud" is very effective in teaching text lookback (Swanson & De La Paz, 1998). Here is a sample dialogue for such a modeling lesson.

"I've read about the Apache Indians and how they lost their land and their forced removal from the plains. The question is asking me to name the most important treaty that resulted in the removal of these Native Americans from their homeland. First, I'll skim the chapter to see if I see a heading about Indians losing land, or Indian removal. The first section heading in the chapter deals with the need of settlers for land of their own, and how most immigrants wanted their own farm. The answer wouldn't be there. The next section is titled, "Moving Into New Lands." The answer may be in that section, so I'll look a bit more closely here. I see one side heading that mentions "Conflict Over Land." A picture above that section shows Native Americans at war with settlers in a wagon train. This is where I'll find the answer. I'll read this paragraph carefully, and look for the mention of any words like "treaties" that might be a clue to the answer."

_____

_____

_____

I have personally used a more structured retelling approach for both reading and listening to lectures in higher level classes called the RTC procedure. RTC stands for "recorder, talker, and checker." Prior to beginning a ten- to fifteen-minute segment of a lecture, I appoint students for the following jobs:

R   a *recorder*, who records the critical information on a poster as I lecture,

T   a *talker*, who will present that critical information to the class at the end of my twenty-minute presentation, and

C   a *checker*, who checks to ensure that the critical information is all covered by the recorder and the talker.

Thus, after I present information for a while, I then have students in the class present the critical aspects of the information I just covered. This ensures participation of the students who are serving in these roles and breaks up the lecture/discussion format. Also, sometimes teachers do not say exactly what they wish to say, and/or students hear something different, so this procedure gives the teacher the opportunity to hear what the students heard and to correct, clarify, or add to that information. This is a fairly simple retelling procedure that teachers from Grade 4 through secondary school can easily implement in inclusive classes.

> Verbally retelling the information from a story, a reading passage, or even a lecture in a subject content area has been shown to increase comprehension among students with learning disabilities in the middle and upper grades.

## A Storytelling Tactic

Closely allied with the retelling tactic described above is the use of storytelling in reading and language instruction (Craig et al., 2001). Storytelling involves the teacher, another adult, or a student in using language to present a narrative to the class. When a teacher is telling a story, the structure of the story itself provides a perfect opportunity for the teacher to "coach" the student and his or her listeners in the structure of narratives. For example, after the teacher describes the characters involved and sets up the story "problem" or plot, the teacher could ask students to predict what may come next (i.e., the anticipated climax). Coaching on story structure can enhance reading across the subject areas because understanding the story structure is a critical reading skill.

There are a number of other advantages in using storytelling in reading and language arts instruction. First, having students of various ethnic backgrounds tell stories offers the opportunity to explore the cultural diversity that is so characteristic in today's classrooms (Craig et al., 2001). Next, teachers may find that students with learning disabilities can demonstrate knowledge of the subject matter more effectively in a storytelling format than on the unit test. Thus, this tactic may well provide teachers in inclusive classes with an alternative testing format. Finally, storytelling involves multiple language capabilities on the part of the student with a learning disability. These include the following:

- language ability
- understanding of story components
- use of facial cues, voice tone, and physical gestures for enhancing the interest level (i.e., "dramatic license")
- understanding of cues from one's audience

These and many other aspects of communications are involved in the act of telling a story. Because of the involvement in these multiple skills, storytelling is truly a "literacy" strategy rather than a "reading" strategy per se. Also this tactic is particularly effective in the differentiated class, as it involves a variety of the multiple intelligences including linguistic and interpersonal intelligence. Teaching Tip 7.13 presents ten tactics that may be used to employ storytelling in your classroom.

## CONCLUSION

In this chapter, perhaps more so than others in this text, the overlap of various strategies is quite apparent. Because reading is a deficit area for many students with learning disabilities, it has become one of the most thoroughly researched areas in the field, and there are numerous instructional strategies that will facilitate differentiated instruction for students with learning disabilities and others in the class. This chapter has presented the growing emphasis on a holistic approach—literacy instruction—that seems to encompass many of the techniques for teaching reading, and although many more specific strategies are available in the literature, the array of strategies presented here does demonstrate

## Ten Tactics for Using Storytelling to Teach Reading

1. Whenever possible, the teacher should use storytelling to illustrate events in history, science, or other subject areas. Rather than telling how scared the soldiers were just prior to the last day of the battle of Gettysburg, the teacher may use a storytelling technique to make that event "real" for the students. Even parts of books read to the students can present these historical facts (e.g., using a few pages of the popular book *Killer Angels* to portray this battle).

2. When using storytelling to illustrate or present events from other subject areas, supplement the storytelling with video, films, or subsequent discussions of the pictures in the subject textbook. Ask about any differences students may have noted between the teacher's story and the pictures in the text.

3. Have students tell stories of various types—stories that really happened or makeup stories—to illustrate concepts. In a lesson on gravity, the teacher may say something like. "Who can tell a funny story from your family about when something fell?"

4. Have several children retell the same story, movie, or television show. Explore with the class the differences in each child's version, without making any student "wrong" or "right."

5. In the middle of stories, stop to check on children's understanding of the narrative. Teachers may use questions such as, "Who can tell me what may happen next?" or "Who can tell me what Tabitha really wants to happen?"

6. Have children use physical movement in telling stories to the class. Have one student tell a story while several other students silently "act out" the story for the class. Use those actors to discuss how emotions may be portrayed or to discuss the feelings of the actors.

7. Use music, rhythms, or chants to tell stories. Some stories involve repeated lines or phrases, and these can be done as a chant by the entire class as the teacher tells the story. This will increase the attention of students with learning disabilities since they will be listening for the opportunity to participate in the chant.

8. Have the students discuss and subsequently demonstrate how they might tell the same story to different groups. For example, telling a story to students at a lower grade level would involve telling the story differently from telling the same story to one's parents or other adults. Students should reflect on what different terms or examples may be used.

9. Expose different students to different parts of the same story and let each student tell his or her part in sequence. Use a video and this same idea, and after each student has contributed his or her part, show the video to the class. Discuss what aspects of the story were omitted, if any.

10. Use drama and role-play to illustrate stories as the teacher tells them. Allow students to sense or feel the roles of the characters in the story.

the types of strategies that general education teachers are using to differentiate instruction for students with learning disabilities in the inclusive classes. These ideas and teaching procedures will greatly assist all students in those classes and are essential for the reading success of students with learning disabilities.

## WHAT'S NEXT?

Although this chapter and text have presented a large number of strategies for differentiating instruction in the classroom, teachers may wonder where to begin. The final chapter suggests how teachers may wish to move into differentiated instruction in their own class.

# Implementing Differentiated Instruction 8

<table>
<tr><td>

**Topics Included in This Chapter:**

✓ Self-Evaluation for Differentiated Instruction
✓ Targeting Students in Need
✓ Initiating Action Research
✓ Developing a Professional Improvement Plan

</td></tr>
</table>

Having explored the strategies and tactics presented in the first seven chapters, teachers may need some suggestions for beginning the process of differentiated instruction in their class. This final chapter is designed to present teachers with some suggestions about how to proceed into this new and challenging way of teaching. This chapter is not intended as a "blueprint" for instructional change because most veteran teachers do not need such a cookbook approach. Also, many veteran teachers may have already incorporated many of these strategies and ideas into their typical classroom routines. Still, teachers may want some ideas on how to proceed. Below are some suggestions for improving instruction using the differentiated instruction model in the inclusive class for students with learning disabilities.

## SELF-EVALUATION AND SELF-CONGRATULATIONS

As a first step in this process, teachers should consider the strategies and tactics that are already in use and congratulate themselves for already using some of these ideas. Although the term "differentiated instruction" is new, many of the strategies and tactics that are applied in the differentiated instructional classroom are not, and teachers already may be doing many of these things. For example, the emphasis on authentic assessment and portfolio assessment has been noted for the past ten years or so, and many teachers are evaluating students using a variety of diverse approaches. Likewise, the self-monitoring strategy is not new, and with decades of research attesting to its efficacy, many teachers are using that strategy already. What is new in the differentiated classroom is a cohesive, well-planned effort to implement all of these effective strategies as necessitated by the individual strengths, learning styles, and multiple intelligences of the students in the class. In differentiation, teachers target their instructional activities to various groups of students based on those learning and multiple intelligences strengths, and this typically results in use of a broader range of instructional tactics and strategies. By using a wider array of innovative, brain-compatible instructional tactics, and planning lessons based on highly differentiated activities for various learners and groups of learners, teachers will see increased participation in the lesson, as well as enhanced achievement for more students in the class.

When undertaking significant change in one's teaching procedures, it is always wise to find reason for self-praise, and a brief summation of the strategies and tactics that one already employs will allow almost every teacher a reason for pride in his or her teaching. Consequently, one of the most important things teachers can do when exploring a new approach is to consciously identify reasons for pride in their current work. Although this text does recommend many adaptations in teachers' instructional efforts, these should be interpreted as ideas to improve a successful instructional technique and not to rebuild a failing career. The teachers that I work with (and I work with thousands each year) are by and large highly skilled professionals who are motivated to seek out enriching modifications for their classroom technique. In that sense, the strategies herein can assist those teachers.

## REFLECTIVE EXERCISE: SELF-EVALUATION AND SELF-CONGRATULATIONS

As a first step, teachers should print out the Bender Classroom Structure Questionnaire (BCSQ) (from Chapter 1) and each of the "ten tactics" lists from the various chapters. With those forms and lists as a guide, teachers should conduct an honest appraisal of how many of those strategies are currently in use in the classroom. In fact, the brief rating procedure below can help teachers determine what tactics to emphasize first. Teachers may do this by asking three questions:

1. What brain-compatible and multiple intelligence strategies and tactics are already implemented? These tactics are implemented already and not included in the rating.

2. Which strategies would be fairly easy to implement next, based on your teaching style and current procedures? Teachers should rate each indicator on this scale, with a 1 for very difficult to implement, 2 for somewhat difficult to implement, and 3 for fairly easy to implement, given my current instructional approaches.

3. What strategies would make the most positive instructional difference for the individual learners in your class? Teachers should rate each indicator on this question with 1 for makes only a little difference, 2 for makes some difference for some students, or 3 for makes an important difference for many learners in my class. For each indicator, merely multiply the ratings for questions 2 and 3 above, and the higher indicators indicate the types of strategies teachers should implement first in the move toward a differentiated classroom.

After the self-evaluation and self-congratulations, teachers may wish to identify one or two of the strategies presented in this self-evaluation and try them. For example, teachers are often motivated to attempt a new strategy because another teacher in the building has tried the strategy and had success with it. Alternatively, teachers sometimes hear of innovative ideas at conferences or learn of new ideas from reading educational journals and then apply those in their own class. Many teachers implement strategies based on a desire to "try something new." There is certainly nothing wrong with this effort at modifying one's teaching style, and there is no time like the present to select several of these strategies and apply them.

# A PROFESSIONAL DEVELOPMENT LEARNING COMMUNITY ON DIFFERENTIATION

## Activities of a Learning Community on Differentiation

After a teacher has considered what differentiated strategies he or she might already employ, that professional will want to find ways to move forward to increase differentiation in his or her classroom. As a first step, that teacher should consider beginning a professional development learning community dedicated to implementation of differentiated instruction. Such a professional development learning community can be of great benefit to individual teachers who wish to increase their differentiated instructional practices, and the initiation of such a learning community can result in positive impact beyond the classrooms of the participating teachers (Kanold, 2006). Over time, other teachers, parents, and/or parent teacher organizations may wish to become involved, thus increasing the overall impact of the group.

The concept of a learning community of professionals dedicated to working together toward a series of professional development goals has become an earmark of high quality professional development in education (Kanold, 2006; Wiliam, 2006). A professional learning community is comprised of a group of dedicated professionals who commit some of their time and effort toward a common goal—in this case, the goal of implementation of differentiated instruction in their classes. Even with only two or three participating teachers, a professional development learning community can have an important impact on the participating teachers and their classes, since support for innovative differentiated instructional efforts is provided by the group. The activities that such a learning community might wish to consider are highly varied and may involve a wide variety of funded and unfunded activities ((Kanold, 2006; Simpson, LaCava, & Graner, 2004). Here are some examples:

- Initiate a "book a month" group in which each member reads one professional development book on differentiated instruction each month, and then presents a summary to the group in a monthly meeting. The group may also choose to read/study/discuss the same book in any given month. Books by Carol Tomlinson, Gayle Gregory, Carolyn Chapman, Rita King, William N. Bender, and others would be appropriate for such study.

- Contact authors of the books used by the study group, and invite them to participate in some professional development at your school. Many professional development presentations are done on a fee for service basis, but you might also consider inviting them to do a "conference call" discussion of 30 minutes about their book. You should inquire of that author about doing this gratis, since you are using their book for your learning community activities.

- Arrange coteaching opportunities for two teachers to work together in a differentiated lesson in one of their classes. This gives each some experience at managing differentiated lessons as teachers first implement this instructional approach, while also providing support from a colleague during the first such lesson. Teachers in the learning community may wish to hold several such joint differentiated classes to get comfortable with the concept and the problems that may arise.

- After the participating teachers are comfortable implementing a differentiated lesson, one or more of them should conduct several demonstration lessons in other teacher's classes. In this fashion, the impact of those participating in the professional development learning community can be extended to teachers who chose not to participate in that community during any particular year.

- Target specific conferences that focus on differentiation and seek funding for participation in those conferences from the administration. In each case, when requesting funding for such conference participation, teachers should commit to the administration to "come back" with some good teaching ideas and share those in a future faculty meeting with all teachers in the school. Again, this will increase the impact of the learning community and the concept of differentiation.

- Undertake a search of the Web and develop a list of helpful and supportive Web sites. While most Web sites attempt to "sell" something, there is also a large amount of free information available on differentiation. For example, on the site: www.teachersworkshop.com, teachers may click on the buttons for "Free On-line Resources" and then "Differentiated Instruction." In that location, teachers will find various lists of brain-compatible songs and chants for use in teaching a wide variety of academic topics. These can be printed out and used in your class when you cover those topics, or adapted as you choose. Also, many sites that focus on multiple intelligences include informal inventories that may be used to teach your students about their own strengths and weaknesses. You should use several topics as your search parameters.

These may include differentiated instruction, multiple intelligences, brain-compatible instruction, etc.

- Structure "mini-retreats" that involve 24- or 48-hour escapes to undertake discussions and planning for differentiation in various classes. You may wish to involve only the participating teachers in the learning community, involve other teachers from other locations, or bring in a facilitator skilled in the areas of differentiation, school reform, and/or group process activities (Childs, 2005).

## Creating a Learning Community on Differentiation

There are many advantages to the networking that result from creating a learning community in your school focused on increasing differentiated instruction (Simpson et al., 2004; Wiliam, 2006). First, teachers in such communities tend to support each other as they move to enhance their instruction, and such support can be critical. Next, organized efforts such as this are more likely to result in financial support from the school or school district. Finally, while all schools are attending to the mandate to enhance learning and improve performance, the establishment of a learning community that focuses the professional development efforts of the school is likely to be one of the most effective ways to move forward on those goals. In particular, an increased emphasis on differentiation, individual learning styles of students, and enhancing student learning via brain-compatible instructional techniques is quite likely to enhance learning and move schools forward in their overall goals (Sternberg, 2006).

In order to initiate such a learning community, two or more teachers should undertake several initial tasks. First they should jointly develop a one- to two-page statement about their desires and goals in relation to forming such a learning community focused on differentiation. This document may be considered (and referred to) as a "Plan for a Professional Development Learning Community." That statement should explicitly state several things, including

- the exact focus of the group, such that appropriate activities might be identified
- the broad goals of the group for the first year of collaboration
- the time commitments each teacher is willing to make (e.g., two hours per month for meetings, and three additional hours for individual study/readings), since that type of information would be useful to other teachers who may wish to join subsequently
- some form of organization. (For example, a "learning community organizer," or a "convener of meetings" might be defined by that document to let others know who is in charge initially.)

Next, those teachers should share that planning document with their administrator in a meeting. The administrator may be able to indicate what types of assistance, if any, the school can provide. The administrator may wish to make suggestions concerning modification of the plan for various reasons. For example, at times it is quite politic to fit such a plan within the larger professional development goals of the school district, since such tailoring of the plan might result in financial support for various activities.

Next, working in conjunction with the administrator, the participating teachers should produce a specific list of activities for the first three to six months. The activities' list should provide some examples of things the group may wish to undertake, and there is no limit to the types of activities that may be undertaken. Again, a clear statement of focus written into the plan should provide guidance on what activities do and do not fit within the learning community's activities.

Finally, the group should share the plan with all of the teachers at the school and with teachers at nearby schools who may wish to participate. Teachers generally know the instructional practices of other teachers at their own school, but it is quite possible that, when sharing this plan with other schools in the district, the developing learning community might discover teachers in other schools who have long implemented differentiated instruction, brain-compatible instructional practices, or multiple intelligence based instruction. Of course, finding such a teacher in a neighboring school provides a hidden resource for the learning community. Also, in this fashion, the size of the learning community would grow, and with additional participants the overall goals and resources are likely to increase. This, in turn, will increase the overall impact of the learning community.

# INDIVIDUAL IMPLEMENTATION OF DIFFERENTIATION

In conclusion, there are many advantages to creation of a learning community in the school that focus specifically on increasing differentiation, and teachers should certainly explore this option with their colleagues. However, individual teachers can also implement differentiated instructional practices on their own, and that would typically involve targeting students in need of differentiation, initiating action research, and developing a professional improvement plan.

## Targeting Students in Need

Of course, when choosing to move toward a more differentiated classroom, targeting strategies for specific students would seem to be most effective. By targeting students first in the change process, teachers are more likely to make a qualitative difference in the lives of their students and, ultimately, in their own enjoyment of teaching. Thus, I recommend targeting one's efforts at instructional modification to specific needs of specific students.

After some reflection on what strategies and tactics are already in use, teachers should consider their relationships to particular students as well as the learning endeavors of those students. Are there students who do not seem to be "making it" on most class activities? Teachers should envision the most recent instructional problems they noted for those students. Perhaps some students seem to need more support in comprehension of their reading assignments. Perhaps other students need assistance in developing self-regulatory skills for organizing their homework assignments. Again, teachers should think of the specific needs of the students and identify those students who need the most assistance. Specifically, teachers must think in terms of one or two specific problems demonstrated with some frequency by particular students and then determine the relative importance of those problems.

## REFLECTIVE EXERCISE: STUDENTS IN NEED

What three students are in the most trouble academically in the class? Are there similarities in their learning processes that the teacher can identify (e.g., a tactile learner, or a learner who needs numerous concrete examples; a learner who needs movement built into the lesson, or a learner who needs to demonstrate his or her competency by a project, performance, or portfolio)? How do these students' problems manifest themselves in the classroom? What subject areas and what types of academic exercises are most indicative of the problems? Write a paragraph about each of the three students, noting these specific needs.

## Initiating Action Research

"Action research" is classroom-based research undertaken by teachers to solve specific learning problems demonstrated by particular students. As described in Chapter 6 of this book, the response to intervention procedure should be considered one form of action research since that procedure involves stipulating a learning problem and bringing appropriate educational interventions to bear on the problem.

The first two sections of this chapter involved consideration of the teacher's classroom organization and instructional strategies that were currently in use, as well as the needs of particular students who may be having trouble. With those considerations in mind, teachers are ready to plan and initiate an intervention project to differentiate the learning in their classes for those students in need. In conducting this type of action research project, teachers move through a five-step process, including the following:

1. Isolate a learning problem of a particular student (describe the learning problem in detail).

2. Select an intervention for that problem and that student (after review of an array of strategies, select a strategy that has proven effectiveness and that the teacher believes may work for that student).

3. State an action research hypothesis and implement the strategy (e.g., the self-management strategy will help this student be prepared for class).

4. Take data to evaluate the effectiveness of the intervention (complete an action research intervention with a minimum of three weeks of data).

5. Evaluate the action research (Did the intervention work? Is it necessary to continue? What other strategies might work if the first strategy did not?).

Using these five steps, teachers can select any of the differentiated instructional strategies in this text and implement an action research intervention. Teaching Tip 8.1 provides a brief form that may be of assistance in considering the problems as well as the possible interventions. However, teachers should

**Identifying a Student's Learning Problem**

Student's Name _____ Date _____

1. Describe the most recent academic difficulty this student displayed.

2. What type of educational activity was the student doing?

3. Was this a problem in motivation (i.e., student not attempting the work) or in the learning process itself?

4. Does the student have a particular learning style or learning strength that could be exploited to address this problem?

5. Does the activity the student was attempting lend itself to a particular strategy described here?

6. Can specialized strategies such as peer tutoring, authentic assessment, or self-management help?

7. Can the teacher state a hypothesis about a particular activity that may work for this student to alleviate this type of problem on similar tasks in the future?

With this information, teachers should undertake an action research project to determine if the strategy or strategies selected above can alleviate the problem for this struggling student.

realize that almost any of the evaluation activities in this book may be of use here also.

### Developing a Professional Improvement Plan

Teachers, like all professionals, are expected to remain constantly updated in their profession, and although the demands on the teachers' time are many and varied, almost all teachers strive to constantly improve their instructional efforts. Thus, teachers

- read professional journals
- take college courses for professional recertification
- attend conferences where innovative instructional ideas are presented
- talk with other veteran teachers about problems that students are having and discuss teaching strategies that may alleviate those problems
- reflect on their instructional efforts constantly in an effort to constantly improve

A professional improvement plan is one step that teachers can take to pull together these various activities and give some cohesion to these diverse professional development efforts. As teachers move to a differentiated classroom, the development and use of a professional improvement plan may help. Teaching Tip 8.2 presents a simple professional improvement plan that may serve as a model for teachers who wish to develop a differentiated instructional inclusive classroom.

## CONCLUSION

With the strategies described herein, coupled with a continual effort to improve one's teaching, a differentiated classroom is within reach of every professional educator today. Not only will one become a more effective teacher, but students with learning disabilities will also benefit much more from the individual instruction that characterizes the differentiated classroom, and this will improve the relationship between the students and the teacher. In turn, by developing a differentiated instruction classroom, teachers typically find that they enjoy their teaching, and their students, even more. In this fashion, all teachers can more concretely enhance the learning and, ultimately, the lives of the students with learning disabilities in their classes, and these students deserve nothing less than the best we educators can offer.

## A Professional Improvement Plan

Name _____     Date _____

School _____

Proposed Professional Development Activities for Academic Year:

_____

I. Professional Knowledge Activities

1. I will read a minimum of 15 journal articles on differentiated instruction and create an annotated bibliography on those articles.

2. I will attend one state conference and seek out sessions on differentiated instruction.

3. I will read two books on differentiated instruction and develop a one-page synopsis on each to share with the faculty at my school.

4. I will create a portfolio over the course of the year to synthesize all of these activities.

II. Initial Tasks Toward Differentiation

1. I will talk with colleagues concerning creation of a professional development learning community.

2. I will reflectively examine my teaching practices to consider where I can increase differentiation.

3. I will reflectively examine the multiple intelligences and learning styles of my students, and make notations for each of them on their learning style preferences.

4. I will implement universal design principles in my classroom as a basis for differentiation.

III. Action Research

1. I will develop two action research projects with two different students between September and December of next year.

2. I will present the results of those action research projects to the principal in January of the following year.

IV. Professional Engagement

1. I will make a 45-minute presentation to our school faculty on differentiated instruction in the spring of next year.

2. I will submit a proposal to present my action research to a state meeting of the _____ (name of the teacher's professional organization here).

# References

Abell, M. M., Bauder, D. K., & Simmons, T. J. (2005). Access to the general curriculum: A curriculum and instruction perspective for educators. *Intervention in School and Clinic, 41*(2), 82–86.

Acrey, C., Johnstone, C., & Milligan, C. (2005). Using universal design to unlock the potential for academic achievement of at-risk learners. *Teaching Exceptional Children, 38*(2), 22–31.

Archer, A. L., Gleason, M. M., & Vachon, V. L. (2003). Decoding and fluency: Foundation skills for struggling older readers. *Learning Disability Quarterly, 26*(2), 89–102.

Arreaga-Mayer, C. (1998). Increasing active student responding and improving academic performance through classwide peer tutoring. *Intervention in School and Clinic, 24*(2), 89–117.

Ashton, T. M. (1999). Spell CHECKing: Making writing meaningful in the classroom. *Teaching Exceptional Children, 32*(2), 24–27.

Ausubel, D. P., & Robinson, F. G. (1969). *School learning: An introduction to educational psychology.* New York: Holt, Reinhart & Winston.

Barry, L. M., & Messer, J. J. (2003). A practical application of self-management for students diagnosed with attention deficit/hyperactivity disorder. *Journal of Positive Behavior Intervention, 5*(4), 238–249.

Baskette, M. R., Ulmer, L, & Bender, W. N. (2006). The Emperor Has No Clothes! Unanswered questions and concerns on the Response to Intervention Procedure. *The Journal of the American Academy of Special Education Professionals. 38*(2).

Beirne-Smith, M. (1991). Peer tutoring in arithmetic for children with learning disabilities. *Exceptional Children, 57,* 330–337.

Bender, W. N. (1992). The Bender classroom structure questionnaire: A tool for placement decisions and evaluation of mainstream learning environments. *Intervention in School and Clinic, 27,* 307–312.

Bender, W. N. (2002). *Relational discipline: Strategies for in-your-face kids.* Needham Heights, MA: Allyn & Bacon.

Bender, W. N. (2005). *Differentiating Math Instruction: Strategies that work for K–8 Classrooms.* (pp. 1–46; 60–134). Thousand Oaks, CA: Corwin Press.

Bender, W. N., & Shores, C. (2007). *Response to intervention: A practical guide.* Thousand Oaks, CA: Corwin Press.

Bender, W. N., Vail, C. O., & Scott, K. (1995). Teachers' attitudes toward increased mainstreaming: Implementing effective instruction for students with learning disabilities. *Journal of Learning Disabilities, 28*(2), 87–94.

Bos, C. S., Mather, N., Silver-Pacuilla, H., & Narr, R. F. (2000). Learning to teach early literacy skills—collaboratively. *Teaching Exceptional Children, 32*(5), 38–45.

Bryant, B. R. (1999). The dynamics of assessment. In W. N. Bender (Ed.), *Professional issues in learning disabilities* (pp. 253–279). Austin, TX: PRO-ED.

Bryant, D. P., Ugel, N., Thompson, S., & Hamff, A. (1999). Instructional strategies for content-area reading instruction. *Intervention in School and Clinic, 34*(5), 293–302.

Burks, M. (2004). Effects of classwide peer tutoring on the number of words spelled correctly by students with LD. *Intervention in School and Clinic, 39*(5), 301–304.

Butler, D. L., Beckingham, B., & Lauscher, H. J. N. (2005). Promoting strategic learning in eighth-grade students struggling in mathematics: A report of three case studies. *Learning Disabilities Research and Practice, 20*(3), 156–174.

Caine, R. N., & Caine, G. (2006). The way we learn. *Educational Leadership, 64*(1), 50–54.

Casebier, A. (2002). *Senate Bill 243: Kentucky revised statutes.* (www.lrc.state.ky.us/research/02rs/sb243.htm).

Chalk, J. C., Hagen-Burke, S., & Burke, M. D. (2005). The effects of self-regulated strategy development on the writing process for high school students with learning disabilities. *Learning Disability Quarterly, 28*(1), 75–87.

Chapman, C. (2000, March 16). *Brain compatible instruction.* Paper presented at a nationwide telesatellite workshop, Tactics for Brain Compatible Instruction, Bishop, GA.

Chapman, C., & King, R. (2005). *Differentiated assessment strategies: One tool doesn't fit all.* Thousand Oaks, CA: Corwin Press.

Chard, D. J., & Dickson, S. V. (1999). Phonological awareness: Instructional and assessment guidelines. *Intervention in School and Clinic, 34*(5), 261–270.

Childs, L. C., (2005). Creating a Galilean leadership shift. *The Journal of Staff Development, 26*(2), 22–27.

Cowan, G., & Cowan, E. (1980). *Writing.* New York: John Wiley.

Craig, S., Hull, K., Haggart, A. G., & Crowder, E. (2001). Storytelling: Addressing the literacy needs of diverse learners. *Teaching Exceptional Children, 33*(5), 46–52.

Darch, C., & Carnine, D. (1986). Teaching content area material to learning disabled students. *Exceptional Children, 53,* 240–246.

Day, V. P., & Elksnin, L. K. (1994). Promoting strategic learning. *Intervention in School and Clinic, 29*(5), 262–270.

Dayton-Sakari, M. (1997). Struggling readers don't work at reading: They just get their teachers to! *Intervention in School and Clinic, 32*(5), 295–301.

Delquadri, J., Greenwood, C. R., Whorton, D., Carta, J. J., & Hall, R. V. (1986). Classwide peer tutoring. *Exceptional Children, 52,* 535–542.

Deno, S. L. (2003). Development in curriculum-based measurement. *Journal of Special Education, 37*(3), 184–192.

Denton, C. A., Fletcher, J. M., Anthony, J. L., & Francis, D. J. (2006). An evaluation of intensive intervention for students with persistent reading difficulties. *Journal of Learning Disabilities, 39*(5), 447–486.

Deshler, D. (2006). An interview with Don Deshler: Perspectives on teaching students with learning disabilities (Interview conducted by Steve Chamberlain). *Intervention in School and Clinic, 41*(5), 302–306.

DiCecco, V. M., & Gleason, M. M. (2002). Using graphic organizers to attain relational knowledge from expository text. *Journal of Learning Disabilities, 35*(4), 306–320.

Dickson, S. V., Chard, D. J., & Simmons, D. C. (1993). An integrated reading/writing curriculum: A focus on scaffolding. *LD Forum, 18*(4), 12–16.

Digangi, S., Magg, J., & Rutherford, R. B. (1991). Self-graphing on on-task behavior: Enhancing the reactive effects of self-monitoring on-task behavior and academic performance. *Learning Disability Quarterly, 14,* 221–229.

Dye, G. A. (2000). Graphic organizers to the rescue! *Teaching Exceptional Children, 33*(4), 72–76.

Elbaum, B., Moody, S. W., Vaughn, S., Schumm, J. S., & Hughes, M. (2000). *The effect of instructional grouping format on the reading outcomes of students with disabilities: A meta-analytic review* [Online]. Available: www.ncld.org.

Ellis, E. S. (1994). Integrating writing strategy instruction with content area instruction. *Intervention in School and Clinic, 29*, 169–179.

Englert, C. S., Berry, R., & Dunsmore, K. (2001). A case study of the apprenticeship process: Another perspective on the apprentice and the scaffolding metaphor. *Journal of Learning Disabilities, 34*(2), 152–171.

Foil, C. R., & Alber, S. R. (2002). Fun and effective ways to build your students' vocabulary. *Intervention in School and Clinic, 37*(3), 131–139.

Forsten, C., Goodman, G., Grant, J., Hollas, B., & Whyte, D. (2006). *The more ways you teach the more students you reach: 86 strategies for differentiating instruction.* Peterborough, NH: Crystal Springs Books.

Fuchs, D., & Fuchs, L. S. (2005). Responsiveness-to-intervention: A blueprint for practitioners, policymakers, and parents. *Teaching Exceptional Children, 38*(1), 57–61.

Fuchs, D., & Fuchs, L. S. (2006). Introduction to response to intervention: What, why, and how valid is it? *Reading Research Quarterly, 41*(1), 93–98.

Fuchs, D., Fuchs, L. S. & Compton, D. L. (2004). Identifying reading disabilities by responsiveness-to-instruction: Specifying measures and criteria. *Learning Disability Quarterly, 27*, 216–227.

Fuchs D., Fuchs, L., Yen, L., McMaster, K., Svenson, E., Yang, N. et al., (2001). Developing first grade reading fluency through peer mediation. *Teaching Exceptional Children, 34*(2), 90–93.

Fuchs, L. S., & Deno, S. L. (1994). Must instructionally useful performance assessment be based in the curriculum? *Exceptional Children, 61*, 15–24.

Fuchs, L. S., Fuchs, D., Eaton, S. B., Hamlett, C., Binkley, E., & Crouch, R. (2000). Using objective data sources to enhance teacher judgments about test accommodations. *Exceptional Children, 67*(1), 67–81.

Fuchs, L. S., Fuchs, D., Hamlett, C. L., Phillips, N. B., & Bentz, J. (1994). Classwide curriculum-based measurement: Helping general educators meet the challenge of student diversity. *Exceptional Children, 60*, 518–537.

Fuchs, L. S., Fuchs, D., Hamlett, C. C., Phillips, N. B., & Bentz, J. (1995). General educators' specialized adaptation for students with disabilities. *Exceptional Children, 61*, 440–459.

Fuchs, L. S., Fuchs, D., & Kazdan, S. (1999). Effects of peer-assisted learning strategies on high school students with serious reading problems. *Remedial and Special Education, 20*(5), 309–318.

Fulk, B. M., & King, K. (2001). Classwide peer tutoring at work. *Teaching Exceptional Children, 34*(2), 49–53.

Gagnon, J. C., & Maccini, P. (2001). Preparing students with disabilities in algebra. *Teaching Exceptional Children, 34*(1), 8–15.

Gardner, H. (2006). *Multiple Intelligences: New horizons.* New York: BasicBooks.

Gardner, H. (1983). *Frames of mind.* New York. Basic Books.

Gersten, R., & Dimino, J. A. (2006). RTI (Response to Intervention): Rethinking special education for students with reading difficulties (yet again). *Research Quarterly, 41*(1), 99–108.

Goleman, D. (2006). The socially intelligent leader. *Educational Leadership, 64*(1), 76–81.

Good, R. H., & Kaminski, R. (2002). *Dynamic indicators of basic early literacy skills.* Longmont, CO: Sopris West.

Greenwood, C. R. (1991). Longitudinal analysis of time, engagement, and achievement in at-risk versus non-risk students. *Exceptional Children, 50*, 521–535.

Greenwood, C. R., Tapia, Y., Abbott, M., & Walton, C. (2003). A building-based case study of evidence-based literacy practices: Implementation, reading behavior, and growth in reading fluency, K-4. *The Journal of Special Education, 37*(2), 95–110.

Gregory, G. H., & Chapman, C. (2002). *Differentiated instructional strategies: One size doesn't fit all.* Thousand Oaks, CA: Corwin Press.

Hallahan, D. P., Lloyd, J. W., & Stoller, L. (1982). *Improving attention with self-monitoring: A manual for teachers.* Charlottesville: University of Virginia.

Hallahan, D. P., & Sapona, R. (1983). Self-monitoring of attention with learning disabled children: Past research and current issues. *Journal of Learning Disabilities, 16,* 616–620.

Hammill, D. D. (2004). What we know about correlates of reading. *Exceptional Children, 70*(4), 452–468.

Harris, K. R., Friedlander, B. D., Saddler, B., Frizzelle, R., & Graham, S. (2005). Self-monitoring of attention versus self-monitoring of academic performance: Effects among students with ADHD in the general education classroom. *The Journal of Special Education, 39*(3), 145–156.

Ihnot, C., Mastoff, J., Gavin, J., & Hendrickson, L. (2001). *Read naturally.* St. Paul, MN: Read Naturally.

Jones, C. J. (2001a). CBAs that work: Assessing students' math content-reading levels. *Teaching Exceptional Children, 34*(1), 24–29.

Jones, C. J. (2001b). Teacher-friendly curriculum-based assessment in spelling. *Teaching Exceptional Children, 34*(2), 32–38.

Joseph, J., Noble, K., & Eden, G. (2001). The neurobiological basis of reading. *Journal of Learning Disabilities, 34*(6), 566–579.

Kameenui, E. J., Carnine, D. W., Dixon, R. C., Simmons, D. C., & Coyne, M. D. (2002). *Effective teaching strategies that accommodate diverse learners* (2nd ed.). Upper Saddle River, NJ: Prentice Hall.

Kanold, T. D. (2006). The flywheel effect: Educators gain momentum from a model for continuous improvement, *The Journal of Staff Development, 27*(2), 16–21.

Keeler, M. L., & Swanson, H. L. (2001). Does strategy knowledge influence working memory in children with mathematical disabilities? *Journal of Learning Disabilities, 34,* 418–434.

Korinek, L., & Bulls, J. A. (1996). SCORE A: A student research paper writing strategy. *Teaching Exceptional Children, 28*(4), 60–63.

Laing, S. P., & Kamhi, A. G. (2002). The use of think-aloud protocols to compare inferencing abilities in average and below-average readers. *Journal of Learning Disabilities, 35*(5), 436–447.

Larkin, M. J. (2001). Providing support for student independence through scaffolded instruction. *Teaching Exceptional Children, 34*(1), 30–35.

Lederer, J. M. (2000). Reciprocal teaching of social studies in inclusive elementary classrooms. *Journal of Learning Disabilities, 33*(1), 91–106.

Lenz, B. K. (2006). Creating school-wide conditions for high quality learning strategy classroom instruction. *Intervention in School and Clinic, 41*(5), 261–266.

Lenz, B. K., & Hughes, C. A. (1990). A word identification strategy for adolescents with learning disabilities. *Journal of Learning Disabilities, 23,* 149–163.

Lenz, B. K., Schumaker, J. B., Deshler, D. D., & Beals, V. L. (1984). *The word identification strategies (Learning Strategies Curriculum).* Lawrence: University of Kansas Press.

Leonard, C. M. (2001). Imaging brain structure in children: Differentiating language disability and reading disability. *Learning Disability Quarterly, 24*(3), 158–176.

Lindsley, O. R. (1971). Precision teaching in perspective: An interview with Ogden R. Lindsley (A. Duncan, interviewer). *Teaching Exceptional Children, 3,* 114–119.

Lipka, O., Lesaux, N. K., & Siegel, L. S. (2006). Retrospective analyses of the reading development of grade 4 students with reading disabilities: Risk status and profiles over 5 years. *Journal of Learning Disabilities, 39*(4), 364–378.

Lovitt, T., & Horton, S. V. (1994). Strategies for adapting science text-books for youth with learning disabilities. *Remedial and Special Education, 15*(2), 105–116.

Lovitt, T., Rudsit, J., Jenkins, J., Pious, C., & Benedetti, D. (1985). Two methods of adapting science materials for learning disabled and regular seventh graders. *Learning Disability Quarterly, 8,* 275–285.

Lyon, G. R., & Moats, L. C. (1997). Critical conceptual and methodological considerations in reading intervention research. *Journal of Learning Disabilities, 30*(6), 578–588.

Maccini, P., & Gagnon, J. C. (2006). Mathematics instructional practices and assessment accommodations by secondary special and general educators. *Exceptional Children, 72*(2), 217–234.

Maccini, P. & Hughes, C. A. (2000). Effect of a problem solving strategy on the introductory algebra performance of secondary students with learning disabilities. *Learning Disabilities Research and Practice, 15*(1), 10–21.

Maheady, L., Harper, G. F., & Sacca, K. (1988). A classwide peer tutoring system in a secondary, resource room program for the mild handicapped. *Journal of Research and Development in Education, 21*(3), 76–83.

Maher, C. A. (1982). Behavioral effects of using conduct problem adolescents as cross-age tutors. *Psychology in the Schools, 19,* 360–364.

Maher, C. A. (1984). Handicapped adolescents as cross age tutors: Program description and evaluation. *Exceptional Children, 51,* 56–63.

Marks, J. W., Laeys, J. V., Bender, W. N., & Scott, K. S. (1996). Teachers create learning strategies: Guidelines for classroom creation. *Teaching Exceptional Children, 28*(4), 34–38.

Marston, D. (2005). Tiers of intervention in responsiveness to intervention: Prevention outcomes and learning disabilities patterns. *Journal of Learning Disabilities, 38*(6), 529–546.

Marston, D., Muyskens, P., Lau M. & Canter, A. (2003). Problem solving model for decision-making with high-incidence disabilities: The Minneapolis experience. *Learning Disabilities Research and Practice, 18*(3), 187–200.

Marzano, R. J., & Marzano, J. S. (2003). The key to classroom management. *Educational Leadership, 61*(1), 6–13.

Mason, L. H., Snyder, K. H., Sukhran, D. P., & Kedem, Y. (2006). TWA + PLANS strategies for expository reading and writing: Effects for nine fourth-grade students. *Exceptional Children, 75*(1), 69–89.

Mastropieri, M. A., Leinart, A., & Scruggs, T. E. (1999). Strategies to increase reading fluency. *Intervention in School and Clinic, 34*(5), 278–283.

Mastropieri, M. A., & Scruggs, T. E. (1988). Increasing content area learning of learning disabled students: Research implementation. *Learning Disabilities Research, 4*(1), 17–25.

Mastropieri, M. A., & Scruggs, T. E. (1998). Enhancing school success with mnemonic strategies. *Intervention in School and Clinic, 33*(4), 201–208.

Mastropieri, M. A., & Scruggs, T. E. (2005). Feasibility and consequences of Response to Intervention: Examination of the issues and scientific evidence as a model for the identification of individuals with learning disabilities, *Journal of Learning Disabilities, 38*(6), 525–531.

Mathes, M., & Bender, W. N. (1997a). The effects of self-monitoring on children with attention-deficit/hyperactivity disorder who are receiving pharmacological interventions. *Remedial and Special Education, 18*(2), 121–128.

Mathes, M., & Bender, W. N. (1997b). Teaching students with ADHD in the elementary classroom: A hierarchical approach to strategy selection. In W. N. Bender (Ed.), *Understanding ADHD: A practical guide for teachers and parents* (pp. 53–78). Columbus, OH: Charles Merrill.

Mathes, P. G., Fuchs, D., Fuchs, L. S., & Henley, A. M. (1994). Increasing strategic reading practice with Peabody classwide peer tutoring. *Learning Disabilities Research and Practice, 9*(1), 44–48.

Mathes, P. G., Fuchs, D., Roberts, P. H., & Fuchs, L. S. (1998). Preparing students with special needs for reintegration: Curriculum-based measurement's impact on transenvironmental programming. *Journal of Learning Disabilities, 31*(6), 615–624.

McConnell, M. E. (1999). Self-monitoring, cueing, recording, and managing: Teaching students to manage their own behavior. *Teaching Exceptional Children, 32*(2), 14–23.

McTighe, J., & Emberger, M. (2006). Teamwork on assessments creates powerful professional development. *The Journal of Staff Development, 27*(1), 38–45.

Meichenbaum, D. H., & Goodman, J. (1969). The developmental control of operant motor responding by verbal operants. *Journal of Experimental Child Psychology, 7,* 553–565.

Meichenbaum, D. H., & Goodman, J. (1988). Training impulsive children to talk to themselves: A means of developing self-control. *Journal of Abnormal Psychology, 77,* 115–126.

Mellard, D. F., Byrd, S. E., Johnson, E., Tollefson, J. M., & Boesche, L. (2004). Foundations and research on identifying model responsiveness-to-intervention sites. *Learning Disability Quarterly, 27,* 243–255.

Miller, M., & Fritz, M. F. (1998). A demonstration of resilience. *Intervention in School and Clinic, 35,* 265–271.

Moats, L. C., & Lyon, G. R. (1993). Learning disabilities in the United States: Advocacy, science, and the future of the field. *Journal of Learning Disabilities, 26,* 282–294.

Monda-Amoya, L., & Reed, F. (1993). Informal assessment in the classroom. In W. N. Bender (Ed.), *Best practices in learning disabilities* (pp. 105–134). Reading, MA: Andover Medical Publishers.

Montague, M. (1992). The effects of cognitive and metacognitive strategy instruction on the mathematical problem solving of middle school students with learning disabilities. *Journal of Learning Disabilities, 25,* 230–248.

Montague, M., & Leavell, A. G. (1994). Improving the narrative writing of students with learning disabilities. *Remedial and Special Education, 15*(1), 21–33.

Moran, S., Kornhaber, M., & Gardner, H. (2006). Orchestrating multiple intelligences. *Educational Leadership, 64*(1), 23–27.

Mortweet, S. W., Utley, C. A., Walker, D., Dawson, H. L., Delquardri, J. C., Reedy, S. S. et al., (1999). Classwide peer tutoring: Teaching students with mild mental retardation in inclusive classrooms. *Exceptional Children, 65*(4), 524–536.

National Council of Teachers of Mathematics. (2000). *Principles and NCTM standards for school mathematics.* Reston, VA: Author.

NCJLD. (2005). Responsiveness to intervention and learning disabilities: A report prepared by the National Joint Committee on Learning Disabilities. *Learning Disability Quarterly 28*(4), 249–260.

Nelson, R., Smith, D., & Dodd, J. (1994). The effects of learning strategy instruction on the completion of job applications by students with learning disabilities. *Journal of Learning Disabilities, 27*(2), 104–110.

NRP. (2000). *Put reading first: The research building blocks for teaching children to read.* National Reading Panel. Washington, DC: National Institute of Health.

O'Connor, R. (2003, December). *Tiers of intervention in kindergarten through third grade.* Paper presented at the national research center on learning disabilities responsiveness-to-intervention symposium, Kansas City, MO (see the discussion of this paper in Marston, 2003).

Palincsar, A. S., & Brown, A. L. (1986). Interactive teaching to promote independent learning from text. *The Reading Teacher, 39,* 771–777.

Palincsar, A. S., & Brown, A. L. (1987). Enhancing instructional time through attention to metacognition. *Journal of Learning Disabilities, 20*(1), 66–75.

Patzer, C. E., & Pettegrew, B. S. (1996). Finding a "voice": Primary students with developmental disabilities express personal meanings through writing. *Teaching Exceptional Children, 29*(2), 22–27.

Pisha, B., & Stahl, S. (2005). The promise of new learning environments for students with disabilities. *Intervention in School and Clinic, 41*(2), 67–75.

Pressley, M., Hogan, K., Wharton-McDonald, R., Mistretta, J., & Ettneberger, S. (1996). The challenges of instructional scaffolding: The challenges of instruction that supports student thinking. *Learning Disabilities Research and Practice, 11*(3), 138–146.

Richards, T. L. (2001). Functional magnetic resonance imaging and spectroscopic imaging of the brain: Application of fMRI and fMRS to reading disabilities and education. *Learning Disability Quarterly, 24*(3), 189–204.

Rock, M. L. (2004). Graphic organizers: Tools to build behavioral literacy and foster emotional competency. *Intervention in School and Clinic, 40*(1), 10–37.

Saenz, L. M., Fuchs, L. S., & Fuchs, D. (2005). Peer-assisted learning strategies for English language learners with learning disabilities. *Exceptional Children, 71*(3), 231–247.

Salend, S. J. (2005). Report card models that support communication and differentiation of instruction. *Teaching Exceptional Children, 37*(4), 28–35.

Santoro, L. E., Coyne, M. D., & Simmons, D. C. (2006). The reading-spelling connection: Developing and evaluating a beginning spelling intervention for children at risk of reading disability. *Learning Disabilities Research and Practice, 21*(2), 122–133.

Scheid, K. (1994). Cognitive based methods for teaching mathematics. *Teaching Exceptional Children, 56*, 540–549.

Schumaker, J. B., & Deshler, D. D. (2003). Can students with LD become competent writers? *Learning Disabilities Quarterly, 28*(2), 129–141.

Shapiro, E. S., DuPaul, G. J., & Bradley-Klug, K. L. (1998). Self-management as a strategy to improve the classroom behavior of adolescents with ADHD. *Journal of Learning Disabilities, 31*(6), 545–555.

Simos, P. G., Fletcher, J. M., Forrman, B. R., Francis, D. J. Castillo, E. M., & Davis, R. N. (2002). Brain activation profiles during the early stages of reading acquisition. *Journal of Child Neurology, 17*, 159–163.

Simpson, R. L., LaCava, P. G., & Graner, P. S. (2004). The No Child Left Behind Act: Challenges and implications for educators. *Intervention in School and Clinic, 40*(2), 67–75.

Smith, C. R. (1998). From gibberish to phonemic awareness: Effective de-coding instruction. *Teaching Exceptional Children, 30*(6), 20–25.

Smith, S. B., Baker, S., & Oudeans, M. K. (2001). Making a difference in the classroom with early literacy instruction. *Teaching Exceptional Children, 33*(6), 8–14.

Snyder, M. C., & Bambara, L. M. (1997). Teaching secondary students with learning disabilities to self-manage classroom survival skills. *Journal of Learning Disabilities, 30*(5), 534–543.

Stanford, P. (2003). Multiple Intelligence for every classroom. *Intervention in School and Clinic, 39*(2), 80–86.

Sternberg, R. J. (2006). Recognizing neglected strengths. *Educational Leadership, 64*(1), 30–35.

Stiggins, R., & Chappuis, J. (2006). What a difference a word makes: Assessment FOR learning rather than assessment of learning helps students succeed. *The Journal of Staff Development, 27*(1), 10–15.

Stipek, D. (2006). Relationships matter. *Educational Leadership, 64*(1), 46–49.

Sousa, D. (1999, April 23). *Motor learning in the classroom.* Paper presented at the teleconference, Brain Based Learning, Atlanta, GA.

Sousa, D. (2006). *How the brain learns* (3rd ed.). Thousand Oaks, CA: Corwin Press.

Sousa, D. A. (2001). *How the special needs brain learns.* Thousand Oaks, CA: Corwin Press.

Stone, C. A. (1998). The metaphor of scaffolding: Its utility for the field of learning disabilities. *Journal of Learning Disabilities, 31,* 344–364.

Swanson, P. N., & De La Paz, S. (1998). Teaching effective comprehension strategies to students with learning and reading disabilities. *Intervention in School and Clinic, 33*(4), 209–218.

Sylwester, R. (2000). *A biological brain in a cultural classroom.* Thousand Oaks, CA: Corwin Press.

Tomlinson, C. A. (1999). *The differentiated classroom: Responding to the needs of all learners.* Alexandria, VA: Association for Supervision and Curriculum Development.

Tomlinson, C. A. (2001). *How to differentiate instruction in mixed-ability classrooms* (2nd ed.). Alexandria, VA: Association for Supervision and Curriculum Development.

Tomlinson, C. A., Kaplan, S. N., Renzulli, J. S., Purcell, J., Leppien, J., & Burns, D. (2002). *The parallel curriculum: A design to develop high potential and challenge high-ability learners.* Thousand Oaks, CA: Corwin Press.

Tomlinson, C. A., & McTighe, J. (2006). *Integrating differentiated instruction and understanding by design: Connecting content and kids.* Alexandria, VA.: Association for Supervision and Curriculum Development.

Utley, C. A., Mortweet, S. L., & Greenwood, C. R. (1997). Peer-mediated instruction and interventions. *Focus on Exceptional Children, 29*(5), 1–23.

Vail, C. O., & Huntington, D. (1993). Classroom behavioral interventions for students with learning disabilities. In W. N. Bender (Ed.), *Best practices in learning disabilities* (pp. 153–176). Reading, MA: Andover Medical Publishers.

Vaughn, S. (2003, December). *How many tiers are needed for response to intervention to achieve acceptable prevention out-comes.* Presented at the National Research Center on Learning Disabilities Responsiveness-to-Intervention Symposium, Kansas City, MO.

Vaughn, S. (2006). A few remarks on response to intervention. *New Times for DLD, 24*(1), 1–2.

Vaughn, S., Gersten, R., & Chard, D. J. (2000). The underlying message in LD intervention research: Findings from research syntheses. *Exceptional Children, 67*(1), 99–114.

Vaughn, S., & Linan-Thompson, S. (2003). What is special about special education for students with learning disabilities? *The Journal of Special Education, 37*(3), 140–147.

Vaughn, S., Linan-Thompson, S., & Hickman, P. (2003). Response to treatment as a means of identifying students with reading/learning disabilities. *Exceptional Children, 69*(4), 391–409.

Vellutino, F. R., Scanlon, D. M., Sipay, E. R., Small, S., Chen, R., Pratt, A. & Denckla, M. B. (1996). Cognitive profiles of difficult to remediate and readily remediated poor readers: Early intervention as a vehicle for distinguishing between cognition and experiential deficits as basic cause of specific reading disability. *Journal of Educational Psychology, 88,* 601–638.

Ward-Lonergan, J. M., Liles, B. Z., & Anderson, A. M. (1999). Verbal re-telling abilities in adolescents with and without language-learning disabilities for social studies lectures. *Journal of Learning Disabilities, 32*(3), 213–223.

Wesson, C. L. (1991). Curriculum based measurement and two models of follow-up consultation. *Exceptional Children, 57,* 246–256.

Whitaker, S. D., Harvey, M., Hassell, L. J., Linder, T., & Tutterrow, D. (2006). The FISH strategy: Moving from sight words to decoding. *Teaching Exceptional Children, 38*(5), 14–18.

White, O. R. (1986). Precision teaching-precision learning. *Exceptional Children, 52,* 522–534.

Wiliam, D. (2006). Assessment: Learning communities can use it to engineer a bridge connecting teaching and learning. *The Journal of Staff Development 27*(1), 16–20.

Winn, J. A., & Otis-Wilborn, A. (1999). Monitoring literacy learning. *Teaching Exceptional Children, 32*(1), 40–45.

# Index

**CORWIN PRESS**

The Corwin Press logo—a raven striding across an open book—represents the union of courage and learning. Corwin Press is committed to improving education for all learners by publishing books and other professional development resources for those serving the field of PreK–12 education. By providing practical, hands-on materials, Corwin Press continues to carry out the promise of its motto: **"Helping Educators Do Their Work Better."**

Council for Exceptional Children

The worldwide mission of The Council for Exceptional Children is to improve educational outcomes for individuals with exceptionalities.

CEC, a non-profit association, accomplishes its mission which is carried out in support of special education professionals and others working on behalf of individuals with exceptionalities, by advocating for appropriate governmental policies, by setting professional standards, by providing continuing professional development, by advocating for newly and historically underserved individuals with exceptionalities, and by helping professionals achieve the conditions and resources necessary for effective professional practice.